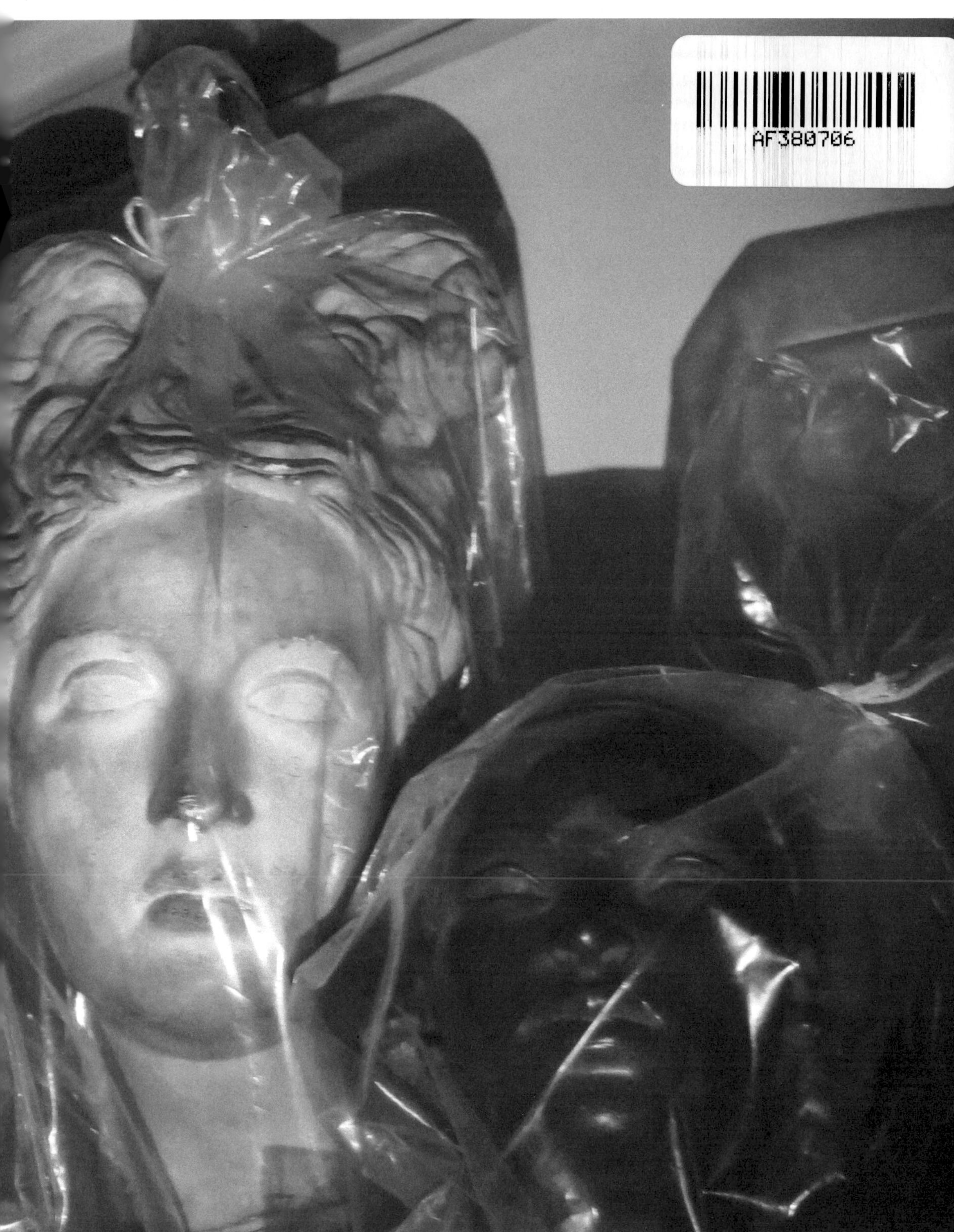

Jimmie Durham & A Stick in the Forest by the Side of the Road

OXYGEN

Have you ever felt that 'you can't breathe' in a museum hall?

In 1972 Franco Mazzucchelli created *Caduta di Pressione*, a conceptual work in which the artist investigates the subtraction of oxygen inside an exhibition hall, as a result of people's breathing, as a subtle but quantifiable modification of the environment. While a diagram illustrates the calculation of the oxygen consumed based on the time spent inside the exhibition, other plaques display phrases that speak of oxygen as vital and indispensable to our survival —but not only ours.

In 2020, during the coronavirus pandemic, Sandra Smith, Head of Collection Care at the British Museum, stated that the museum's halls, without the moisture of the millions of bodies that usually pass through it every year, are suffering, and so are the exhibits: "the objects on display in the museum have been used to breathing along with the visitors. If the visitors are not there, the museum too will be in oxygen debt" (Cimoli 2021).

And then, in the summer of 2020, George Floyd's cry before being killed by two policemen in Minneapolis —"I can't breathe!"—becomes the shout of many people around the world who begin (and in many cases continue) to demand redistribution of power, speech and justice, especially in public spaces, through representations that acknowledge the structural role of racism in shaping institutional narratives and the very structure of our society. Museums, architecture and monuments more than ever take centre stage (Amselle 2017, Raicovich 2021). They become the theatre and main object of the urgency to undo the syntax of the world (as Italo Calvino would say), and to rewrite it from scratch.

So, have you ever felt that you 'can't breathe' in a museum room? What does that mean, literally and metaphorically?

The museum is a place where one normally feels safe. This seems so obvious to us that it doesn't even occur to us (I am speaking from the point of view of the public, while museum workers often suffer from extreme precariousness and feel anything but safe).

Or at least, this was an absolute certainty until the attack on the Jewish Museum in Brussels in 2014, and the attack on the Bardo museum in Tunis in 2015. Until the claims of movements such as 'Decolonise our museums (and every dang Institution)', a movement born in 2015 by 'culture workers who debunk and denounce supremacist iconographies and publicly-funded bureaucracies that sanction their use'. Perhaps, then, more than a safe space the museum is, for some people, a reassuring place, where a very high level of control builds a certain illusion of security, not only regarding objects, people and spaces but also, and even more so, with regard to the narratives and epistemologies that underpin them.

The museum, far from being a universal dispositive, is one of the heterotopias of European modernity, which have historically articulated the dimension of power through knowledge, through the construction of places simultaneously inside and outside space, inside and outside time. The museum has provided the imaginative and performative resources, the cognitive horizons and the practices useful for the construction of the modern European citizen, established as a 'universal' subject, always in relation to a subordinated otherness that defines difference. It constructed 'imagined communities' (Anderson 1983) in a national and colonial sense through a series of oppositions (inside-outside, self-other, nature-culture, visible-invisible), at a time when Europe was defining itself at the height of scientific, technological and 'civilisational' progress. In doing so, it also defined and naturalised a specific regime for the habitation of its spaces, with respect to the objects on display and the bodies of the visitors. It has conveyed a series of habitus (Mauss 2017), that is, a series of dispositions and behavioural norms, which the 'good' visitor has incorporated to the point of feeling them as 'natural'. Today, this museum model is definitely in oxygen debt.

MIRROR

The museum is the colossal mirror in which we in Europe have represented and recognised ourselves. This operates also through the reflection of the image of other cultures, which we have put on display while at the same time constructing their invisibility. This is the paradoxical peculiarity of the museum, which like every archival device produces visibility and invisibility at the same time. It displays something, while at the same time hiding something else. In this sense, the museum seems to resemble a kind of reality-generating hallucination—a mirror, in fact.

Who among us today recognises oneself in this mirror? Probably those who feel they belong to the imagined community that the mirror-museum constructs through its apparatus. This brings out the tautological aspect of this process: I recognise myself if I belong, I belong if I recognise myself.

What if the people, the communities, who recognise themselves in the objects in the museum, do not recognise themselves in the way those objects and their culture are told or shown? That will only be a distorting mirror in their eyes.

What if the specific *sensescape* that the museum has historically constructed and handed down, based on the European sensory model of the five senses (assumed to be universal, although it is not at all) with an absolute priority given to a totally disembodied sight, had never been 'adequate'? What if the preservation of objects in museum collections was not necessarily, universally, a priority? Perhaps looking at it from another angle, the museum's attitude to conservation/cataloguing/exhibiting would appear to us as a sort of patrimonial compulsion (Amselle 2017) that responds to the same accumulative obsession that also underlies the capitalist system that has built our specific model of development. These are questions that profoundly challenge our epistemologies, rooted in the museographic, ethnographic and scientific knowledge that we possess (i.e. that we have historically constructed), and that push us to imagine alternative solutions in practices, displays, narratives, and the very identity of contemporary museums.

I am writing from the perspective of a person outside the museum. I am not a museum worker, but I have often worked with museums, through external curatorial projects, always done together with other people (and this makes a radical

difference). Always trying to work with the museum, not on the museum. And this also makes a radical difference.
I have never considered the museum a simple 'object of study', but a stratified place where a hegemonic discourse is articulated, translated, sometimes contested and re-mediated by the people who work in it, and by the people who pass through it and question it as a public or as directly interested subjectivities (such as the people belonging to the source communities of the objects collected in ethnographic museums). A place that is the bearer and producer of fundamental identity processes, which as such is always itself 'exposed': exposed, as a space of enunciation, to its own vulnerability, to the possibility of being interrupted, questioned, contradicted, contested, usurped, reinvented. Therefore, the perspective from which I write is external to the museum 'machine', but certainly not 'objective'. On the contrary, I write from a partial, positioned and strongly 'compromised' perspective: as a museum visitor; as an insider in another infernal machine like the university (which shares many dynamics with the museum, both being powerful devices of knowledge production); and as a Euro-descendant woman, heir (despite myself) to a toxic colonial setting, which continues to haunt our institutions and reproduce itself in their practices.

GHOSTS

Some museums are haunted, writes Michael Taussig (2004).
Most ethnographic museums are born out of colonial
routes and their 'bittersweet spoils' of genocide and de-
predation, yet these museums often remain silent about
why those objects are there, how they were acquired, and
what kind of knowledge was historically constructed through
their representation.

Agamben (2009) writes that spectrality is a form of posthumous life, made up of the marks that time engraves on
things. Etymologically, *spectrum* is 'the means of seeing'. So
it is more than an image (*phantasma*): it is a vision, a projection, something that allows us to see something else,
and beyond. Like a foggy mirror, in which something never
stops happening: *spectrum-speculum-spectaculum*. If we
were to listen to these spectral echoes, to their voices,
perhaps we would be able to better understand the way in
which many of the urgencies of our contemporary world,
inside and outside museums, are linked to this past that
does not pass and remains, in its ghostly posthumous life,
to torment the present.

It seems that in relation to colonial history, most European
countries have developed pathologies of memory (Ricoeur
2004): they remember too little, and badly, in a kind of active
forgetting, an escape through oblivion. It is all about not
wanting to remember, or wanting to remember in a 'certain
way'. What Ricoeur calls 'selective forgetting' has organised in many of these countries the strategies of memorial-
isation with respect to what and how to remember, building
archives and imaginaries that are now being reopened and
critically questioned.

As for Italy, the myths of 'Italians, good people' and of
a 'minor' colonialism compared to that of other European
countries, and of being well considered by the colonised
themselves, have been elaborated for at least thirty years,
between the end of Fascism (and the formal closure of the
colonial occupations) and the opening of historical archives
containing documents related to our presence in Ethiopia,
Eritrea, Libya, Somalia (but also in Albania and Greece).
This occurred with a guilty and strategic delay only in the
eighties of the twentieth century. In all those years of
documentary silence, it is said that Italians 'removed' their
colonial history, but I believe that it is not so much a matter
of removal, like the erasure of an event from one's
consciousness, but, rather, of 'repression', to remain in

psycho analytic terms. Repression occurs when the traumatic event is not erased from consciousness, but simply moved to another 'place', to another affective constellation. Thus, the violent and racist root of colonialism has been erased in order to move that complex event into the realm of the exotic, of paternalism, of the 'place in the sun'. All this has continued to produce certain imaginaries about ourselves and others, which today shape those racist and violent impulses towards difference (in the intersectional sense, understood as any otherness linked to racial, geopolitical, gender, class positions considered outside the norm). It allows us to understand the continuity of colonial forms of domination after the end of colonial administrations (Grosfoguel 2017).

When I think of the word 'post-colonial', I think of that post- not so much in the sense of 'subsequent to' but in the sense of 'posthumous', of something that was generated by an event in the past, but continues to take place in a later time. To live in post-colonial societies is to inhabit a temporality that is interrupted, conflictual and in perpetual flux, full of fractures but also of continuity, living in a permanently altered space-time, where coloniality continues to act through an intricate intersectional system of privileges and oppressions, which we have interiorised to such an extent that we perceive it as 'normal', both on a transnational level and on a local level (in our cities, in our homes, in our workplaces, in museums and public spaces, in our social relations), even in our intimacy.

We need to understand this temporality, to penetrate what Belgian artist Vincent Meessen calls "colonial hauntology" (Gregos and Meessen 2015); to trigger in every possible way a process of the emergence of the repressed, the denied, the misunderstood, through its reinscription in the present, to which it continues to belong, and to do so in all possible places, from museums to street names, to our family archives, to cultural consumption, to our fantasies and the forms (the cultural imaginaries) with which they are expressed, to the everyday intimacy of gestures, idioms, games. We need to give substance to and recognise these ghosts that are returning to claim their reasons.

STUFF

I am sure that certain objects feel uncomfortable behind the showcase of a museum. The museum has historically cannibalised objects, especially the ethnographic museum with its primal scene of colonial complicity. What does the museum really know about these objects, which some European has appropriated in often illicit ways? The transparency of museum showcases is an illusion—as is the presumed innocence of display. It masks the appropriative gaze of colonial Europe on otherness, that need to construct an otherness against which to define and confirm itself.

Colonialism has undoubtedly been 'material' and sensorial. Bodies, objects and entire ecosystems have always been at the centre of the colonial project, often sharing the same status: racialised and sexualised bodies to be disciplined and exploited; raw materials, artefacts and works of art 'to be saved'; food products, photographs, documents, bodies and pieces of bodies, seeds and plants. This is an economy that is also perceptive, sensorial, involving not only sight but also sounds, smells, tastes and touch. The museum, as a key institution of European-colonial modernity that classifies and controls the cultures of the world, has imposed not only its own construction of knowledge but also its own sensory hierarchies inside, on objects, and outside, on the public. In a way, the ethnographic museum involves a doubling (cleaned up and aseptic, but not without violence) of colonial space. In the colonial world, the logic, epistemologies and values of the coloniser (colonial psychopathology, Fanon would say) are imposed with meticulous order and inflexible rules on the colonised people. Similarly, in the museum space, objects are doubly colonised, both at the narrative level (presented as authentic specimens of a culture, with an attribution of value linked to epistemologies totally different from those of those who produced and used that object) and at the exhibition level, because in the empire of sight that is the museum they are colonised by the gaze in a normative mode of perception (Classen and Howes 2006).

In classical ethnographic museums, the collection of art or ethnography must be subject to certain criteria: the 'best' art or the most 'authentic' artefact; objects that are exemplary or representative of culture; the prestige (local, national, 'universal') of owning a certain object or a certain collection in one's 'heritage'; the tendency to separate art (of superior quality) from culture (ethnographic), generally within a notion of linear or unitary History (of the nation, of humanity, of art) and without fractures (Clifford 1988; Price 1989).

The ethnographic object inside the museum thus appears in some way 'civilised' while remaining 'other', relocated in the visual-rational regime of the museum, and so the populations it represents will also be symbolically 'disciplined', that is, immobilised, frozen in the representation that the museum constructs for them through objects that now speak the language of the museum: "touchless, speechless, and smell-less" (Classen and Howes 2006).

In every archive, however, there is always something missing. Every archive, being linked to the past and necessarily to do with memory and its projection into the future, is at the same time an opening and a separation, a wound. Indeed, there is no archive without cracks (Mbembe 2016). The archive is made up of layers of presences and absences, of babble, shadows and ghosts, as much as of materiality and evidence. It is difficult to grasp the significance of the invisible, the unaccountable and the untold, the unrecognised, the removed, within the ordered and rigorous grammar of what is instead illuminated, affirmed, ordered and presented. But if we look at it closely, the archive is all a crack, a meticulous order always looking out over the conflict and chaos that we recognise at its margins.

There is something that remains unarchivable. There are bodies (with their objects) that cannot enter museums, because they have drowned and lie at the bottom of the Mediterranean, or lost on the paths between the borders of nations increasingly marked by impassable boundaries and walls. These are enormous archives of death, but also of aspirations, life projects, imagination, desire. Certain objects, certain bodies, writes Mbembe, escape the museum, because the museum cannot understand their radicality without immobilising them, domesticating them in a classificatory order, rendering them inoffensive, neutralising their 'potential for scandal'. So perhaps it is precisely because these objects and bodies escape the museum that they manage to retain their radicality.

Perhaps, writes Mbembe, this is essentially the function of the museum, a function of cult, especially in the secular societies of the West. It is possible that this function is necessary for the very survival of society, just as the function of forgetting memory is necessary (Connerton 1989).

These objects, these bodies, in order to preserve their power of scandal, "should not enter the museum", writes Mbembe; instead, they should continue to haunt it with their absence, or with their spectral presence. They should be "everywhere and nowhere", their appearances should always take place "in the form of a break-in and never an institution" (Mbembe 2016). Their story provokes and invites us to a radical effort of imagination, aimed at founding an institution with an unprecedented form, as yet to come, a place of radical hospitality for the stories and bodies of the "damned of the earth".

In the 1970s, with the Democratic Psychiatry movement in Italy, Franco Basaglia managed to render legal the closure of mental asylums. As places of violence, restraint and social control, there was no concern for curing people; on the contrary, madness was produced. The madness was in the institution itself, and so it was necessary to disempower it and imagine another model, another device, another space (Foot 2014), another modality of care and custody. In a similar vein, Clémentine Deliss calls for a "post-ethnographic museum", anomalous and anachronistic (Deliss 2020). Mbembe calls it an "anti-museum": it is not an institution at all, but the figure of another place, that of radical hospitality. As a place of refuge, the anti-museum also conceives of itself as a place of rest and unconditional asylum for all the "damned of the earth" as the witnesses of the sacrificial system that has been the history of modernity, a history that the archive finds difficult to contain.

WHOSE HERITAGE?

At the end of the 1990s, on the pages of the journal *Third Text*, Stuart Hall asked to whom heritage belongs (Hall 1999). If heritage is linked to the preservation and representation of art and culture that bear witness to the history of a national community, it comes to be "the material embodiment of the spirit of the nation". Such a powerful pedagogical vocation is aimed not simply at governing, but extends to how the state, indirectly and remotely, induces and solicits appropriate attitudes and behaviour in its citizens (governmentality). It inculcates in every citizen the embodiment of his or her culture of belonging and the social norms derived from it. So, asks Stuart Hall, who is heritage for? Only for those who 'belong' to an identity imagined and postulated in the past as culturally homogeneous, unified and traditionally secured in the 'origins' of the nation? Those who do not see themselves reflected in the mirror of the 'national heritage' can never properly 'belong' to that community. It is interesting to reread these reflections more than twenty years later, in a post-colonial (but not decolonialised) Europe, with a social and cultural fabric that is far from homogeneous, indeed clearly intercultural, marked by mobility and migration from former colonies and other parts of the world (Modest 2019).

However, following Stuart Hall, if we think of the identity of a community as "an on-going project, under constant reconstruction", and the museum as a mirror that proposes the image of that community through its display, the museum and cultural heritage appear to be at the centre of an unprecedented challenge and possibility. This is especially accentuated in the colonial heritage that haunts European ethnographic museums. The recognition of the role that cultural diversity has historically played in the formation of national identity (and of the violence inherent in this process) leads to a contextual redefinition of possible, legitimate, modes of belonging to the community by people from different backgrounds. It proposes a radical renegotiation of the ownership of heritage itself and transforms the sign of historical appropriations into a new form of justice.

For this reason, it is crucial to finally open a serious debate (even a conflictual one) on the issue of the restitution of colonial heritages, as is finally happening in several countries. Literally, restitution means returning an object to its legitimate owner, but it also means re-establishing the object in its context and the uses and meanings considered

proper to that context. In other words, it means allowing
a process of symbolic re-appropriation of the object that
has been dislocated, decontextualised, re-signified and
inserted into a different symbolic order by the power of the
European gaze. Returning these objects does not therefore
mean returning them to their previous state, but, rather,
re-investing them with a social and historical function. Such
a gesture has an ethical dimension when the restoration of
reciprocal relations between the parties is not carried out
in an asymmetrical modality. The act of restitution explicitly
acknowledges the illegitimacy of the object's possession by
its current owners, and with it the will to operate not only
a recognition but also a 'reparation' of that injustice.

The implications are therefore not only legal but also
political and symbolic. For it opens up a profound reflection
on the colonial past, and the way it has contributed to the
construction of the heritage of Western museums. But it is
also a question of operating an epistemological reversal
and recognising the existence of different (legitimate) interpretations of 'cultural heritage', a concept that is, in any
case, purely European and far from universal in itself. It
means to respond to material culture, to the attribution of
certain values to objects, to the relationship between people
and things, respecting individual and collective identities.
The model of a centralised museum, devoted to the preservation and display of heritage, is only one of the possible
configurations for the location of heritage in social space.

Similarly, the fact that the primary interest of the museum
lies in preserving and maintaining the integrity of the objects in the collection is not necessarily its unique scope:
it is not the intrinsic 'nature' of museums. On the contrary,
we are dealing with the expression of an ideological, epistemological and political framework—corresponding to
a precise model of sensory interaction in the museum—
that considers preserving the objects in the collection
for the future more important than interacting with them
physically in the present (Classen and Howes 2006).

The process of restitution is also a valuable opportunity
to demystify the universalised and normalised notions of the
Western museum as the only 'scientifically' correct ones.
It is hard for us to conceive, but conservation is not a universal museum priority. What may be more important is the
power of cultural heritage to be experienced, to participate
in the ongoing and vital process of narration and reconstruction of memories and in the reinvention of the self,
even outside the museum.

TO HEAL

How, then, to heal the colonial wound? "Kill the museum!"
declared Alpha Konaré, former president of Mali and
president of ICOM (International Council of Museums), who
in 1992 declared: "it is about time that we questioned the
fundamental basis of the situation and 'killed'—I repeat
killed—the Western model of the museum in Africa in
order for new methods for the conservation and promotion of our heritage to flourish" (Deliss 2020).

The body of the museum is a toxic, sick body that
needs urgent treatment, writes Clémentine Deliss. The
colonial museum acts through a necropolitics that poi-
sons the objects and the metabolism of the institution.
Imagining systems of care through radical interventions
and slow pedagogical operations, or accompanying it to
death: there are no other options.

In the documentary *Reflecting Memory* (2016), the
artist Kader Attia, who has been working for years on the
concept of 'repair', reflects on how much the recognition
of an absence brings with it the need to put what is missing back in its place, just as in the case of the phantom
limb, which needs to return to existence, even if only
through its evocation with a mirror, to calm the physical
pain caused by the non-recognition of the lack at the level
of the body schema. A similar mechanism operates at the
level of the mutilated memory of a community, as in the
case of colonial memories: removed, rejected, unrecognised, unspeakable.

It is not enough to return the spoils of colonial heritages,
because the structure of the museum (and of the society
of which it is an expression) remains haunted by coloniality.
If the museum really acts as a mirror, perhaps through it we
respond to the recognition of the mutilation, the wound, and
experiment with collective processes of healing, leading to
practices of re-appropriation and redistribution.

How to disturb and bring out the ambiguities implied in
the transparency of many contemporary museum narratives?
It is necessary to show collections, archives, captions,
museum spaces as discursive and relational fields, as
expressions of certain power-knowledge arrangements.
In this process, who are the subjects allowed to speak and
who risk always remaining the 'objects' of the discourse,
even if they are asked by the museum to deal with its
heritage? How to avoid forms of tokenism and what
Simona Bodo calls "predatory participation" (Bodo 2022)?

It is necessary to avoid the paternalistic gesture of 'giving voice' to a subject who remains nevertheless other, and instead trigger a reciprocity of gazes, even if that involves radically questioning the museum narrative and its authority. It is necessary to question the monological authority of the museum, transforming it into a critical space of awareness and radical questioning: why are those objects there? What stories and memories do they carry? Whose memories? From what point of view do they bear them? Who is invited to listen to them, and who is not? What wounds do they tell? Is it possible to exhibit a wound? Is it possible to heal it in a museum?

What is the 'imagined community' of an (ethnographic) museum in our cities today? The concept of representativeness at the basis of the definition of the museum as a 'public' place must necessarily open up as identities are marked by ever more intense processes of transculturation. If movements are growing that cling violently to a presumed purity to be preserved (the various 'America first', 'Italians first') this only reveals that the concept of citizenship is everywhere at the centre of inclusive redefinitions and powerful conflicts.

Ethnographic heritage itself is merely the outcome of a historical and political process, the product of appropriation and/or exchange, in most cases from an asymmetrical and colonial perspective. It is not the repository of an indisputable value and narrative, nor is it a testimony to 'scientific progress' and national prestige. The museographic strategies of accumulation, cataloguing, exhibiting, preserving, and the definition of scientificity on which our knowledge is based, are inscribed in "particular histories of domination, hierarchy, resistance and mobilisation" (Clifford 1997). These structures refer to political, economic and cultural relations imbued with coloniality, which are neither permanent nor unchallengeable. Rather, they need to be acknowledged and deconstructed, to some extent unlearned, in order to make room for new processes, practices and decolonised knowledge. We need to question what we are most used to, what may even seem ordinary to us, because asking certain questions can help us to overturn points of view born in a specific set-up of colonial hegemony, which have then been naturalised and become normative: "why has it seemed so obvious until recently that non-Western objects should be kept in European museums, even if this meant that no valuable specimens would be seen in their country of origin?" (Clifford 1988).

The objects of an ethnographic collection, whether legitimately acquired or not, can never be fully owned by the museum: they remain subjects of historical and political negotiation. What would change if museums loosened their sense of centrality and authority, and saw themselves as specific places of transit, intercultural boundaries, conflict and communication between different communities?

The task of an ethnographer, in the contemporary diasporic and postcolonial world of discrepant movements, conflicts and modernities, is to continue to be a cultural critic. Engaged in the operation of defamiliarising the reassuring places of normative knowledge, such as the museum, this involves examining the cracks, working incessantly in the margins (Clifford 2003, hooks 2020). The outcome is to render the boundaries porous, provoking change and opening up. This exposes the precariousness of (one's own) knowledge and promotes the critique of any stable interpretative authority, above all by voices previously unauthorised to speak.

It is here that artistic processes and procedures take place and acquire sense by giving body and visibility to those spectres that remain invisible in the museum. To return to know (re-cognise) the colonial roots of our identity and open up a new awareness means to question narratives that have become normative. It means to register the relational, intimate, affective, violent and appropriative structure of colonial relations in the past making the present. To navigate and negotiate this fluid and disquieting archive will mean both recognising what perhaps cannot be translated into a museum display, and preserving the power of the questioning that arrives from such an impossibility.

REFERENCES

Giorgio Agamben, *Nudità*, 2009

Jean-Loup Amselle, *Il museo in scena: L'alterità culturale e la sua rappresentazione negli spazi espositivi*, 2017

Benedict Anderson, *Imagined Communities: Reflections on the Origin and Spread of Nationalism*, 1983

Slmona Bodo, 'Requiem per il museo samaritano? Una provocazione', in Agenzia CULT https://www.agenziacult.it/notiziario/requiem-per-il-museo-samaritano-una-provocazione/ 3 January 2022 (accessed 21 April 2022)

Anna Chiara Cimoli, 'Prefazione', in Giulia Grechi, *Decolonizzare il museo: Mostrazioni, pratiche artistiche, sguardi incarnati*, 2021

Constance Classen and David Howes, 'The Museum as Sensescape: Western Sensibilities and Indigenous Artifacts', in *Sensible Objects: Colonialism, Museums and Material Culture*, eds. Elizabeth Edwards, Chris Gosden, and Ruth B. Philips, 2006

James Clifford, *The Predicament of Culture: Twentieth-Century Ethnography, Literature, and Art*, 1988

James Clifford, *Routes: Travel and Translation in the Late Twentieth Century*, 1997

James Clifford, *On the Edges of Anthropology*, 2003

Paul Connerton, *How Societies Remember*, 1989

Clémentine Deliss, *The Metabolic Museum*, 2020

John Foot, *La repubblica dei matti*, 2014

K. Gregos and V. Meessen, *Personne et les autres*, Catalogue of the Belgian Pavilion at the 56th Venice Biennial, 2015

Ramón Grosfoguel, *Rompere la colonialità: Razzismo, islamofobia, migrazioni nella prospettiva decoloniale*, 2017

Stuart Hall, 'Whose Heritage? Un-settling "The Heritage", Re-imaging the Post-nation', in *Third Text*, Vol 13, Issue 49, 1999

bell hooks, *Elogio del margine*, 2020

Marcel Mauss, *Le tecniche del corpo* (trans. and ed. Michela Fusaschi), 2017

Achille Mbembe, *Politiques de l'inimitié*, 2016

Wayne Modest, 'Introduction: Ethnographic Museums and the Double Bind', in *Matters of Belonging: Ethnographic Museums in a Changing Europe*, eds. Wayne Modest, Nicholas Thomas, Doris Prlić and Claufia Augustat, 2019

Sally Price, *Primitive Art in Civilized Places*, 1989

Laura Raicovich, *Culture Strike: Art and Museums in an Age of Protest*, 2021

Paul Ricoeur, *Ricordare, dimenticare, perdonare*, 2004

Michael Taussig, *My Cocaine Museum*, 2004

This booklet is published on the occasion of documenta
fifteen (Kassel), 18 June – 25 September 2022

Giulia Grechi was invited to write this essay as part
of the publication *Jimmie Durham & A Stick in the Forest
by the Side of the Road* with Jimmie Durham and Bev
Koski, Elisa Strinna, Hamza Badran, Iain Chambers,
Joen Vedel, Jone Kvie, Maria Thereza Alves, Wilma
Lukatsch, Giulia Grechi, Alessandra Marino Al-Mishlab
(ISBN 978-3-7533-0260-7, NUR 640)

Text: Giulia Grechi
Images: © Leone Contini, 2019
Editor: Iain Chambers
Proofreader: Nicola Gray
Design: Karoline Swiezynski, inspired by Will Holder's
design for *Past Imperfect* by Bik van der Pol, which
shaped the collective solution of this publication

Printed and bound in Belgium by Cassochrome with
supervision of ArtLibro Trudy Dorrepaal. Published
in an edition of 500 individual booklets (documenta
fifteen) to be collated in an edition of 1000 books
distributed by Verlag der Buchhandlung Walther und
Franz König, Köln. First published by Verlag der
Buchhandlung Walther und Franz König Ehrenstraße 4,
D-50672 Köln

Bibliographic information published by the Deutsche
Nationalbibliothek – The Deutsche Nationalbibliothek
lists this publication in the Deutsche National-
bibliografie; detailed bibliographic data is available
at http://dnb.d-nb.de.

*Jimmie Durham & A Stick in the Forest by the Side
of the Road* has been generously supported by
documenta fifteen.

This publication has been realized in
the framework of documenta fifteen,
June 18 – September 25, 2022

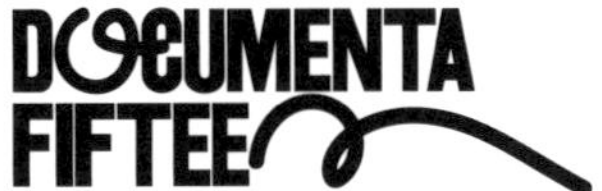

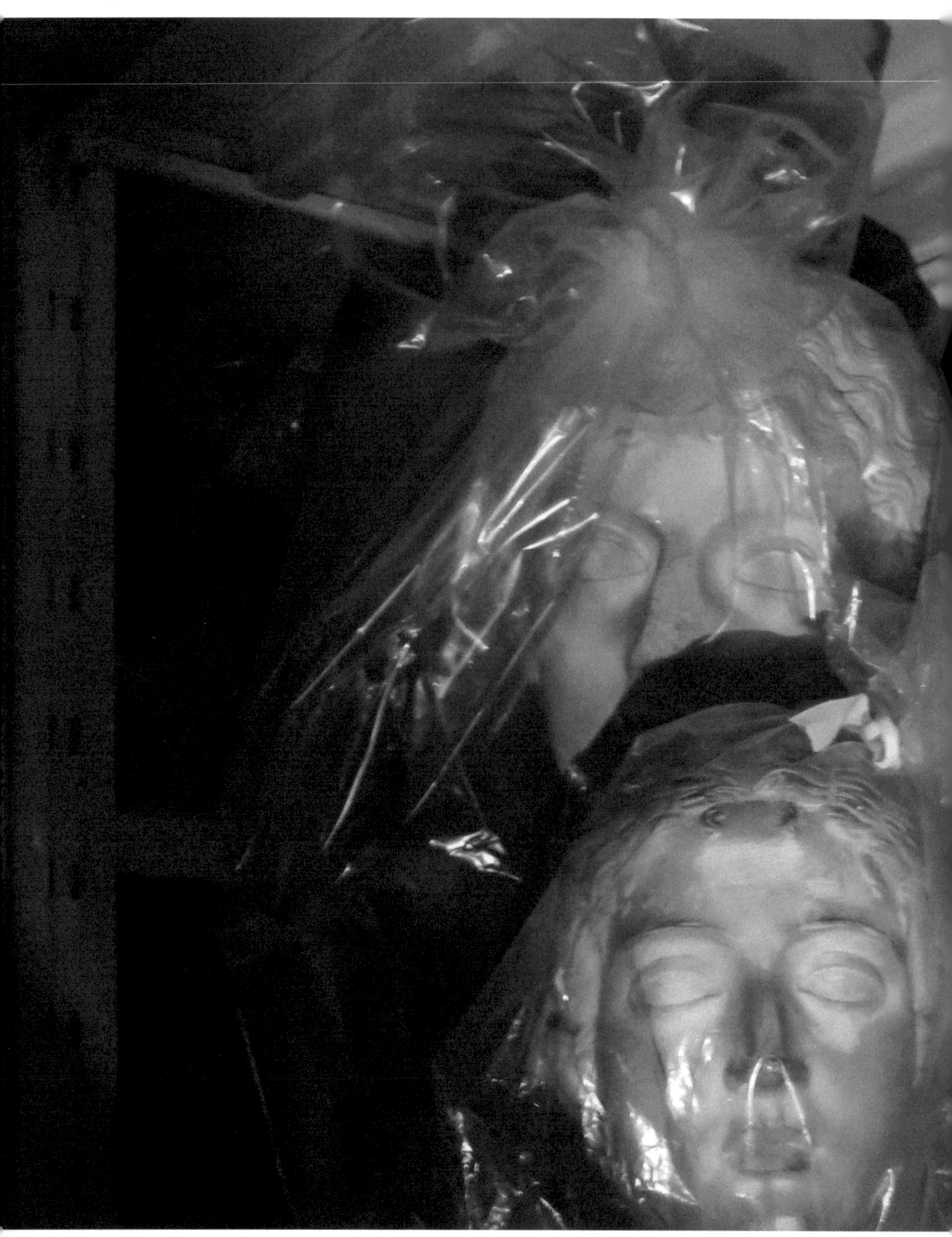

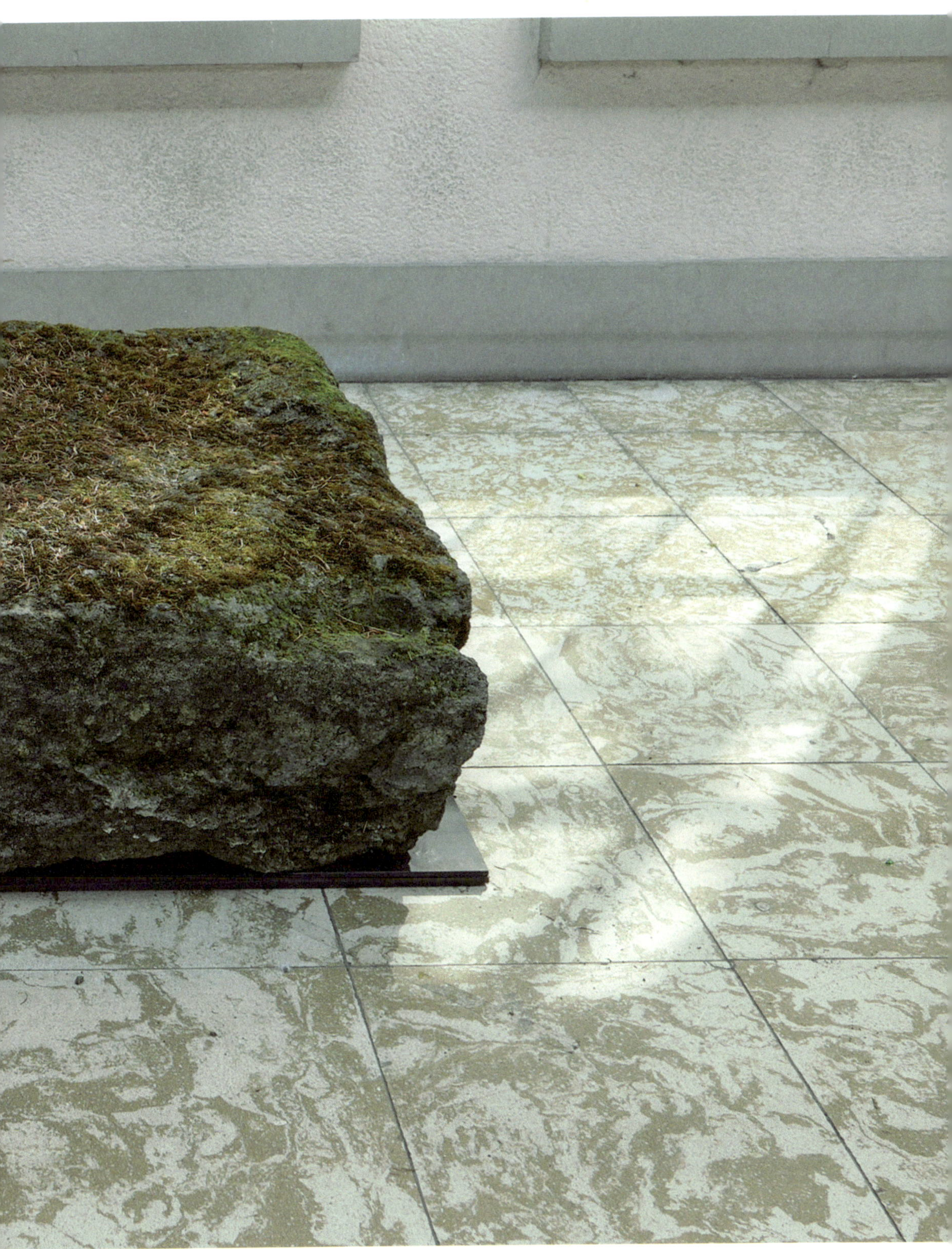

Jimmie Durham & A Stick in the Forest by the Side of the Road

Text by Milena Høgsberg

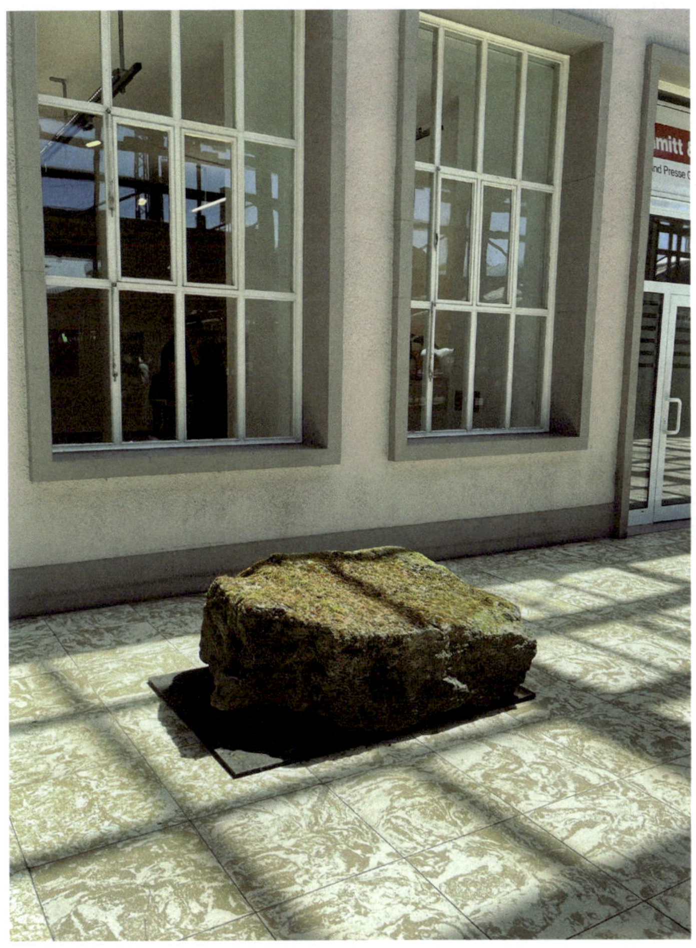

a

Learning from lichens on a rock and other collectives

It's 10 p.m. I look around to ensure no one is watching as I uncap my water bottle and pour water over the surface of a massive rock sitting inside Kassel Central train station. The Norwegian artist Jone Kvie has asked me to check in on the patches of lichens growing on top of this volcanic tuff rock that makes up his main contribution to documenta fifteen. Titled *Here Here VI* (2022), Kvie's work is part of a larger presentation by the nine artists that have formed the collective Jimmie Durham & A Stick in the Forest by the Side of the Road. Although the Documenta guides at the station have been

Text by Milena Høgsberg

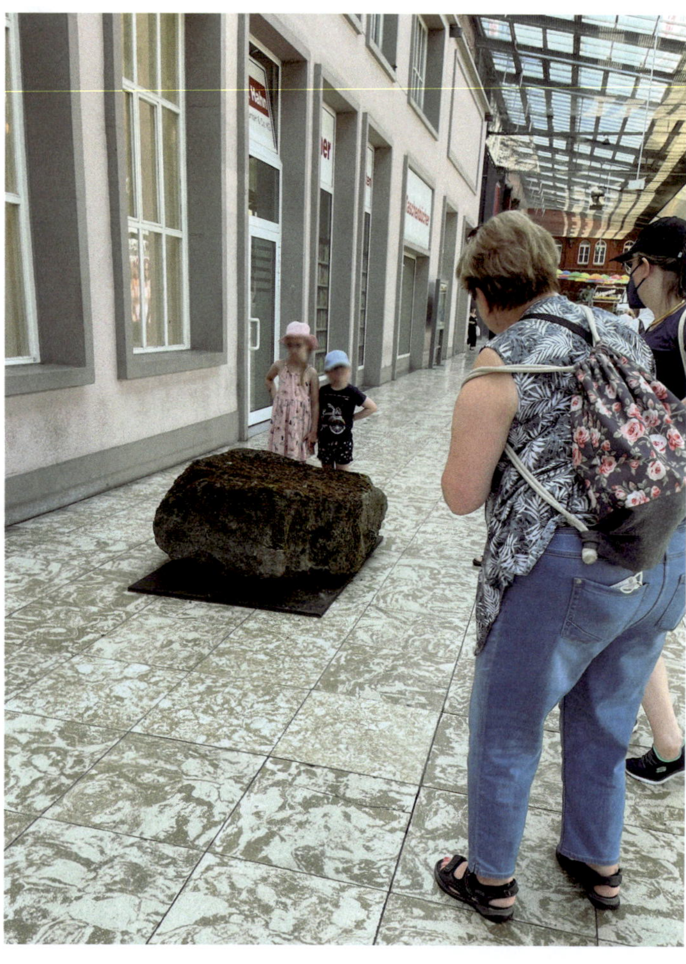

following the artist's instructions to spray the rock three times
a day, I find the vegetation on the top dry and lifeless. I return the
next day during opening hours only to find no improvement.
I wonder if the lichens have already died. For the past weeks, the
temperature in Kassel has been steadily around 27 degrees Celsius,
the sun burning through the glass roof, turning the *Bahnhof* into an
unventilated greenhouse. I strike up a conversation with the guides
in my broken German, pulling up a picture on my cellphone that Kvie
has texted me, showing the lichens green and animated, their
trumpet shapes perked up among the moss and pine needles that
cover the tuff's surface. Eager to help, the conscientious guides
agree that the watering regimen has to be adjusted. We share an
almost tender moment gathered around the rock, while the guide
who has gotten the dedicated water dispenser from the back

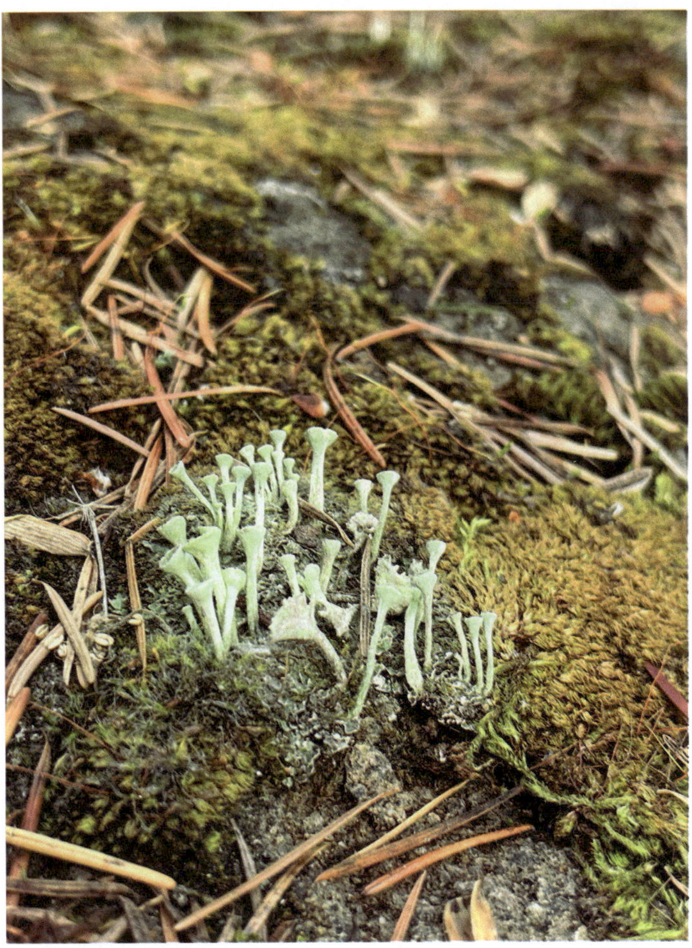

carefully hydrates the vegetation on the rock. It is silently understood that we are collectively caring, not just for a work of art and
the artist's intentions but for a natural entity that provides shelter
for other living life forms.

As I later learn, lichens are, among many wondrous things, very resil-
ient, capable of lying dormant for long periods in order to survive
far more extreme weather conditions than what they are experiencing here. The small patches on the volcanic rock are, in fact,
a sort of micro-ecosystem—a world within the world. Lichens are
not plants, but composite, multi-cellular organisms. They are
composed of algae, cyanobacteria, and fungi, which create
a symbiotic partnership, something more complex than what they
could have individually expressed. According to Wikipedia, there are

Text by Milena Høgsberg

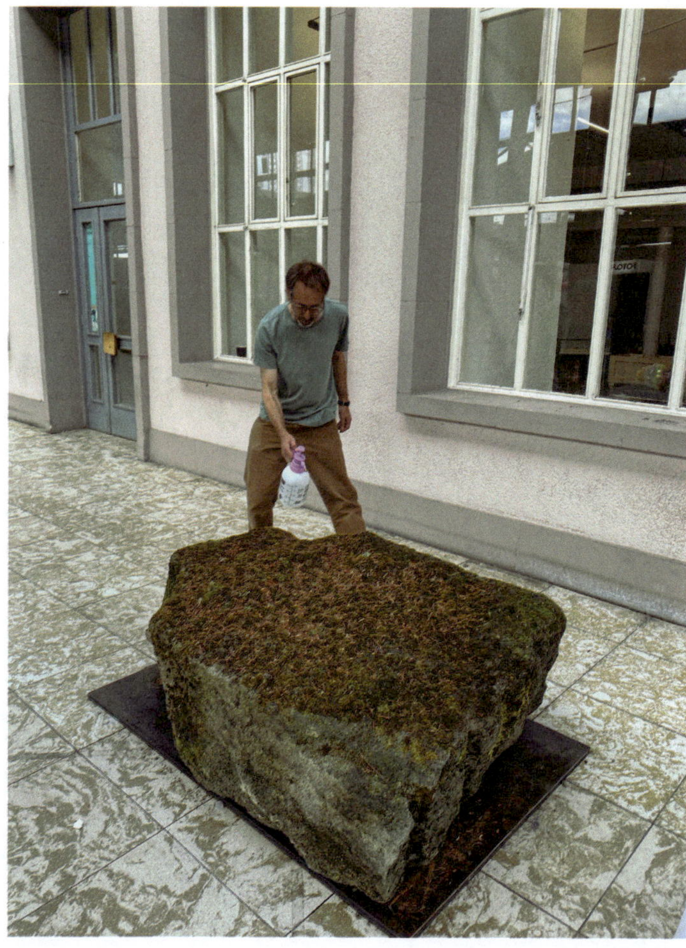

more than 13,000 species of lichen. They are self-sufficient and create their own nutrients. The relationships these organisms form are mutually beneficial, and the 'house' they build offers dwelling places to other life forms, opening up to yet another network of collaborations. As such, lichens seem to embody many of the core ideas of the collective, where individual practices give way to something beyond the individual. As Merlin Sheldrake writes in the chapter 'The intimacy of strangers', in his moving book, *Entangled Life: How Fungi Make Our Worlds, Change Our Minds and Shape Our Futures:*

> Lichens are places where an organism unravels into an ecosystem and where an ecosystem congeals into an organism. They flicker between 'wholes' and 'collections of

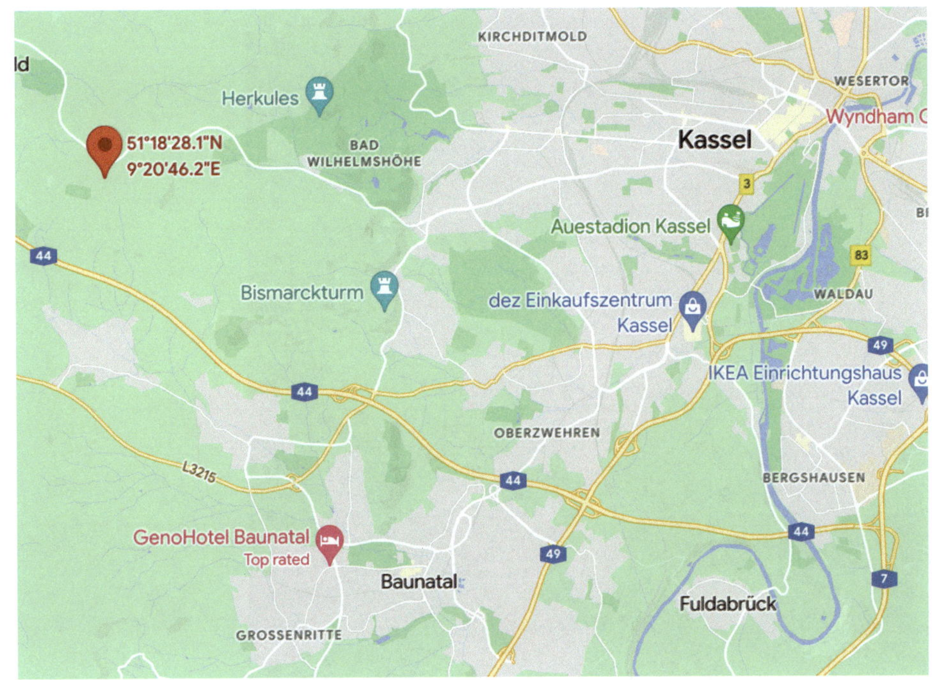

parts.' Shuttling between the two perspectives is a confusing experience. The word individual comes from the Latin meaning 'undividable.' Is the whole lichen the individual? Or are its constituent members, the parts, the individuals? Is this even the right question to ask? Lichens are a product less of their parts, than of the exchanges between those parts. Lichens are stabilized networks of relationships.

Like the parts joining to create lichens, the artist Jimmie Durham understood that an individual artistic practice could be enriched through sustained, mutually beneficial dialogues with other artists. Kvie's decision to exhibit the volcanic rock as found, without any intervention, and to borrow it from the local quarry rather than buy it, grew out of an attempt to stay connected to the spirit of

Text by Milena Høgsberg

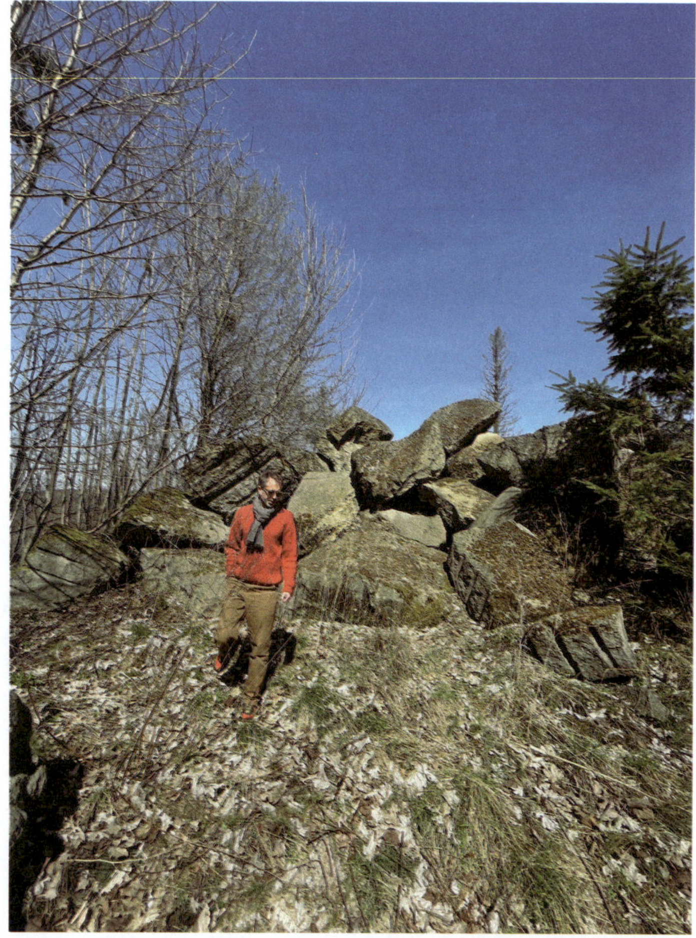

thoughts, conversations, and ideas he had shared with Durham over twenty years, and more recently with the eight artists who Durham had invited to form a collective before he fell ill. When Durham passed away in November 2021 at the age of 81, the group lost not only a treasured friend and fellow artist but also the connective tissue between individual members and extending to the wider network of ideas and conversations of documenta. For Kvie, bringing a large volcanic rock with live vegetation into a transit hub and inviting people to pause, touch, or rest on it, felt like an authentic response to the prompt first given by the Indonesian collective ruangrupa to Durham 'to bring what you do' to Kassel, an invitation he had then extended to his cohorts. The curatorial concept of Lumbung — a focus on the practices that give rise to artworks and the sharing of resources in the quest for collective

9

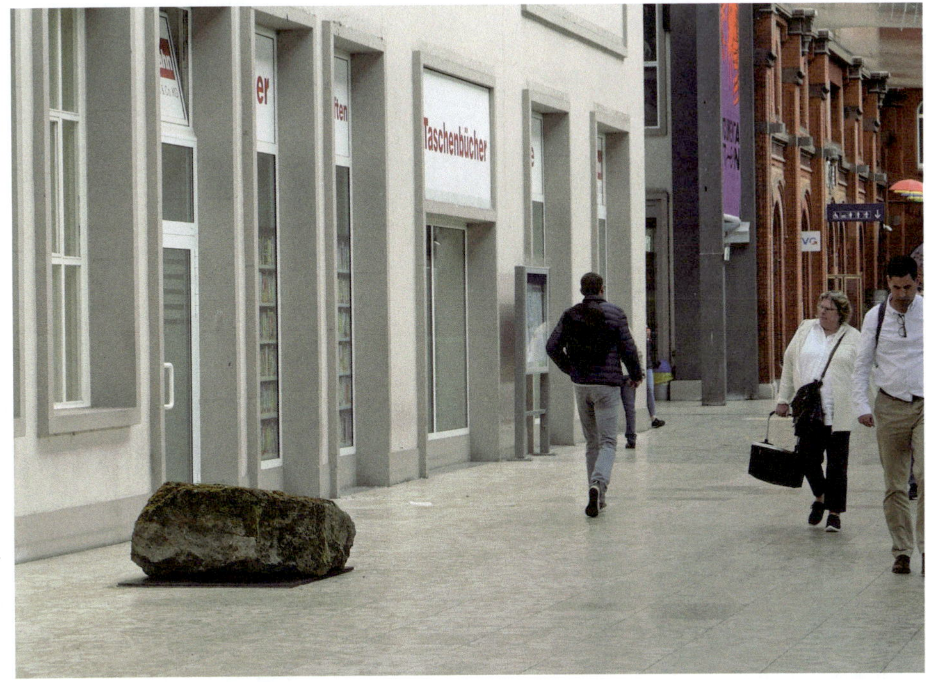

learning—seemed a natural extension of his and Durham's conversations over the years about sculptural making. Looking around the local quarry in Druseltal (which supplied the tuff, a porous and impractically erosive rock, used, for example, to build the Hercules Monument in Kassel), Kvie was particularly drawn to a pile of discarded rocks, deemed unworthy of use as building material. As the rock was placed at the station, he surrendered to the fact that there was nothing he could meaningfully add; the rock was perfectly capable of gesturing to a world that extends beyond human perception.

The use of a found natural object is not new to Kvie. For the past decade, he has been making sculptural works that include found natural materials, often paired with a cast or fabricated element, as

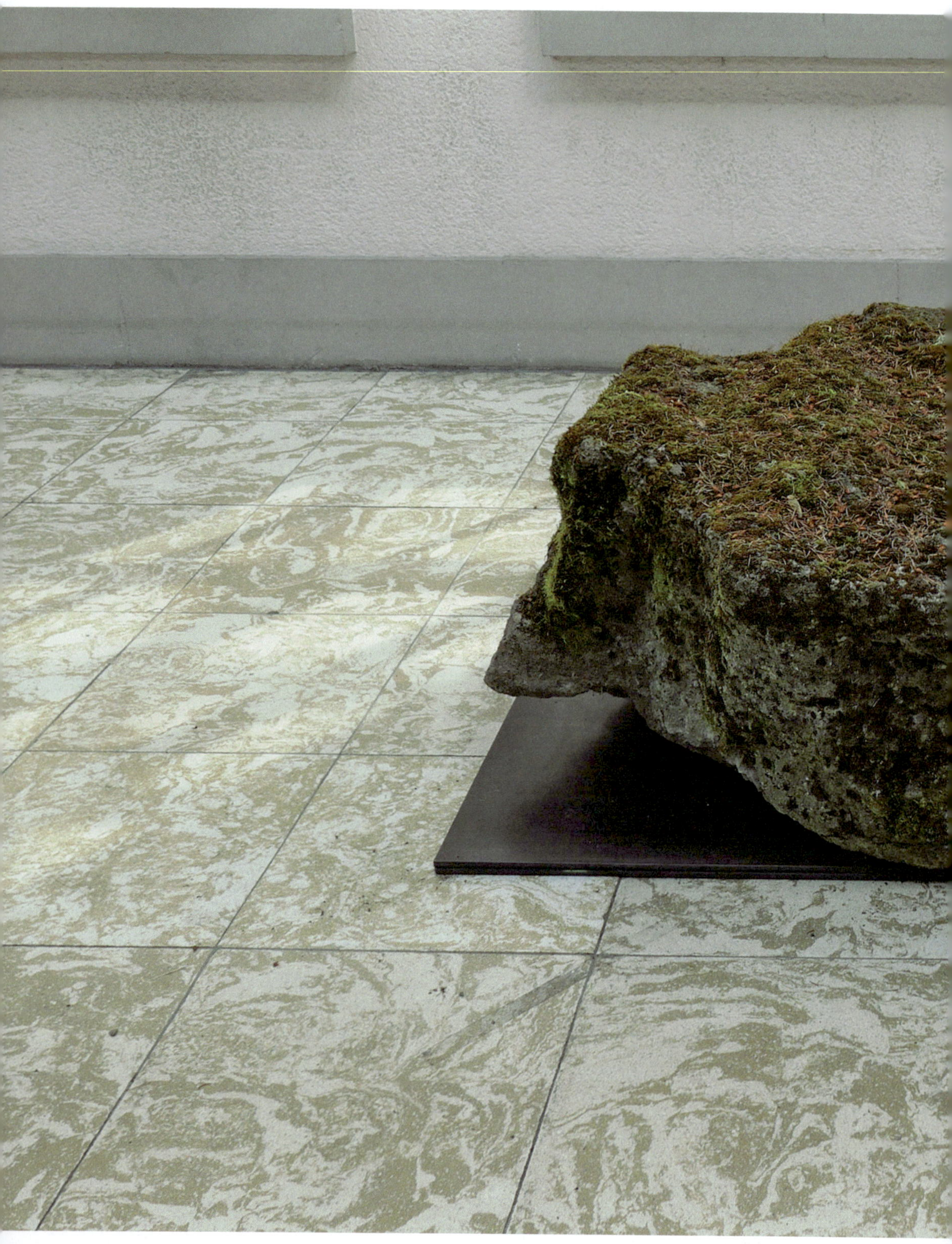

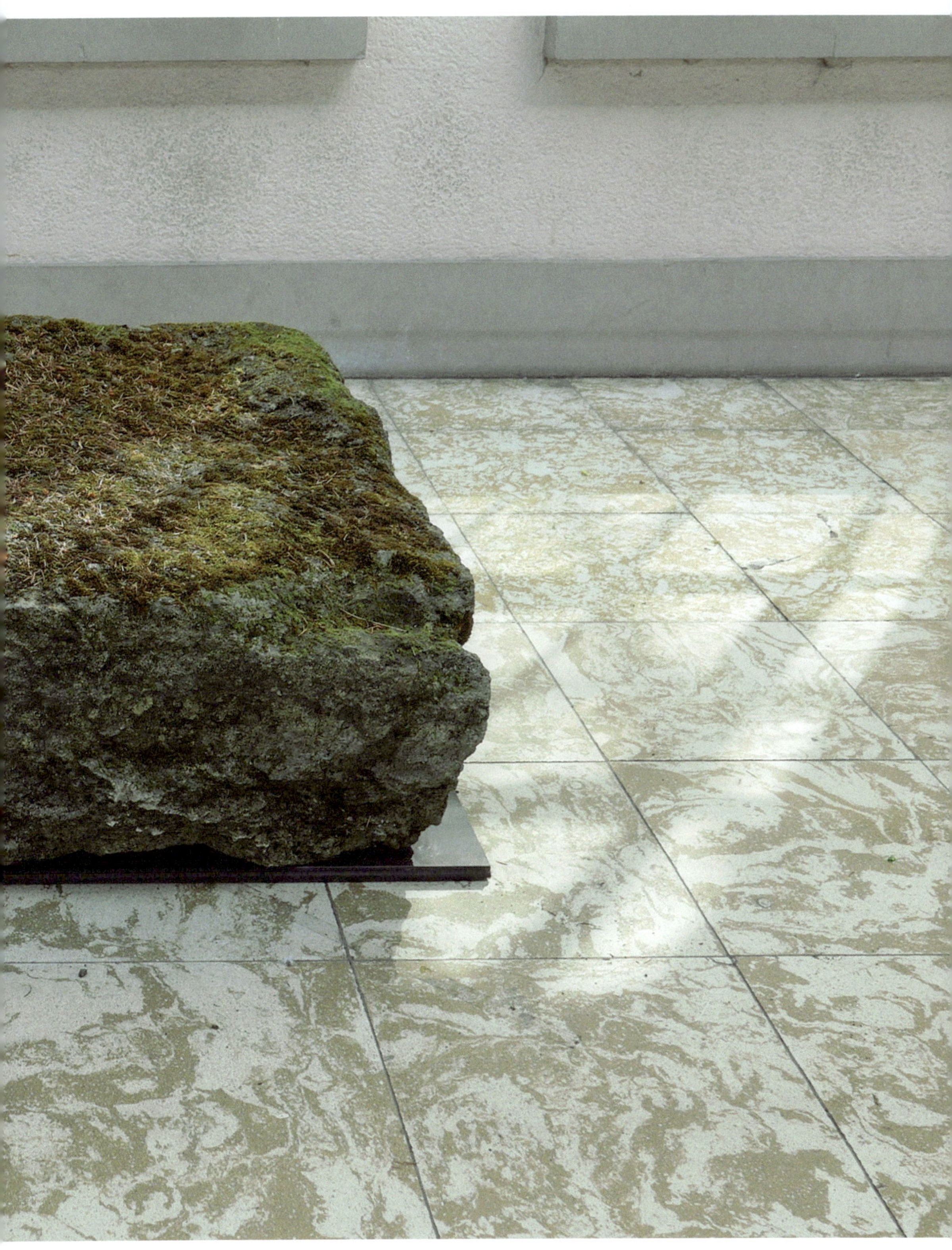

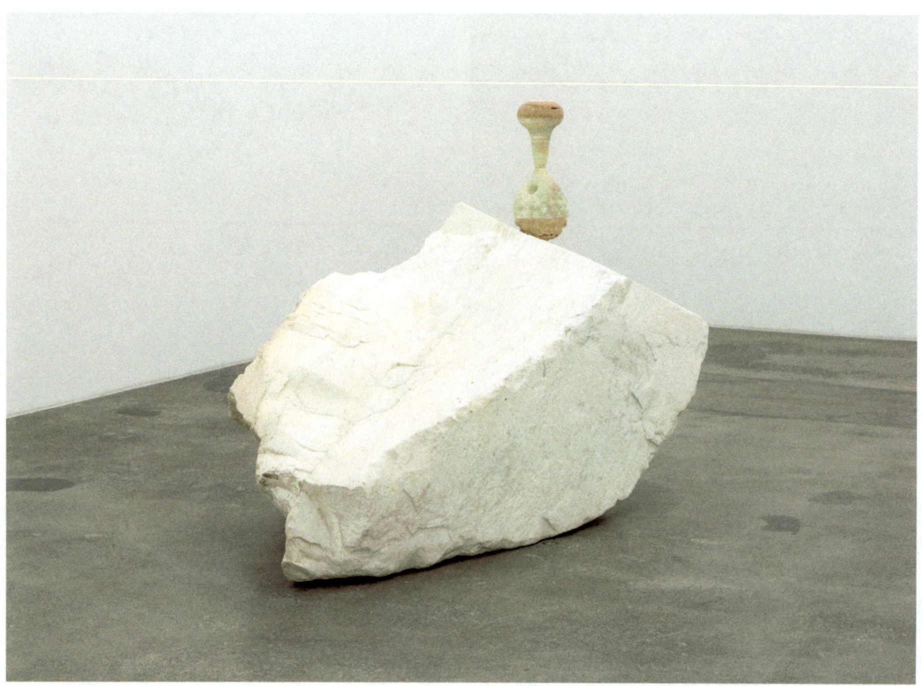

See Magnus af Petersens,
'Jone Kvie: A Glossary' in
Jone Kvie: Here Here,
Stavanger Kunstmuseum/
MUST 2019

1

in *what comes after certainty* (2020). The careful contemplation
and deliberation of objects over time is at the core of his sculptural
practice. In recent years, his work has settled into its own, arriving
at a quiet and subtle complexity derived from an intuitive balancing
of materials, or as his friend Jimmie Durham put it, a 'way of being
intelligent with the things around you.' In Kvie's recent body of
work, it is clear that he has honed a practice where looking,
thinking, making, and situating merge, and the final work allows
both natural and fabricated to be experienced in new ways by an
unhurried viewer. The artist's works are the result of a sustained
engagement with materials on multiple levels—physical, chemical,
and temporal.[1] Kvie has a deep regard for materials, from the basalt,
formed and shaped by volcanic eruptions that gesture to geolog-
ical time, to human makeshift objects, created as temporary

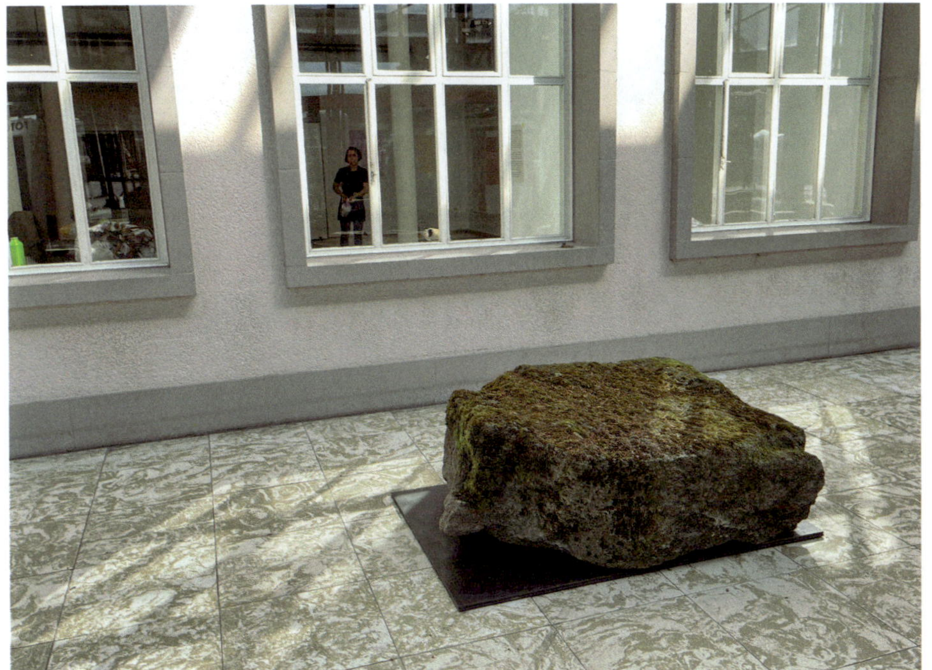

solutions with a limited life span. He practices with an awareness
that all materials have relations to other materials and continuously
interact with and change each other, and with our bodies as we
inhale their particles, forming new relationships. Jimmie Durham
understood and respected this about him. Kvie's humble approach
was one of the traits Durham highlighted to me when the three of
us met in January 2021 to discuss Kvies' practice. Although joining
us from Berlin by screen, Durham's presence and his deep regard
for Jone's being and practice was palpable as he unfolded his
appreciation in a poetic comment:

> There are very many sounds in the world, all sorts of sounds,
> and there are very many human voices in the world, and there
> is very much language in the world, and there are very many

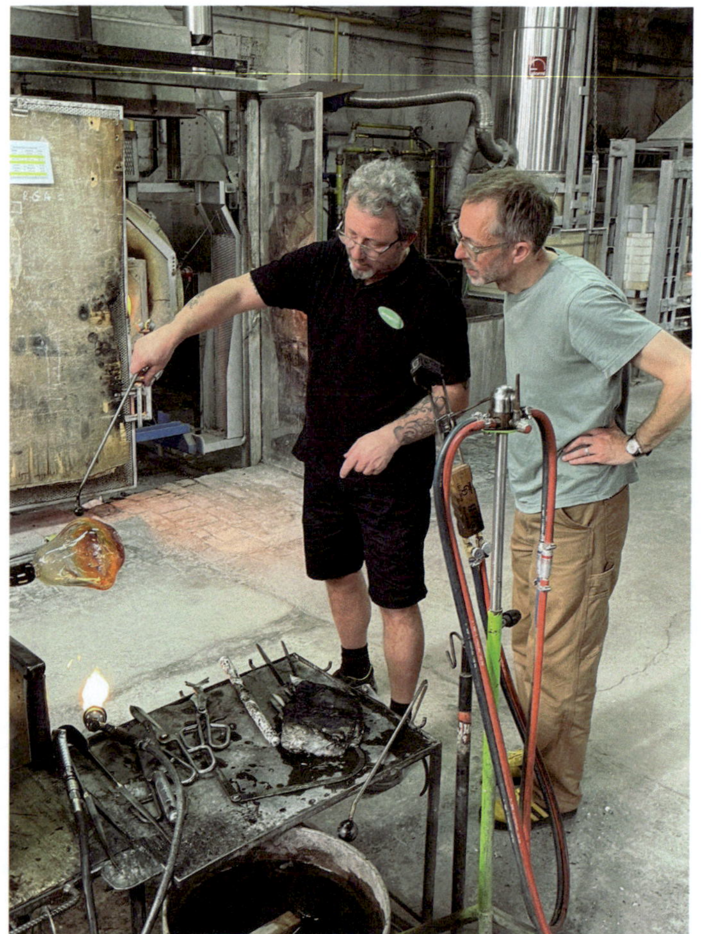

Jone Kvie in conversation with
Milena Høgsberg and Jimmie Durham,
Nils Stærk Gallery, Copenhagen,
January 2021 https://nilsstaerk.dk/
videos/jone-kvie/667-jone-kvie-
in-conversation-with-milena-
hogsberg-jimmie-durham
2

> words in the world. So for any of us to think to add more
> words in the world… we have to be careful. I never am, but
> Jone always is careful. He doesn't say very much, and he
> never says it very loud, and he never says it very adamantly or
> forcefully, but *if* he didn't say it, we would be sorry… I feel,
> Milena, that it's better if you talk in the world, and I feel
> it's better if Jone talks in the world. For us, making sculpture
> in the world is like that.[2]

For Kvie, every work he produces is made with an underlying awareness of the implications of adding an artwork to a world already
filled with things and matter; what justifies the presence of a work
is that it carefully contends with our relationship to the material
world, including the many aspects that we still understand too

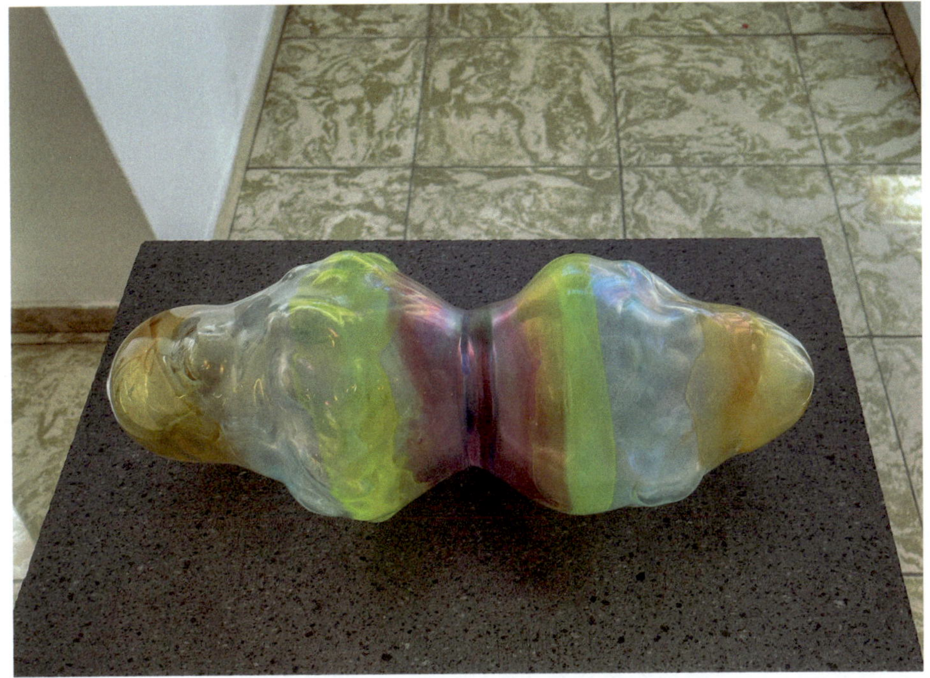

little. This is also why a part of his sculptural work remains devoted to the contemplation of the mysterious structures of the universe and our place in it through the means available to him. Inside the exhibition space at documenta showing works by other members of the collective, Kvie has placed a colorful glass sculpture on a metal pedestal. Titled *A Moment of Clarity* (2022), the work is inspired by photographs of nebulae—giant explosions of interstellar gasses— captured by the Hubble Space Telescope. The work was made in collaboration with an experienced glass blower, who translated the artist's sketch and instructions into a physical object. As with Kvie's previous works that grapple with cosmic phenomena, *A Moment of Clarity* aims to hold a space both for the human longing to understand and the absurdity of trying to materialize a phenomenon that precludes the possibility of direct experience.

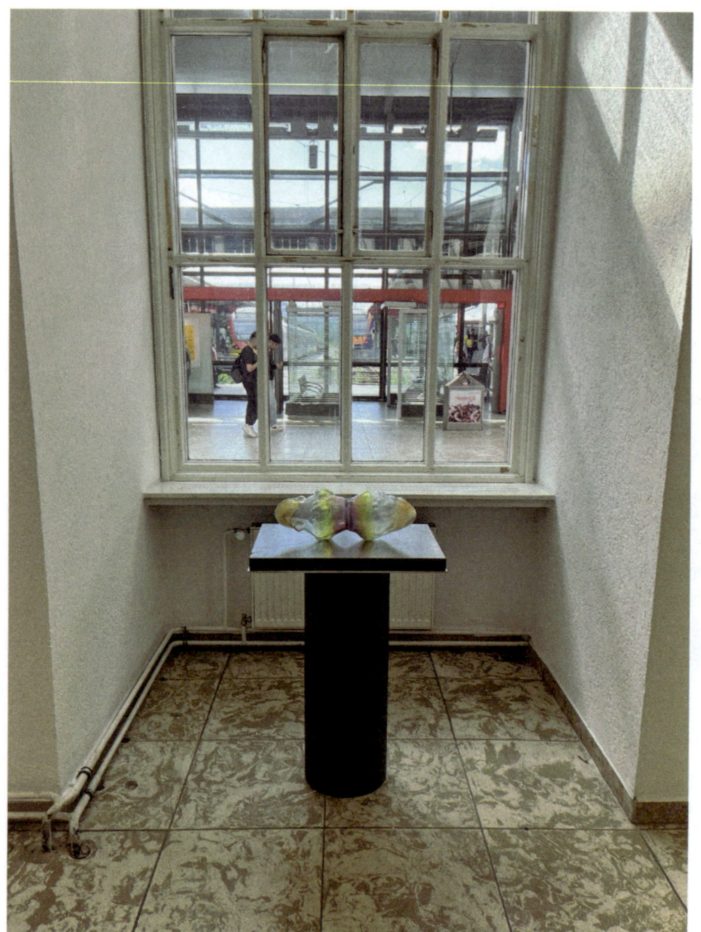

m

Webb, an international program
led by NASA with its partners,
ESA (European Space Agency)
and CSA (Canadian Space Agency)
have published images here:
https://www.nasa.gov/image-
feature/goddard/2022/nasa-
s-webb-reveals-cosmic-cliffs-
glittering- landscape-of-star-birth
3

As I am writing this, the first detailed images of nebulae taken with
Hubble's successor, the James Webb Space Telescope, have been
released by NASA, a humbling reminder that human life is such
a small, small component of the bigger picture.[3]

As I circle back to the rock after viewing the other works by Jimmie
Durham & A Stick in the Forest by the Side of the Road, I am moved
to discover that the lichens have perked up again, their delicate
green color and dusty cups elevating above the rock surface in all
their natural elegance. Just like lichens, collectives challenge us to
go beyond the limitations of individuality and the perspectives we
impose onto the world. They also operate with an awareness that

n

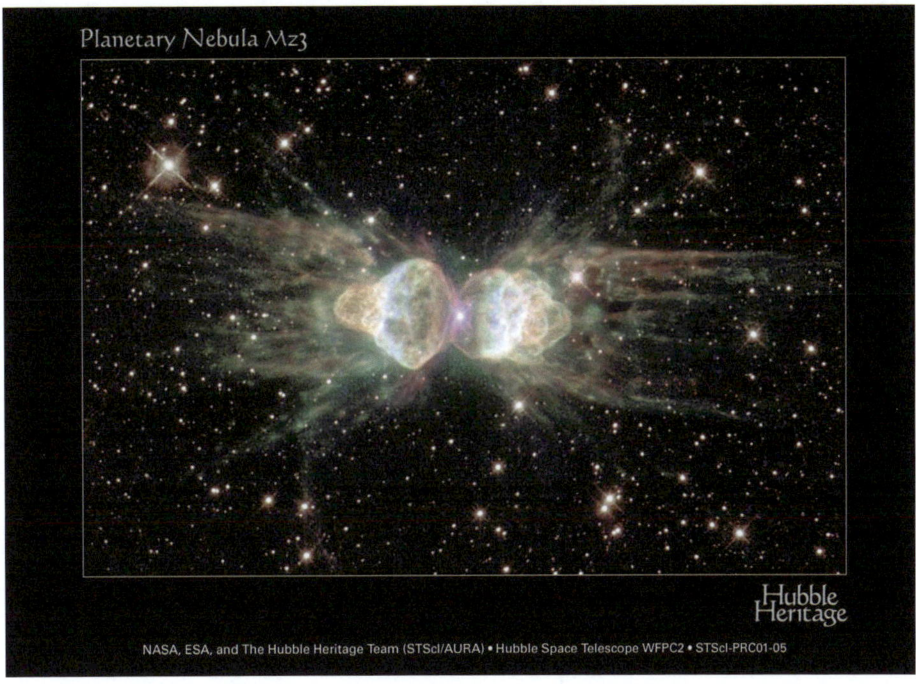

we are part of larger networks and continuously engage in interactions that shape and change us and which extend to more-than-human worlds.

Situated in a space where people are constantly in transit, leaving, arriving, or waiting to go elsewhere, passers-by might only discover the rock as a physical entity, while the ubiquitous complex networks unfolding on its surface might well go unnoticed. Yet, the microbes and fungi that make up part of the lichens exist in everything. The human body and the surrounding world are made up of millions of organisms that work together, and human life would not exist without the collaboration of these friends, working behind the scenes.

Text by Milena Høgsberg

Images

a   *Here, here VI* (2022). Volcanic Tuff-rock, lichens, moss,
pine needles. Appr. 50×120×100 cm

b   From the opening of documenta fifteen, at the KAZ-venue, Kassel
Hauptbahnhof, June 2022

c   Some of the lichens growing on the surface of the rock

d   Jone Kvie watering the moss and lichens
(Photo: Maria Thereza Alves)

e   The site in Kassel, where the rock was found
(Photo: Johannes Choe)

f   Kvie looking at discarded tuff-stone, Druseltal, Kassel
(Photo: Johannes Choe)

g   Installation view, Kassel Hauptbahnhof

h/cover   *Here, here VI* (2022). Volcanic Tuff-rock, lichens, moss, pine needles.
Appr. 50×120×100 cm

i   *what comes after certainty* (2020). Marble and Onyx. 114×185×90
cm (Photo: Malle Madsen)

j   Installation view, Kassel Hauptbahnhof

k   Glassblower Andrea Salvagno and Jone Kvie working on *A Moment of
Clarity* at Berengo Studio, Murano, April 2022 (Photo:
Linus Bonduelle)

l   *A Moment of Clarity.* Handblown glass, volcanic stone, aluminum,
iron. 110×43×63 cm

m   *A Moment of Clarity,* installation view at KAZ, Kassel Kauptbahnhof.

n   Planetary Nebula MZ3, the so called Ant Nebula. Image by the Hubble
Telescope, 2008. (Photo: Nasa)

References

Magnus af Petersens, 'Jone Kvie: A Glossary' in
Jone Kvie: Here Here, 2019

Merlin Sheldrake, *Entangled Life: How Fungi Make Our Worlds, Change Our Minds,
and Shape Our Futures*, Penguin Audio edition, 2020.

This booklet is published on the occasion of documenta
fifteen (Kassel), 18 June – 25 September 2022

It is part of the publication *Jimmie Durham & A Stick
in the Forest by the Side of the Road* with Jimmie Durham
and Bev Koski, Elisa Strinna, Hamza Badran, Iain
Chambers, Joen Vedel, Jone Kvie, Maria Thereza Alves,
Wilma Lukatsch, Giulia Grechi, Alessandra Marino
Al-Mishlab (ISBN 978-3-7533-0260-7, NUR 640)

© 2022 Jone Kvie and Verlag der Buchhandlung
Walther und Franz König, Köln

Text: Milena Høegsberg
Images: © Jone Kvie and BONO, Norway
Editor: Iain Chambers
Proofreader: Nicola Grey, Bryne McLaughlin
Design: Karoline Swiezynski, inspired by Will Holder's
design for *Past Imperfect* by Bik van der Pol, which
shaped the collective solution of this publication

Courtesy: Works courtesy of NILS STÆRK
(Copenhagen), Elastic Gallery (Stockholm), OSL
Contemporary (Oslo) and Galleri Opdahl (Stavanger).

Printed and bound in Belgium by Cassochrome with
supervision of ArtLibro Trudy Dorrepaal. Published
in an edition of 250 individual booklets (documenta
fifteen) to be collated in an edition of 1000 books
distributed by Verlag der Buchhandlung Walther und
Franz König, Köln. First published by Verlag der
Buchhandlung Walther und Franz König Ehrenstraße 4,
D-50672 Köln.

Bibliographic information published by the Deutsche
Nationalbibliothek – The Deutsche Nationalbibliothek
lists this publication in the Deutsche National-
bibliografie; detailed bibliographic data is available
at http://dnb.d-nb.de.

Disclaimer: In making *Jimmie Durham & A Stick in the
Forest by the Side of the Road* we have quotes, images
and texts taken from various resources. Information
concerning the original authors and sources have been
credited as detailed as possible. Despite these efforts,
some sources nevertheless could not be identified.
Please contact the author in case of questions
or objections. The ideas and opinions author unless
stated otherwise.

Jone Kvie's two projects for documenta fifteen were
produced with the generous support of Arts Council
Norway and Office for Contemporary Art, Norway.

*Jimmie Durham & A Stick in the Forest by the Side
of the Road* has been generously supported by
documenta fifteen.

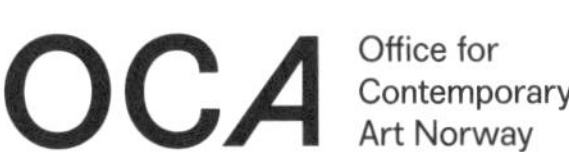

This publication has been realized in
the framework of documenta fifteen,
June 18 – September 25, 2022

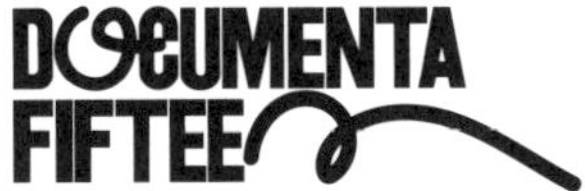

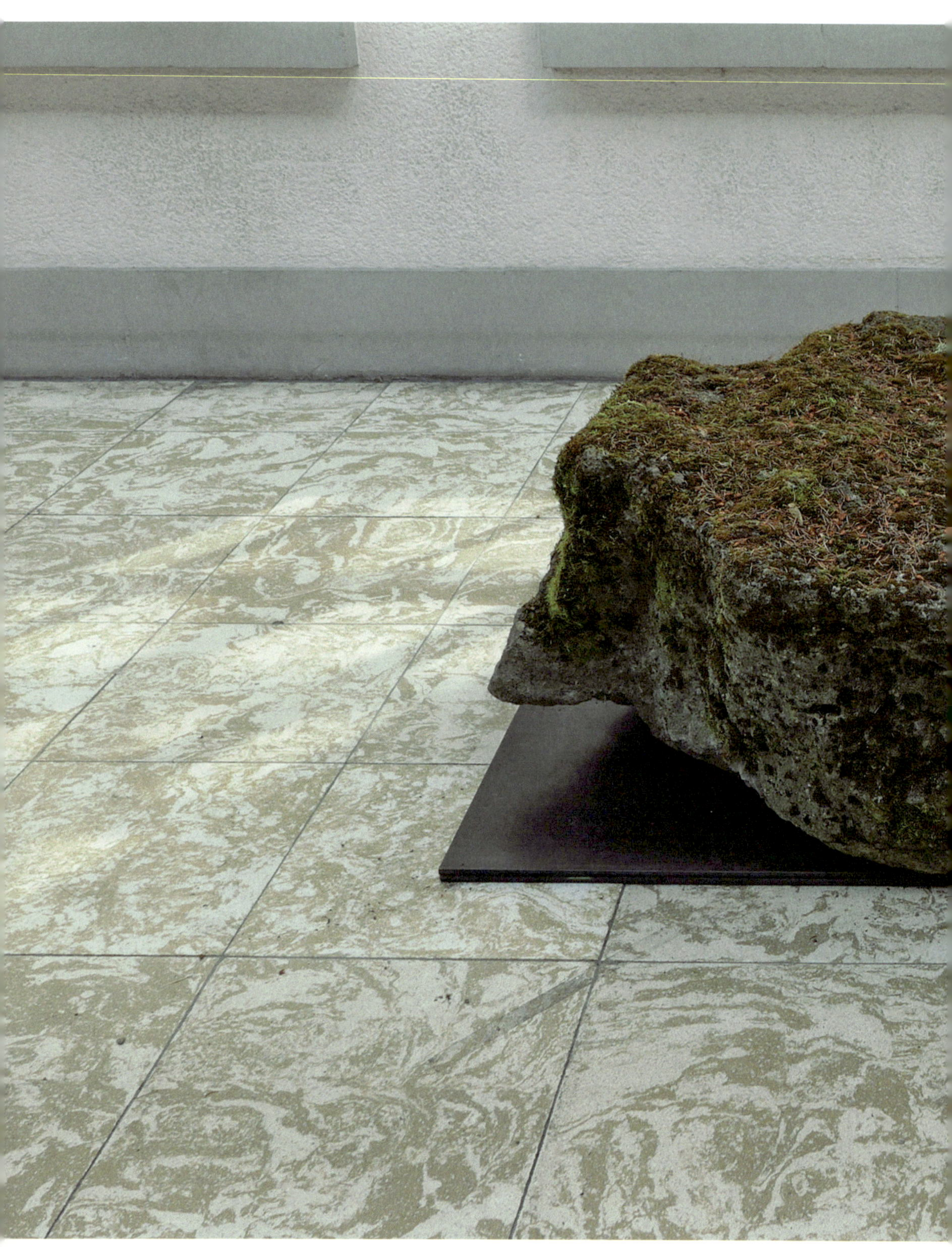

published 15 September 2022

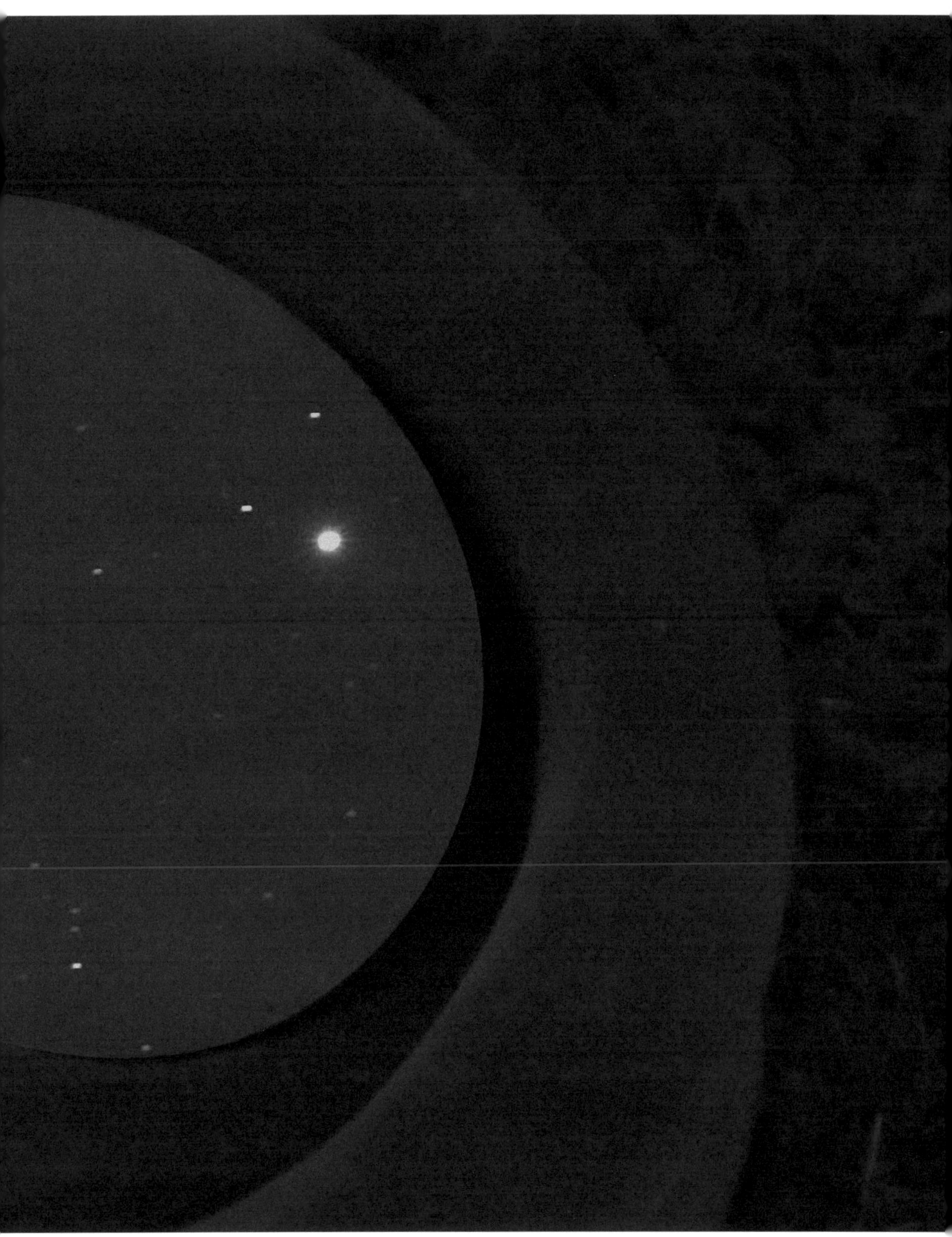

Jimmie Durham & A Stick in the Forest by the Side of the Road

Astroenvironmentalist constellations. Beyond (b)ordering ecologies

Astroenvironmentalist constellations. Beyond (b)ordering ecologies

Just as none of us is outside or beyond geography, none of us is completely free from the struggle over geography. That struggle ... is not only about soldiers and cannons but also about ideas, about form, about images and imaginings.

Edward Said

Cosmic ecologies

In her essay 'The interstellar voyage' in the edited collection *Future Feminisms* (2019), Lidia Curti quotes Nolan philosopher Giordano Bruno and African American science fiction writer Octavia Butler side-by-side to talk about the multiplicities that make up and continuously change the world. In an unlikely pairing, Bruno and Butler are brought closer to each other by their rebellions against the power of authorities and by their capacity to transcend their own space-time to seek new knowledge, and investigate life in its cosmic dwelling. Bruno postulated the existence of an infinity of worlds in the cosmos, each star bursting with its own life forms. Butler registered the interconnections between different domains—the multiple tangles that make up life. In her *Parable of the Sower*, we read: "Seed to tree, tree to forest; Rain to river, river to sea; Grubs to bees, bees to swarm. From one, many; from many, one; Forever uniting, growing, dissolving—forever

Changing" (Butler 2019, 315). Both Bruno and Butler refer to the actions that connect the very small, as seeds, to the very big—the planet, creating self-sustaining ecological networks.

Ecology, for philosopher Isabelle Stengers, is a word for tangles. The seed and the tree, the rivers and the seas are not simply connected by temporal relations that transform one into the other. Plants and water, flowers and pollinators are entangled in a web of multiple associations that enable life. As a science, ecology registers these multiplicities, traces dependencies and modes of co-operation. It observes the laws that underpin these connections, such as the law of symbiosis (Stengers 2010, 33). Lynn Margulis's microbiology talks about symbiosis as "inter-living", or a mode of creating alliances among differing life forms (Margulis 1998, 106–7). At the microscopic level, Margulis coined the term 'symbiogenesis' to address the role of symbiosis in evolution: mitochondria are the trace of the merging of two bacteria into a single cell that determines the partnership at the basis of multicellular forms of life. Too often, these relationships of co-operation are thought of as simply confined to Earth. Beyond the critters living in proximity in earthly environments, symbiogenesis is also a function of cosmic relations. Relations among different celestial bodies are crucial to the emergence and survival of life on Earth: "symbiogenesis was the moon that pulled the tide of life from its oceanic depths to dry land and up into the air" (Margulis 1998, 111). The biological dependency of Earth on other planetary bodies in the solar system enables planetary survival. The Moon's tides and the Sun's light are central to sustaining life on Earth, with their microbial exchanges and chemical connections.

The emergence of an environmentalist approach to outer space needs to account for and stay with the trouble of this interdependence. Astroenvironmentalism sees ecological relations as a cosmic matter. Not only celestial dynamics, but forms of pollution, whether space debris or biological contamination, join Earth and space into the same fold. Tending to how humans relate to space, and attempting to move away from the utilitarianism that has commodified environments and their complex webs of life, requires a new imagination. It is no surprise that imaginaries of off-Earth geographies, displayed in arguments about space use for resource extraction and settlements, seem to repropose old colonial tropes such as discourses about *terra nullius*—territories that call for new forms of occupation. However, the same imaginaries also underpin environmentalist arguments, wrapping conservationist proposals in colonial resource and wilderness thinking. In this frame, Earth is thought of as limited and self-enclosed, as if the thin layer of the atmosphere was a border that neatly divides the blue oasis of our planet from the uninhabited void of space, scattered with barren rocks. Here, I focus on how this imaginary can be a barrier to a more just relationship with our place of cosmic dwelling.

Entrepreneurs of the New Space Age have explicitly embraced the aspiration of creating a multi-planetary civilisation. The promise of expansion towards new lands is supported by the assumption that space is a vast, untapped resource. The desertic landscape of Mars, for example, can be disciplined and rendered into productive land for future human colonies. In a video by the Italian collective locose, *Pointing at a New Planet* (2020), this promise of expansion is embodied in Elon Musk's travelling pointer finger, which is superimposed upon the red Martian landscape. A 3D-model of Musk's severed hand is seen increasingly pointing forward, towards more distant lands, while his most famous statements and tweets become the lyrics of a karaoke song that makes up the video's soundtrack. A musical karaoke brings to the fore the paradox of current discourses on space travel and colonisation: they predicate the necessity for humans to expand into outer space because of the destruction they have created on their own planet. The soundtrack captures the urgency to 'become a spacefaring, multi-planet civilisation', while the visual field is filled with the barren landscape, there to be colonised.

In the New Space Age, the possibility of salvation from the environmental catastrophe fuels fantasies of space colonisation. However, a deeper reckoning is needed to untangle the relationship between colonial enterprises, modes of environmental exploitation and the current state of earthly crisis. The environmentalist argument that 'there is no planet B' has been co-opted by space entrepreneurs to promote these exit fantasies. The invitation to cherish the special status of Earth in the solar system, as the only planet known to us as harbouring life, has given rise to unexpected proposals. Amazon founder Jeff Bezos has famously suggested that with humans living in space, maybe in pods in orbit, Earth could finally be preserved and become the equivalent of a big national park. This proposal completely overlooks how humans are enmeshed within ecological relations of interdependence that sustain the very life on Earth that is worth preserving. However, the proposal of creating parks in the solar system is far from incidental or isolated. Advocacy organisations like For all Moonkind have vowed to create parks or delimited zones to protect human heritage in space, starting with safe-guarding those landing sites on the Moon that have come to populate cultural imaginaries of space. Parks or heritage sites need to be encircled and defined as areas of specific and scientific interest.

Parks call for acts of enclosure that can transform waste-lands into settlements, into well-maintained or 'useful' spaces. Space environments are thus co-opted within geographies defined by binary oppositions and acts of border creation that separate opposites: wastelands/ resources; core/frontiers; centre/peripheries. These bina-ries are engrained within a colonial cartographic mindset and reinforce anthropocentric and Eurocentric views of what constitutes environments worth protecting. Such images are ubiquitous: they populate the scientific litera-ture on space, the culture of space industry settings, and the law. The *Treaty on Principles Governing the Activities of States in the Exploration and Use of Outer Space, including the Moon and Other Celestial Bodies* (also called the Outer Space Treaty, or OST) from 1969 remains the main governance mechanism of space law. Its language is part of this cultural repertoire that consolidates a spatial division between a centre and its others. According to Article I, "the exploration and use of outer space shall be carried out for the benefit and in the interests of all countries and shall be the province of all mankind" (United

Nations 2002). If activities in space are cast as 'the province of mankind', space becomes a 'province'—or an expansion—when it is occupied and used.

Giuditta Vendrame's art installation produced for the CCA Fellowship Program Exhibition in Kitakyushu (Japan) in 2018 takes its cue from the OST and is named *The province of all mankind*. The installation, made of modular concrete blocks, places vertical towers reminiscent of rockets and other space objects in the otherwise empty space of a museum room. The blocks are erected and point to the sky, as in a show of phallic power. The artist's commentary says:

> Erecting, mining, colonising, settling are all recurring verbs. They connect outer space to the same muscular principles of exploitation we have perpetuated on Earth throughout centuries of predominantly white colonial power.[1]

In creating the space as a province, value is cast upon earthly cores. From the active centre, drawing new borders defines territories to colonise, and lines of control create peripheries or wilderness.

1 See http://giudittavendrame.net/The-province-of-all-mankind

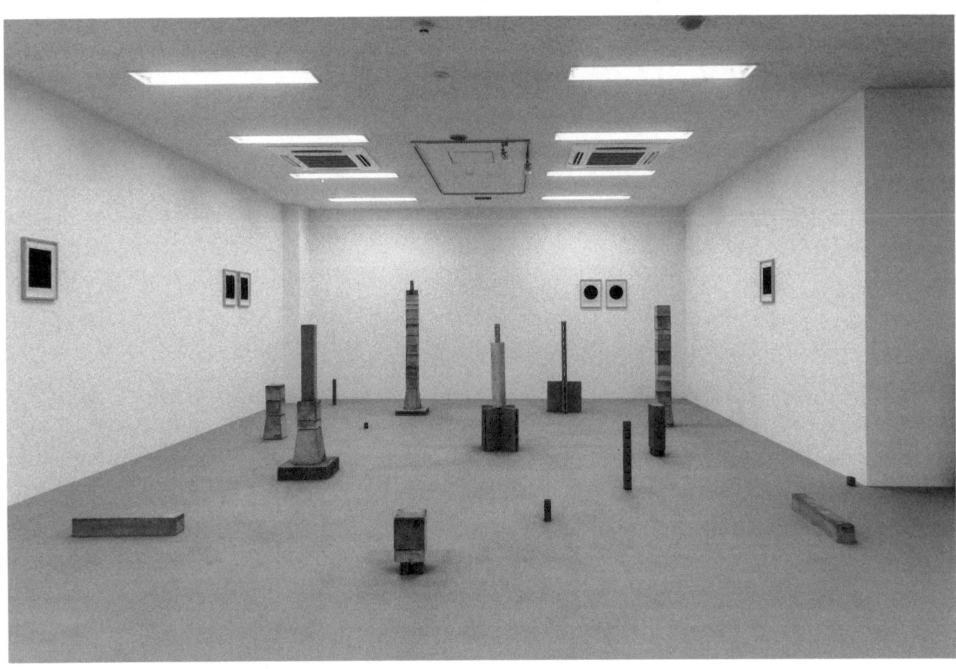

Giuditta Vendrame, *The province of all mankind*, 2018, Installation view at CCA Fellowship Program Exhibition, © Giuditta Vendrame CCA Kitakyushu

Bordering wilderness

The line that draws new borders is an ordering device that attempts to tame and classify the diversity of outer space environments. Colonial imaginaries are tools of territorial control: (b)ordering expresses the possibility of environmental governance in outer space to become a harmful extension of earthly politics. Borders divide the core from the rest. If spaceship Earth is the core and the atmosphere a border, all that lies beyond that limit is often cast as homogenously untamed wilderness.

The wilderness analogy has been endorsed and heavily used in space ethics since the 1980s, when Eugene Hargrove published the pioneering collection of essays *Beyond Spaceship Earth* (1986). In the book, most of the essays in the section on environmental ethics refer to space as wilderness. More recently, this image has resurfaced as an alternative to the reliance upon the frontier metaphor in the space sector. In creating an imaginary for astroenvironmentalist thought, NASA consultant Linda Billings resorted to wilderness as an alternative to the metaphor of the 'last frontier'. She suggested that the more apparent colonial connotations of the frontier metaphor in the settler history of the United States could be displaced by endorsing wilderness as a description of space:

> Treating the solar system like a wilderness to protect rather than a frontier to exploit could keep nuclear weapons, nuclear power, humanmade debris, and environmental hazards out of space and prohibit private and sovereign property claims. The point... would be to avoid making the same mistakes in space as we have on earth. (Billings 2006, 434)

Spatial thinking has a performative power. Here the promise implicit in the exchange of frontiers with wilderness seems to be not repeating mistakes made on Earth. Unfortunately, however, the environmental discourse of protecting wilderness has also been historically coterminous with colonial exploitation, the expropriation of lands, and genocide.

The concept of wilderness is nothing inherently benign (Cronon 1996, 79). The very ideology of wilderness can be 'in contrast' with what it wants to protect. For example, the creation of national parks as protected wilderness on Earth has been predicated on a model of territorial occupation that attempted to erase Indigenous people's ties to their lands and displaced ecological knowledge that did not belong to European centres. A long, critical tradition of critiques of wilderness from Indigenous, postcolonial and Global South perspectives has powerfully questioned wilderness as a Western construct. The Indigenous scholar Fabienne Bayet has shown that wilderness posits humans and nature as fundamentally separate. There is a failure to account for relational understandings of home and homelands, as well as their place in the cosmos: "To Indigenous peoples the land is no abstract wilderness. The whole of Australia is an Aboriginal artefact." (Bayet 1994, 28).

Wilderness is a colonial construct—one with a long history and a global reach. Indian historian Ramachandra Guha (1989) has argued that national parks and wilderness preservation are specifically North American preoccupations, and are ineffective and even counterproductive tools for dealing with environmental challenges in the Global South. Their establishment, and the exclusionary nature of drawing borders around protected areas, are infused with the legacies of colonialism and racism. Bordering practices marginalise not only people but also non-settler or non-proprietary conceptions of relating to the land. For example, they are obstacles to the movement of pastoralist societies and they disavow the existence of lands that are not privately owned but customarily used for common grazing. Despite these critiques, parks and preservationist policies became tenets of environmentalist arguments.

The prospect of creating 'planetary parks' reproposes this exact model for space. In policy and science, these are delimited areas on celestial bodies that are chosen because of their "scientific, historical or aesthetic importance" (Cockell and Horneck 2006, 256). Planetary parks have been suggested as a way to preserve space wilderness. They are similar to National Parks and work by controlling the types and frequency of activities that become permissible in tightly enclosed areas. Astrobiologists Charles Cockell and Gerda Horneck, who first suggested parks as a mode of environmental governance, have pinpointed some suitable candidate areas to become Martian Parks, such as the Olympus Mons. In this hypothesis, the perimeter of parks works as a border, out of which other practices become acceptable. Foreseen external practices include the transformation of land through labour. Parks are the vehicle for the expansion into outer space of a type of territorial management that is deeply entrenched with John Locke's doctrine of property, with its centrality to colonial thought and practices.

On Earth and in space, parks privilege a colonial–capitalist relationship with nature, functioning as mechanisms of colonial territorialisation and primitive accumulation. Interestingly, early wildlife preserves in Africa were dubbed as "rich men's playgrounds" (Rashkow 2014, 819). With outer space becoming the new billionaires' playground, the establishment of parks raises questions about the capitalist co-optation of wilderness within the persisting inequalities of postcolonial modernity. Planetary Parks may delimit spaces where the use and extraction of resources is heavily managed. However, that implicitly means condoning capitalist extraction on a cosmic scale and creating the need for power structures that support bordering practices beyond Earth.

In brief, national parks have not protected our planet from the catastrophic consequences of anthropogenic activities. Quite the contrary, they have been part of colonial modes of control that were in keeping with the European exploitation of colonised environments. In the same way, planetary parks are unlikely to protect otherworldly environments from permanent changes derived from pollution and settlements. Wilderness thinking reinforces two attitudes towards environments: idealising areas for their high environmental value, and dismissing them as wastelands. These are two sides of the same colonising discourses and practices, in which acts of occupation and the creation of waste sustain each other.

Thus, parks are emblematic of how astroenviromentalism endorses Western epistemologies that deny the complexity of environmental relationships and see planets as territories that can be parcelled out and bounded. Planetary parks suggest that permanent changes can be made to parts of an ecosystem, but these changes can be controlled and delimited through acts of border creation. Under the guise of an environmentalist argument, this hypothesis entertains a settler future in outer space and legitimises colonial claims to property and extraction. Addressing the issue of colonialism in space requires a paradigm shift, a transformation that goes beyond simply expanding hegemonic environmentalist discourses beyond our planet. What is needed is a 're-constellation' of astroenvironmentalism through key strategies, such as resistance to extractivism, anthropocentrism and exclusionary bordering practices predicated upon European and Western privilege.

Alien Horizons

The artistic gaze on outer space has provided precious opportunities to deviate from existing forms of environmentalism, which are heavily rooted in dominant scientific thinking and reproducing the separation of nature and culture. In her *The Wilding of Mars* (2019), artist Alexandra Daisy Ginsberg shows a view of Martian deserts blooming with plant life. A computer simulation projected on four or twelve screens mediates views of millennia of growth of earthly flora happening within one hour. This perspective on wilderness proposes a future of plants without humans, thus displacing the anthropocentrism of the New Space narratives of salvation. It also shows that the seeding of cross-planetary wilderness may not be part of a terraforming project (i.e. the transformation of other planetary environments into earth-like systems), but, rather, result from the migration and extra-terrestrial expansion of other life forms. Overthrowing the primacy of humans as cosmic subjects, a commitment to alien horizons, requires becoming attuned to how environments are made through the disparate activities of different entities "co-shaping" (Haraway 2016) and of "intra-actions" (Barad 2007).

This environmental future without humans, which displaces colonial mastery, is a vision that emerges side-by-side with other types of futurisms. Afrofuturism has long paved the way to representations of outer space that make room for a possible retreat from the unjust histories and exclusionary character of earthly politics. From Alabama-born jazz musician Sun-Ra to the Detroit-based duo Drexciya with their imagination of underwater worlds, outer space environments have been both settings and enablers of new possible relationships which are human, more-than-human and environmental. Rather than providing a mere background, outer space is an unexpected geography for alien relationships that exceed the normativity of capitalist, colonial, racist and hetero-patriarchal logics.

A recent example of a critique of the hetero-patriarchy is provided by Portuguese artist Pedro Neves Marques's project *Vampires in Space*, exhibited at the 2022 Venice Biennale, which focuses on the interplanetary travel of a family of vampires. At Palazzo Franchetti, this three-screen film installation displays the journey of vampires carrying life to an exoplanetary twin Earth. Vampires are the perfect beings to travel to the stars because in space it is always night. But they are also a fundamental figuration of human excess that provides an entry point to discuss social processes of normalising bodies and relations. In this case, a figuration was redeployed to explore non-binary and transgender experiences. Outer space environments, with their darkness and otherworldly features, harbour plural realities; these displace representations of the European, white, heterosexual male norm of humanity.

Palestinian artist Larissa Sansour's video *Space Exodus* (2009), often shown alongside the installation of her *Palestinauts*, vinyl sculptures of cartoon astronauts, projects the Palestinian experience of displacement into space. On a lunar landscape, Sansour, dressed as an astronaut with Palestinian embroidery on one of the sleeves and the flag on the other, takes a historic step. A Palestinian flag is pitched in the lunar soil, provoking a sense of absurdity. For the artist, the film is an autobiographical statement about the impossibility of accessing Jerusalem, with the Moon being more accessible. The barren landscape of the Moon contrasts with the colours of the Palestinian flag and sparks a question about the arbitrary value cast upon environments. Counter-intuitively, this exodus or interplanetary travels are not an escape. On the contrary, they bring outer space into the fold of earthly political, social and environmental processes. Old borders defining individual and collective experiences are rewritten in narratives that see outer space environments in a continuous relationship with the Earth.

These alien horizons enable reflections on the nexus between territorial claims, the politics of occupation and the promise of extraction, which connect the earth with the sky. Once one overcomes the simplistic view of outer space as a wilderness to be conquered or transformed into value, other questions emerge, such as: what environments are worthy of interest? Who are the subjects that are to provide stewardship? For whom does the sky represent the possibility of a more just environmental future?

British artist Bethany Rigby's *Mining the Skies*, an installation about the politics of outer space extractivism exhibited at the Venice Architecture Biennale in 2021, adds to these the question of 'How will we live together?'. This work that displays the materiality of extraterrestrial minerals, with metallic meteorites and simulants of extraterrestrial soil, also includes extracts in morse code from the Outer Space Treaty, the Moon Agreement and the US Space Act that relate to the ownership of space resources. Applying these international treaties and national laws is contradictory and contested, bringing to the fore the inevitability of conflicts in the definition of both new and ecological relations in space. International law is at a standstill; Western knowledge and postcolonial power dynamics subsume environmental relations into battles for new colonies and resources. What languages, imaginaries and perspectives can usher in a commitment to environmental justice that is anticolonial, non-anthropocentric and attentive to the possibilities of multispecies cohabitation? What constellations are being formed?

New constellations

In his *Negative Dialectics*, the philosopher Theodor Adorno dwells on the idea of constellations. Constellations are clusters of thoughts that signify a concept (Adorno 1983, 163). Gaining awareness of a constellation is a bit like decoding a sequence that allows new light to be shed on a concept. If astroenvironmentalism is the concept in question, the continuous references to frontiers, borders and wilderness are traces of the colonial roots of its epistemology. Mainstream environmentalist discourses do not deconstruct the abstraction of planetary boundedness, or displace 'the planet' enough to allow for the emergence of other imaginations of living with multiple ecologies on the ground, in the lower Earth orbit and beyond. On the contrary, they risk reproducing universalist narratives of what types of environments count as worthy of protection, and who are the subjects to be entrusted with protecting them. These views that separate humans and nature, in turn, affect and justify enclosures of outer space environments for capitalist extraction, their use as stations for more anthropogenic technologies and as dumping sites for waste. As exemplified by Earth's environmental crisis, this utilitarian ideology constitutes a significant barrier to a more just and future-oriented relationship with our dwelling place. Bordering processes, the encircling of parks and the use of wilderness thinking cannot be tools for environmental justice in outer space. If astroenvironmentalism condones resource extraction, it becomes a form of ethics that serves the interests of capitalism and enables the continuation of a system of oppression that transforms labour and life into profit.

Astroenvironmentalism needs to be 'reconstellated' with ideas, images and analogies that bring about non-extractive practices. Embracing ethics concerning planetary contamination and environmental justice involves listening to worldviews and voices that have historically been oppressed and marginalised in the production of scientific thought. Writing about Aboriginal cosmological thought in Sky Country (Australia), the collective intellectual work of Bawaka Country greatly contributed to this endeavour. They insisted that the image of spaceship Earth and its totalising narratives, together with the idea that colonising space environments can be made to benefit humanity as a whole, have the power to conceal our planetary histories of injustice and racism. This erasure risks reproducing forms of environmental injustice that envision space as a dumping ground for pollution and ecologically harmful activity. Against this image of Spaceship Earth, and its binary division between inside and outside, the invitation to listen to Sky Country presents non-Indigenous audiences and advocates of colonisation with a view of environmental relations where "The Land, Sea and Sky Country are all connected, so there is no such thing as 'outer space' or 'outer Country'— no outside" (2020, 2).

This intimate cosmic connection displaces the image of Earth as an enclosed globe, or a 'sealed vessel' separated from space. Artist Elisa Strinna's renditions of the *Ojo estelar* (Starry Eye), a technology to study the stars in pre-Columbian cultures, point to this same interconnection. The technology consisted of a round basin placed in front of a stone seat. The astronomers could study the night sky reflected in the water-filled basin. Due to the difficulty of recovering the archaeological remains of the *Ojo estelar*, Strinna, in collaboration with the Community Museum of the Xico Valley, in Chalco, Mexico, in 2015, reconstructed a prototype. In the basin, the water and the stars become one, pointing to a continuity between cosmic and earthly matters. Ecologies, on and off Earth, are entanglements of different beings but also of life and non-life. Such connections fundamentally resist thinking of space as a colonising enterprise of occupation and primitive accumulation.

Anticolonialism in space must oppose the imaginaries and practices of territorialisation, resource extraction and the exclusionary power of the tales that subsume all humans and all environments under one Eurocentric norm. An anticolonial agenda must make room for a wide range of repertoires of resistance to extraction, a relational ethos and broader ecologies of knowledge. A route for this undertaking is to work on art–science collaborations that can displace the need for bordering practices that

divide and conquer, and to resignify borders as connections. In this sense, the title of a Cisco-NASA partnership
to create one of the largest wireless networks of sensors
launched in 2009 provides me with a generative image:
Planetary Skin. The 'skin' here refers to the encircling
of the Earth by data transmitted from a myriad of data
points and sensors, whose erratic trail questions the existence of a self-evident outer layer of Earth coinciding with
the atmosphere. In *Biospheres*, Dorion Sagan and Lynn
Margulis suggest that the atmosphere is more like a giant
circulatory system than a static border, as it supports the
movement of a wide range of chemicals across the planet
(Sagan and Margulis 1989, 13). We continually breathe
out gases in the atmosphere, actively contributing to the
flow of chemicals and organic compounds that support
Earth's dynamic harmony. In other words, the atmosphere
is part of the same complex matter that makes up our
planet: "Many very unusual, highly unstable chemicals exist
in Earth's air. These include all sorts of organic compounds
from the scent of magnolia flowers to butyl mercaptan, the
spray of skunks. Our complex atmosphere reflects the diversity of organisms living on the surface" (Sagan and Margulis
1989, 19).

In this sense, the ecological feedback loops and the
complex interactions that materially constitute life urge
us to question what borders can obstruct, protect
or halt. Just as human and animal skin is teeming with life
of different microbial communities, making it a dynamic
ecology, so planetary skin could be understood as other
than a shield protecting the individuality of Earth. Instead,
it could stand for the plurality and interrelatedness of life
as an active player in cosmic symbioses, such as referencing the dependency of life on Earth from several cosmic
processes, including tidal waves and solar energy, crucial
to the development of early living organisms.

Thinking of planetary (s)kin has allowed me to enlist the
work on ecology by Margulis and Stengers as cohabitation with difference in this cosmic reconstellation. Locating
symbiosis on the planetary skin suggests focusing
on the complex relations that make up life while recognising that the bio-centricity of some scientific thought

is reproducing an antiquated binary—life/non-life—in which
the latter is considered less worthy. Instead, ecological
thinking brings about the relationality intrinsic to what
Jennifer Gabrys calls "becoming planetary"—a way of living
on the planet "otherwise" (Gabrys 2018). Making kin can
be part of this re-constellation, which proposes the planetary in terms of visible interactions between different
organisms and the co-dependency of organic and inor-
ganic substances. In this sense, *(s)kin* provides more
dynamic views of the possibilities of cosmic dwelling
and prompts us to think about ecologies as being,
by definition, 'intra-planetary'.

REFERENCES

Theodor W. Adorno, *Negative Dialectics*, 1983

Karen Michelle Barad, *Meeting the Universe Halfway: Quantum Physics and the Entanglement of Matter and Meaning*, 2007

Fabienne Bayet, 'Overturning the Doctrine: Indigenous People and Wilderness. Being Aboriginal in the Environmental Movement', *Social Alternatives* 13 (2), July 1994

Bawaka Country, including A. Mitchell, S. Wright, S. Suchet-Pearson, K. Lloyd, L. Burarrwanga, R. Ganambarr, M. Ganambarr-Stubbs, B. Ganambarr, D. Maymuru and R. Maymuru, 'Dukarr lakarama: Listening to Guwak, talking back to space colonization', *Political Geography* 81, August 2020

Linda Billings, 'To the Moon, Mars, and Beyond: Culture, Law, and Ethics in Space-Faring Societies', *Bulletin of Science, Technology & Society* 26 (5), October 2006

Octavia E. Butler, *Parable of the Sower*, 2019

Charles S. Cockell and Gerda Horneck, 'Planetary parks—formulating a wilderness policy for planetary bodies', *Space Policy* 22 (4), November 2006

William Cronon, ed., *Uncommon Ground: Rethinking the Human Place in Nature*, 1996

Lidia Curti, ed., *Femminismi Futuri: Teorie, Poetiche, Fabulazioni*, 2019

Jennifer Gabrys, 'Becoming Planetary', *E-Flux Architecture*, 2018 www.e-flux.com/architecture/accumulation/217051/becoming-planetary/

Ramachandra Guha, 'Radical American Environmentalism and Wilderness Preservation: A Third World Critique', *Environmental Ethics* 11 (1), Spring 1989

Donna J. Haraway, *Staying with the Trouble: Making Kin in the Chthulucene*, 2016

Eugene C. Hargrove, ed., *Beyond Spaceship Earth: Environmental Ethics and the Solar System*, 1986

Lynn Margulis, *Symbiotic Planet: A New Look at Evolution*, 1998

Ezra D. Rashkow, 'Idealizing Inhabited Wilderness: A Revision to the History of Indigenous Peoples and National Parks', *History Compass* 12 (10), October 2014

Dorion Sagan and Lynn Margulis, *Biospheres: From Earth to Space*, 1989

Isabelle Stengers, *Cosmopolitics*, Posthumanities 9–10, 2010

United Nations Treaties and Principles on Outer Space, 2002

This booklet is published on the occasion of documenta fifteen (Kassel), 18 June – 25 September 2022

It is part of the publication *Jimmie Durham & A Stick in the Forest by the Side of the Road* with Jimmie Durham and Bev Koski, Elisa Strinna, Hamza Badran, Iain Chambers, Joen Vedel, Jone Kvie, Maria Thereza Alves, Wilma Lukatsch, Giulia Grechi, Alessandra Marino Al-Mishlab (ISBN 978-3-7533-0260-7, NUR 640)

© 2022 Alessandra Marino Al-Mishlab and Verlag der Buchhandlung Walther und Franz König, Köln

Text: Alessandra Marino Al-Mishlab
Cover image: © Elisa Strinna, *A Hole in the Universe–Ojo estelar prototype; The Sky Beyond Venice*, print on satin paper, 70×70 cm; courtesy Elisa Strinna
Editor: Iain Chambers
Proofreader: Nicola Grey
Design: Karoline Swiezynski, inspired by Will Holder's design for *Past Imperfect* by Bik van der Pol, which shaped the collective solution of this publication

Printed and bound in Belgium by Cassochrome with supervision of ArtLibro Trudy Dorrepaal. Published in an edition of 250 individual booklets (documenta fifteen) to be collated in an edition of 1000 books distributed by Verlag der Buchhandlung Walther und Franz König, Köln. First published by Verlag der Buchhandlung Walther und Franz König Ehrenstraße 4, D-50672 Köln.

Bibliographic information published by the Deutsche Nationalbibliothek – The Deutsche Nationalbibliothek lists this publication in the Deutsche Nationalbibliografie; detailed bibliographic data is available at http://dnb.d-nb.de.

Disclaimer: In making *Jimmie Durham & A Stick in the Forest by the Side of the Road* we have quotes, images and texts taken from various resources. Information concerning the original authors and sources have been credited as detailed as possible. Despite these efforts, some sources nevertheless could not be identified. Please contact the author in case of questions or objections. The ideas and opinions author unless stated otherwise.

Jimmie Durham & A Stick in the Forest by the Side of the Road has been generously supported by documenta fifteen.

This publication has been realized in the framework of documenta fifteen, June 18 – September 25, 2022

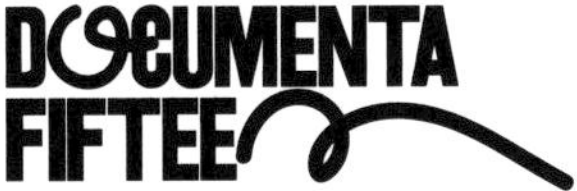

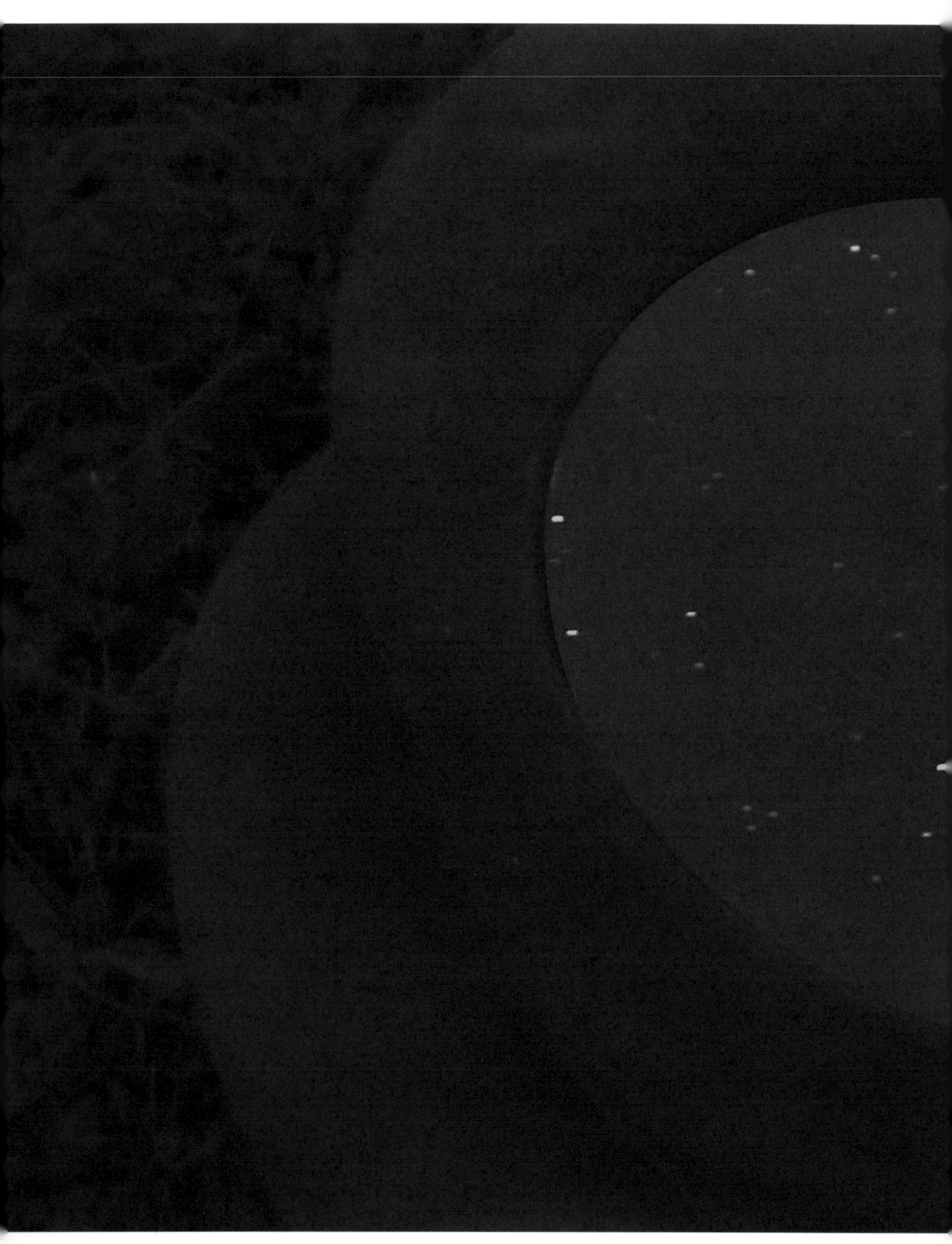

published 15 September 2022

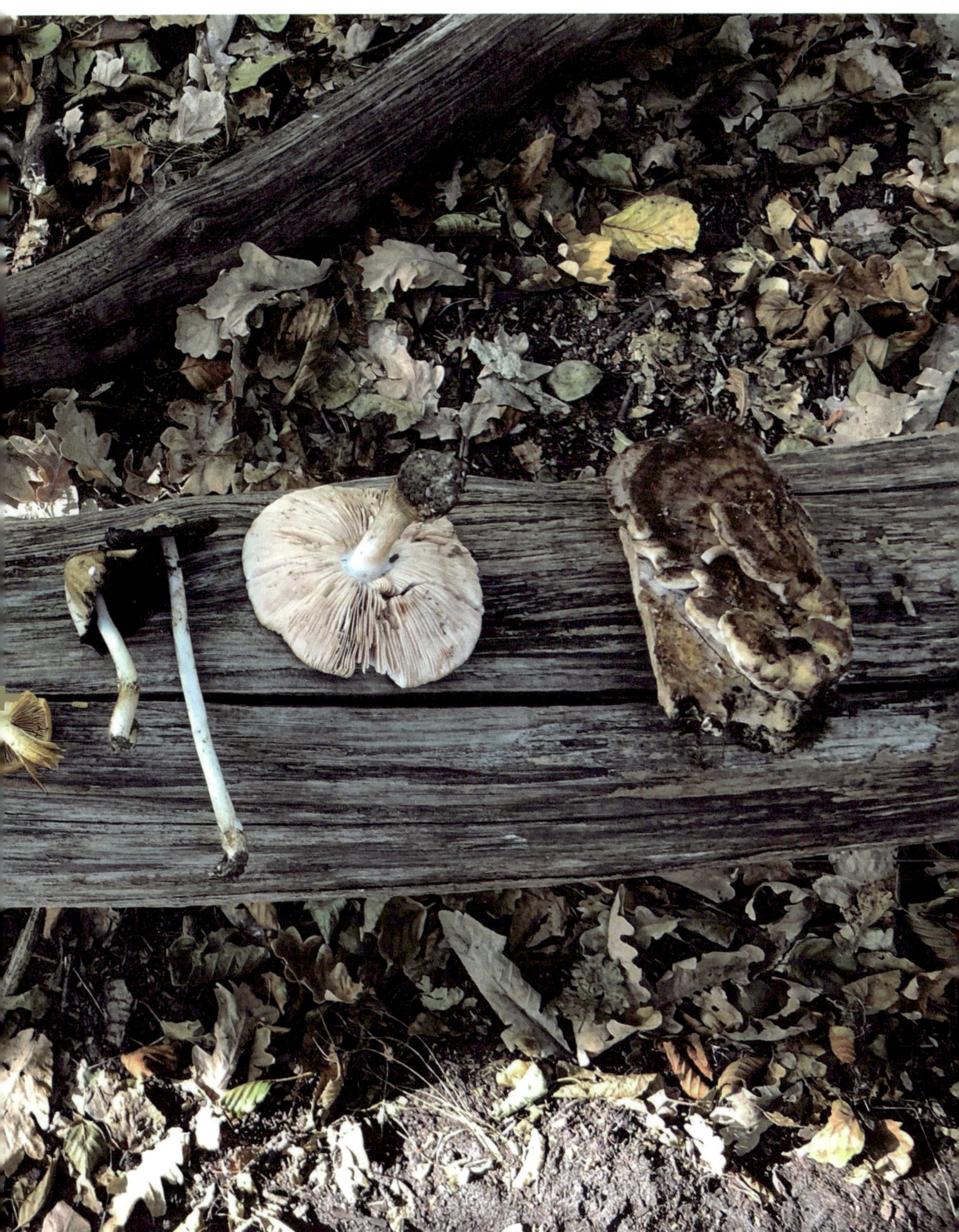

Jimmie Durham & A Stick in the Forest by the Side of the Road

A SHORT INTRODUCTION TO THE PROJECT

As my project within the collective *Jimmie Durham & A Stick in the Forest by the Side of the Road* is wandering around the many ways to memorise and honour Jimmie Durham, I decided to centre it around the joy and pleasures of spending time together whilst sharing some bites, sips and life. And after all, it was through Jimmie that I learned that working and cooking in parallel, always and everywhere, is just the way to make things work out, as well as make them as tasty as possible at the same time. Sitting and being surrounded by pleasant smells and nicely prepared food, people start to share time and times. Histories, memories, recipes, and all other sorts of stuff are on the table.

Isn't it true that space and time and their histories are shaped through food, and through processing what we experience whilst sitting together? Even (or especially?) the lack of food or of ingredients can bring our histories closer together, and possibly open up potential spaces for recognising the common ground.

I understand food and time as taking pleasure in what nourishes us; *plaisir* as an ingredient that we give to ourselves and to the language which connects each other. It is all about the HOW TO EAT AVEC PLAISIR.

In the conversations that I had with various actors in the food world in the context of documenta fifteen, I focus on expanding our gastrosophical understanding, our imaginations and our specific way of dealing with recipes as formulations, with traditions and their (re-)interpretations, with taste as a carrier of memories, with ingredients as inspiration for positive change. To what extent could examining food and the memories coming with it also make historical trauma tangible and allow for possibilities of non-Western constellations to know?

Knowledges and ways to know each other are colonised, when acted upon each other to divide and re-establish colonial differences. Knowing structures flatten out plurality, multiplicity and the joy of variety and cornucopia, just as, alongside, the human microbiome and digestion system is dying for the same reasons and logic at work. By seeing both as connected and intertwined, we could recognise food and eating habits as more than biological duties but as methods of memorisation through digestion—a social, historical and possibly decolonial methodology of responding.

It is through the richness of ingredients, the unfolding of their stories, the how to eat with pleasure that we can experience other ways to sense and enjoy recipes, to celebrate tastes and textures, to give complex life/meaning to preparation time. Eating and food histories can enable us to experience and enrich our connectedness as our microbiome, and through that can destabilise Western ways of reducing complexity and producing tasteless and indigestible stuff. By taking time for understanding food stories, we might change the vision of telling histories past and ahead. So, listening, and a good portion of sticking around, are the main ingredients for both tasty, delicious and just food as well as rich and just history.

This talk with food psychologist Jocelyne Reich-Soufflet from Frankfurt/ Main (Hessen) goes off into the world of how to eat with pleasure and how to enjoy the richness without starving the future. What does it require to enjoy eating, and to value eating in community? What, how and where is our food coming from, where does it belong, and how could our questioning affect the potential to decolonise our imaginations of the common ground?

HOW TO EAT AVEC PLAISIR

Thinking Art Through One's Stomach

An exchange of thoughts between
Jocelyne Reich-Soufflet and Wilma Lukatsch about enjoyment,
memories and the sensuality of sharing

Jocelyne Reich-Soufflet (JRS) In our preliminary talk, you brought up the subjects of enjoyment and desire relatively quickly, and I had to ask myself what the difference between the two was. In French, after all, the two words are the same. That's how it starts. Enjoyment as a positive sensory perception—we French people call it *le plaisir*—which can be physical as well as mental. Whereas desire is more closely tied to the need or wish to do something. So, you can have a desire for enjoyment or take enjoyment in desire. [*laughs*] A nicely laid table creates desire. It creates the desire to do something. And then we'll be able to receive the food with our capacity for enjoyment.

And then I asked myself, what would be the opposite of enjoyment? Could it be inattentiveness? After all, enjoyment is closely tied to attention. So, could its opposite mean an absence of attention? Or are there good and bad forms of enjoyment? That is obviously a question that comes to mind. Or maybe there are different realities of enjoyment? Again, I rather think so. Or maybe there are even misunderstandings in the interpretation of enjoyment. These are all important aspects, and I believe that without the capacity to consider enjoyment, we will ultimately never find our way through the food jungle. Which is to say that for me, enjoyment is a very important directional sense.

Wilma Lukatsch (WL) Yes, I find that to be a helpful description, understanding enjoyment as a sense of direction. There's something freeing in it, I think. It could help us to move more freely, and be more free of judgement, in the huge and now totally hyped-up topic of food.

JRS Yes, it's a sense of direction, and therefore it's not for nothing that the industry has flavour architects that help us literally grasp enjoyment. It is not so easy to do that, and so you need flavour architects because otherwise you wouldn't be able to get it right. It all seems very complicated. And I ask: is it sickening if we suddenly stop being able to enjoy food? That's also an important question, and one that's being asked more and more. Or do we need a food enjoyment coach? [*both laugh*] Yes, yes, I have to ask that. Or does enjoyment simply mean feeling something, experiencing something?

I think that enjoyment is very often shrouded in fear. As in the nutrition tables we have in this country, with warnings like: 'You mustn't eat too much meat or chocolate, or you'll get fat. Or sugar, for God's sake!' and so on. Taking pleasure in food is almost a kind of sinful cheating.

But from a purely historical point of view, I think it's important to examine the idea of enjoyment, because it came along so recently. The gastronomy field has long been concerned with certain values. 'Gastro' means belly, and 'nomia' are, ultimately, values. And the enjoyment of food was only meant for a select audience. At the end of the 19th century, this expanded somewhat. It was no longer just a concern of the elite but opened itself up for the wider masses. And then, of course, there was a lot of overstimulation. I find that a very important topic as well, because enjoying food has something to do with small amounts, not with the pressure to consume. It's not about overstimulation, and it's also not about overabundance. In the end, it's about something very simple. And I believe that hasn't played a very large role.

The film *Babette's Feast* is an important film for our topic. It is based on a short story by Karen Blixen about a very renowned chef who assumes household cooking duties for a very ascetic Protestant community. Babette brings in all these wonderful goods from France. She cooks for days, but because enjoyment and *plaisir* are forbidden in this pietistic community, they eat it all without even changing their facial expression. The company for which Babette hosts the feast speak without speaking, sing without singing, are mechanical and resemble a still life, while in comparison Babette prepares the food, and the moment she takes a quail out of the oven, for instance, something alive emerges. Suddenly, a General at the feast, a man of the world, recognises the extraordinary quality of the food, and he praises it, and all of a sudden everyone sitting at the table begins to loosen up, drinking a little more wine and giving themselves over to the pleasure. So, in their togetherness, the company at the table could allow themselves this sensual enjoyment. But they needed specific permission. While there is little exchange in this community at the beginning, words and gestures take on an impact after the meal. It is an insanely good film that makes it clear that enjoyment is about a certain sensual perception. The food surely evoked certain memories in the General, while the rest of the society hadn't experienced anything of the sort and so wouldn't have those associations. I'm talking about this because you were also asking about the role of imagination. It is obviously the case that the enjoyment of food is something that we develop *peu à peu*, that we can teach ourselves, and which needs to be allowed by us in order to become possible.

WL So, it has something to do with learning and a possibility to develop oneself?

JRS It has something to do with learning and with permission. We need to have memories of certain dining experiences, maybe also embedded in a particularly pleasurable situation, perhaps where food enjoyment is combined with pleasure, without prohibition. That's the kind of impulse that suddenly arises via the General. He recognises certain flavours in a certain dish, and that serves as a kind of ignition. Food enjoyment is something very physiological, too. Of course, it has to attract me physiologically, not repel me. And at the same time, it is also something very psychological.

And then later in the 20th century, when they started mixing science into it, that's when the fear came along: what if people suddenly began thirsting for more food enjoyment [*laughs*]; and what if someone basically always anticipated a lack of such pleasure and therefore tried to stockpile it and developed a food addiction?

Of course, that didn't quite fit in with science, which tries to regulate everything. It's been found—if you look at certain eating disorders, for example—that when people eat very restrictively because they have been taking no enjoyment in food, or have lost the desire to eat (anorexia is not just the loss of appetite, but the loss of desire), that, in fact, an enormous greed can arise and one can no longer hit the brakes. So, it's not by indulging in pleasure that we develop this addiction, but rather by suffering from a lack of it. But it's really not medically navigable. Food enjoyment is a very ambivalent topic, a subject that perhaps is actually related to art, insofar as I find it resists any attempt to evaluate it. To that extent, it remains ambivalent.

And people really wondered if someone could become a slave to this passion. It was examined by lots of people, again and again, and they kept saying that if someone suddenly got fat, for example, it was because they enjoyed food too much. Until they realised, of course, that it was the pressure to consume that lay behind it, not an addiction to enjoying food, not at all. But it was so easy to connect the two. That's not it, though. Food is political, and politicians are always trying to control our eating habits. The Nazis had strict rules about it, for example. Enjoying food became sinful, and I suspect a connection to an inhibition of pleasure during that era. During World War II, food served in the evening had to be cold—nobody in Germany was allowed to properly cook at night. The kitchen was only used at midday, and your dinner was thrown together on a board. You would eat your sandwich straight off that board. They tried to present this evening meal as a particularly healthy one, along the lines of the motto 'A hot supper is unhealthy'. But that's something that was only promoted in Germany. [*IVL laughs*] In other countries, it's different. So, this type of evening meal is a historical tradition in Germany, and I suspect that the concepts of obedience, purity and eating leave little room for enjoyment. When values are suddenly politically constructed and asserted, pleasure becomes difficult and a system of oppression arises. So, it was hard for Germany to institute different values and create more room for pleasure after World War II. I have now been living in Germany longer than in France, and I found out early on that German gastronomy has been shaped by external attributions. But for each of us, as eaters, it's important to know that the enjoyment of food and its development is always tied to a questioning of ourselves and our own history. And from a sociological point of view, this enjoyment comes from sharing. Kitchen gardens have always been shared between people. And it's an important idea, that savouring and enjoying food is always related to a shared *plaisir*.

You also raised the question of the spatial as well as the temporal aspects of enjoyment. It's true that you could bring the concept of space into it. The table is a space; the kitchen, too. And so, I think, is your place setting as well as the plate. These are all spaces, all fantastic spaces. And there's also a time dimension, which is even a bit more pronounced here in Germany. They say '*Guten Appetit*' before they eat here, but they also like to say '*Mahlzeit*' ['mealtime'].

The word itself contains time, the time dimension, perhaps also time for enjoyment. In any case, *Mahlzeit* is a special moment. We don't say 'mealtime' in France, for example, nor in Italy or Spain, because it's obvious.

I was once invited to talk about the theme of food enjoyment in connection with obesity. This was in a clinic that mostly treats people who are overweight. And there, too, the concept of enjoyment came up. I provocatively asked: should overweight people actually be excluded from these concepts of space and time? It is a very important point, because we know that many people who are overweight think to themselves: 'I'm so fat that I shouldn't eat in front of other people. I mustn't let them see me enjoying food.' Because for many people, it's quite clear that if an overweight person is eating a scoop of ice cream, then it shouldn't be surprising that they look the way they do. And then sometimes that person says, in the face of all that repulsion and denigration, 'Well, why don't I just get myself four scoops!' Then it leaves the realm of enjoyment and goes more towards the realm of self-defence. As you see, food enjoyment is quite complex, and it is a very nice concept that unfortunately, at least in science, has acquired a bad aftertaste.

What might also be of interest to you, since you were asking about concepts of memory and recollection, is that eating without mindfulness leaves no trace in one's memory.

WL   So, if you eat something while you're doing or thinking about something else, it's like you hadn't eaten?

JRS   For your memory, exactly. Whereas conscious eating leaves a mark. That is why it's a big treat, this eating together, this savouring together. Because the more experiences I have accumulated in my memory, the better I am practically able to model my own enjoyment of food—because in the end we all eat differently, and we all enjoy food differently—and the freer I am. I think enjoying food really has a lot to do with freedom. These are some important additional thoughts.

And the concept of pleasure also plays a large role in the psychology of resilience. That is also an important point for you, perhaps, because it's about people integrating beauty into their lives. And with this integration of beauty, we can regulate emotions much more easily. It's connected to sensual perception, in that when I feel guilty, when I have a bad conscience, when I feel I'm behaving in a sinful way, that's an affect. And that affect, the hurt, causes a reduction in sensory perception.

WL   Of course, there are many aspects that we could go deeper into. My own approach to the topic is based on my experiences in the context of my art history studies and research, regarding the possibilities of a decolonial approach to art histories, and methodologies. These are questions about the dimensions of historical and colonial injustice and the possibility of its epistemic shift. From there, and with Jimmie Durham in mind, I have begun exploring the topic of food enjoyment, companionship at the table, hospitality. I understand the presence of eating with each other as an invitation to share enjoyment along our differing experiences of taste as historical conditions. Insofar as sharing food is intertwined with the task of remembering, it is also tied to the question of how to remember, the methodologies to remember following a shared 'mealtime' or common 'lunch break'. In which ways can we weave theses memories into a common narration? Also, how do I take care of these stories at my own stove, so to speak? How do I proceed with these fresh enjoyments I've experienced? How do I process the memories of ingredients, recipes, histories, etc., or of specific textures, colours, smells that I may not have been familiar with before? In other words, how do I deal with the historical significance of a shared meal, and how can I become aware of them being related to my own stories and experiences? Experiences, for example, like what someone was and wasn't allowed to eat in their family; what was available and what wasn't; what was merely dreamed of and present as a missing ingredient. So, I'm also concerned with achieving a clearer understanding of the respective eating communities in which we find ourselves today as historically charged spaces, ones that come with a responsibility—albeit a responsibility that wants to be experienced as enjoyment for each single Other. Here we come to the theme of mindfulness that you brought up earlier, as well as that of listening. I find that interesting, as well as what you were saying about the largeness—or better, the smallness—of meals that are enjoyed. The enjoyment comes in the little, not the excess. That makes sense to me immediately. For example, take the phenomenon of looking at a magnificent display in a bakery window. You marvel at the richness of the assortment, all the different ways that the items are formed, rolled, glazed, etc. To me, that is a tremendous joy, and not because I want to buy everything or eat everything. I mean, one could, but it would not...

JRS ... you wouldn't be able to savour it.

WL Yes, exactly. But the thought pathways that are set into motion upon that sight are huge and incredibly rich. And then it basically only takes one bite to align your imagination with reality, and sometimes you don't even need that. Even just mindful viewing and perceiving can be a part of 'mealtime' and a shared enjoyment of food, I believe. I'm also mentioning this because you said in an interview with a nutritionist that scarcity is beneficial to our creativity. We're not talking about the kind of scarcity that arises from an emergency or war situation, but, rather, about an emancipatory moment in a world where our tables are bending more and more. When everything is available, then our imagination atrophies, if I'm understanding you correctly. And scarcity could be imagined not as a state of deficiency, but as a wealth of possibilities to be creative—with recipes, for example. Doesn't this kind of creativity also fit under the umbrella of food enjoyment?

JRS   Absolutely. I think that, in the end, pleasure is almost always connected to imagination. It is my imaginings of what I could perceive as pleasurable. It doesn't always have to be directly related to something I'm doing right now. For me, pleasure isn't reality (*Realität*); rather, pleasure is a functional reality (*Wirklichkeit*) because it has functional effects.

WL   How do you differentiate reality from functional reality?

JRS   Functional reality functions in your reality, and reality is reality. In other words, you're here in reality. Functional reality is this interview that exists between us. And I think that's already something special. And with mental images, with our imaginations, it's only right that we're searching for beauty; we're looking for the experience in the pleasurable quest, the pleasurable expectation that we might make ourselves mashed potatoes on Sunday because it is only on Sunday that we'll be able to get the milk or the potatoes. Pleasure means I'm attracted to something. It doesn't necessarily mean it's there right now. But I'm allowed to be attracted. And you said it correctly before, that we're living in a society where, on the one hand, there are many stimuli, but, on the other, there is not necessarily a free space for pleasure. Because freedom for pleasure means paying a little attention to these internal and external registers. We have internal registers inside us, where, for example, our stomach tells us something, our intestines tell us something, our body reports to us about a need for something—that's one thing. But we also have external registers: Am I allowed to do this? Or let's say there was something you liked to eat... I recently had a guest who told me that when he was a child, he developed a taste for raw liver because it helped him recover from a serious illness. He had a very bad blood disease, and they gave him raw liver to get better, and to this day he says it's a pleasure to eat. But he knows full well from external registers that it's not something he can enjoy everywhere, because other people's conceptions of liver don't coincide with his own. The conception that came from his experience is that in this raw form, liver isn't only healthy but something to be savoured. And most people don't have that. They only know cooked liver. Some people only eat liver if it's extremely well-done; others even have an absolutely repulsive image of offal in general. And that means he treads very carefully around these external registers. So, yes, it's not only internal registers that are active in food enjoyment; we also have these external registers, those which I already named while I was talking about obesity. That's one topic, but you could also bring it up another way. For example, when I was a girl, I always loved eating raw meat as tartare. But when I moved to Germany, straight after graduating high school, and I ate my first bite of raw minced meat in front of friends, they all looked at me and said: 'You know, that's really unhealthy.' [*laughs*]

WL   I have shared that same experience, because we used to eat that on bread for supper in the GDR quite a lot.

JRS   *Tartarbrot*, yes!

WL   Ground meat, with very thinly sliced raw onions and some chives on top, if at hand.

JRS   Yes! Exactly! How delicious!

WL   I love it too. And then the Berlin Wall fell, and they started saying: 'Oh, salmonella, you can't eat that anymore.' And now that you're bringing it up, I'm just now realising that I never ate a 'minced-raw-meat-bread' after that, not for 20 years.

JRS   Yes, yes, there is an inhibition around it.

WL   Yes, I completely forgot about it.

JRS   The inhibition arises simply because the external registers are telling us something else. And in the end enjoyment is part of my reality, because enjoyment really has something to do with autonomy. But it also has something to do with dependence. It is sociologically interesting, for example, that during the Mao Zedong era in China it was only permissible to eat among others, never alone. The Chinese could only share what they had. There was no other way. It's a new thing now that a Chinese person can eat his soup alone. Before, it was only possible with company. People would meet in the fields so they could share the little that they had to eat with each other. It was simply enormously important sociologically. And therefore, it has something to do with autonomy and something to do with dependence. It's got something to do with the fact that we're not only drawing from our internal registers, our own wealth of experience, our own memories, but that we can see very well how it's received by those around us. For example, I'm crazy about eating oysters. But I still remember how, during my first seminar years ago, I told my students—of course this was a little gag, but I told them: oh, I'm so excited, because today we're going to be doing a seminar about the subjects of food enjoyment and mindfulness and this evening at six someone's going to come by with a surprise for us. A surprise, you say? Yes, he'll be bringing some fresh oysters... [*feigns horror*]

WL   This was in Germany?

JRS   Yes, of course [*laughs*]. If someone said that in France, the most that would happen is someone would go chill the wine. [*Both laugh loudly*] And it was so funny, because obviously I couldn't afford to order that many oysters; they're simply far too overpriced here. But I realised that, anyway, the experience couldn't be shared. Only two or three people from the whole seminar would have stayed and the others would have left. That wouldn't have been such a bad thing, and we would have enjoyed the oysters either way. But we wouldn't have enjoyed them as much because we would have had the feeling that the others were being excluded. And of course, we'd then all take that into consideration. So, enjoyment also requires a sensitive approach. That is very important, in order for us to enjoy something.

WL   It is truly an important ingredient, so to speak.

JRS   Yes, it is a mindfulness ingredient, a very limited one. *Plaisir* is limited. And when it isn't limited, when someone basically has an addiction to enjoying food, it will lead to pain. I mean, it is also limited insofar as not everyone likes eating the same things. From a purely philosophical viewpoint, food enjoyment can only be argued about [*laughs*], similar to taste. It's also an experience that takes place entirely in the present; we can't hold onto it. Maybe we can capture the experience of enjoying food in our memory. But in any case, it's limited.

WL   Thinking of food enjoyment as something which is limitated means that in a certain way, enjoying food is a state of exception.

JRS   Yes.

WL   And perhaps the art, then, is happening in the moment when we savour something—an oyster with a glass of wine, for example, or, who knows, some bread with raw mincemeat... [*both laugh*]

JRS   Yes, right, you've got it... a *Tartarbrot*!

WL   Now you've really brought back memories for me.

JRS   I had no idea that people in the former GDR liked *Tartarbrot* that much.

WL   I don't want to overstate it, but we really did eat *Tartarbrot* for dinner very often.

JRS   But that's great. It's wonderful!

WL   It was also cheap and easy to put together: you just put the meat through the grinder, threw in an egg and some finely chopped onions, some herbs if you had them, mixed it up with your hands and you were done. The recipe is adaptable to anything you had in the fridge or garden to add, no?

JRS   Yes, and it was a lot better than this sausage with phosphates, you know. It was something very special.

WL   I need to ask around and find out whether anyone's still eating it.

JRS   Yes, yes! But be that as it may, perhaps the real question is whether it's really the desire, the waiting for it, that's the main source of pleasure? That's why we really don't need much to savour something. And that's why I said pleasure is a functional reality. It functions. Something's happening there. There's an effect behind it. And of course, that requires... so you notice when you're baking and imagining the way you'll put the ingredients together, that there's an inner freedom that you have, an absence of dependence. You're not baking just so you can eat it all.

WL   No, right, it is not about that.

JRS   Just by thinking about it, you know it's not that. Because then the pleasure turns into necessity. And that won't do.

WL   Yes, agreed. After all, the joy that comes from imagining combinations of ingredients and the actual quantities that are produced in my kitchen seem almost detached from one another. But let's quickly go back to the aspect of enjoying food as something extraordinary, as something out of the norm. Because then one question would also be, how do we get back to a 'normal' state by healthy means, in order to rebuild our concept of food enjoyment? How do you build enjoyment back into your everyday routine beyond these extraordinary moments of pleasure? You just said that the downside of freedom is a dependence that can gradually develop, and which one should naturally try to avoid. How do we get that, this movement between the two moments?

JRS   Exactly. I believe it has something to do with a sort of inner freedom. Viktor Frankl, a wonderful psychoanalyst, wrote the following sentence that is spot-on: "Between stimulus and reaction there is a space. In this space lies our power to choose our reaction. In our reaction lies our development and our freedom." If I'm correctly sensing the meaning of these words in the context of our topic, then inner work can help us feel this space and design it anew. I find that very important, because we can also do that with regards to mindful care, or the expansion of our own perceptions. And that, in the end, would be the thing that actually enables an inner freedom. This inner freedom naturally reduces dependence, because addiction only arises out of urgency. Say you wanted a piece of chocolate right now, and I told you I could bring you something, and you said: 'Oh no, I've got some at home and I'm looking forward to coming home and having a glass of milk with chocolate.' Then it's about a desire for chocolate, a perception of the fact that it would bring you joy. Or if you thought to yourself right now: 'Ahh, I could make myself a really nice *Tartarbrot*.' Then you'd surely do that in the next few days, as soon as you had the opportunity. But there's no urgency to it. And addictive behaviour is a response to an urge—that is,

I feel an urge and I go straight away to a drawer, open it and take something out. But then it's not about enjoying the food, it's about responding to that sense of urgency. We're not looking for beauty. We're not seeking an experience. We're just looking for an immediate reaction to a stimulus that's come up. I must have this now, so I'll do that. And I believe that when we're talking about enjoyment, then it's about something else.

WL   Enjoyment is the creation of a space.

JRS   Yes.

WL   And addiction is the absence of that space.

JRS   Exactly. And of course, this freedom requires a very high level of sensitivity: What do I associate with pleasure? I called it a functional reality—what functions for me as enjoyable? I believe that is quite an individual question. You were also talking about how the history of a dish had an effect; the images that I have, they have an effect. It also makes a difference whom I am talking to about it. For example, I was once asked to give a lecture on food, but to stick purely to dietary topics without going into psychology. I told them that enjoying food could not be regulated. It won't do. Enjoyment is free of that. Enjoyment has something to do with freedom, it requires an inner freedom. How one ultimately codifies this freedom is another story. But there, I noticed that I could only answer questions about enjoying food by saying: 'Pleasure doesn't go according to plan, it can't be regulated.'

WL   And isn't that the most wonderful thing! [*laughs*]

JRS   That's what's great about it, yes. And then I realised that we can't separate people's symptoms from themselves. We can't attempt to treat someone without seeing the person behind the symptoms. It's just not possible. And then I also see that there are strong political forces trying to regulate the issues of food and illness without wanting to look at the motivations behind them, why someone does what they do. And I find that we can't separate the enjoyment of food from the eater. It's not connected to a type of food, the enjoyment—it's connected to an enjoying person.

WL   That is perhaps also what I was trying to describe with my questions about digestion and digestibility and indigestibility.

JRS   Maybe some imagery will help. I am of the opinion that what we're eating is the world. We're eating plants, animals, minerals, and in the end, nourishment is me having to let something from the outer world into my inner world. And the digestibility of something has to do with whether I allow that outer world to enter my inner one at all. And if you take this mental image, of the integration of the outer world into the inner one, then it leads to the possibility that through this integration, they can both find each other again. Let's see, I know the concept of delegated enjoyment as an eating disorder symptom—when people cook for others but don't eat anything themselves, that's delegated enjoyment. But in analytical language, it's a form of perversion. They cook, they cook a lot, and then they just let other people eat it. So, enjoyment also has a perverse side [*both laugh quietly*]. It is really a tough nut to crack.

WL Then to a certain extent, the question also arises: is enjoyment even attainable at all? Or is it more of a dream or ideal that can perhaps only exist in the tiniest of micro-moments, like you see with freedom or love? There are these tiny moments in life where you're almost bursting with happiness, because you feel so wholly embraced and carried. But just a little later, you again start feeling like you're all alone in the world. And then you've got to actively remind yourself to reactivate your own imagination.

JRS Exactly, and maybe that's the connection. Maybe defining enjoyment is an art in itself. To define enjoyment for oneself is an art, that's what I think.

WL So is managing to savour the act of talking about enjoyment.

JRS Yes. Again, I believe—and maybe this is the point—that things are even more limiting than what we discussed earlier. We were talking about how when something's not limited, it leads to pain. In other words, if I ate an unlimited amount of something I really liked to eat, I would no longer find myself in the realm of enjoyment but on the border of pain. There are also people who say: 'Yeah, but I love it so much I just can't stop eating it.' That's the problem. Enjoying food always has something to do with limitation, with the capability to limit oneself. And then there's maybe one other thing that's important. It also has to do with harmony, with mindfulness, and perhaps it's got to do with caring in our bodies and in our psyches. Yes, that's quite a sensitive value.

WL So, a type of self-care.

JRS Absolutely.

WL That means, for example, cooking because I like to cook and I like to eat.

JRS Yes, and because you're doing something good for yourself.

WL But of course; I also especially like having company.

JRS Yes, that is tied closely to our basic needs. On the one hand, the need for lightness, for relaxation, but, on the other, the need for connectedness via sharing something with someone, and also the need for security. Of course, I won't cook meals that I'm afraid might poison me, but those I feel I can rely on. That creates security. And I'll do it because I'm autonomous, because I've learned to get by that way. Enjoyment is very much tied to our basic psychological needs. I wouldn't separate the two. And there's also always a context for enjoyment. You can't talk with just anyone about it, in the same way that you can't talk to everyone about everything. It's not because it is an intimate topic—it does have an intimacy, but it's something else. It needs to be listened to. It doesn't have to be shared immediately, but it has to be heard so that I can understand myself when I explain enjoyment. And therefore, you can't talk about enjoyment with everyone. And I think that in the space where people might be reading this text, it needs a certain context, an invitation to enter one's own reflections and one's own experience of enjoyment while listening.

WL If we're expanding the topic of enjoyment so widely, then my aim is to think about, experience and fan out the facets and possibilities of enjoyment with you. I also definitely enjoy recipes, formulas, certain tastes and certain peculiarities and their stories. But the subject is also connected to unease. For example, I experienced that in Brazil, where certain ingredients have fallen victim to a systematic colonial forgetfulness and erasure. But how can one, and a settler nation in particular, re-remember recipes or specific techniques or uses?

JRS Yes, I believe this aspect actually gets to the heart of the matter. When you enjoy food, memory is also involved because you've already experienced the dish before. Or you have an idea of what you're about to experience, and because of that your psyche will stage something to try to get it back. If I had to name one of my favourite foods as an example, I'd think of Comte, because first of all it's a cheese that was often around in my childhood but that I didn't particularly like as a child. I knew my parents loved it, but to me it wasn't that special or extraordinary a cheese. But at some point, I read about the cheese, and at some point I also saw where it came from, and I said to myself, that's unbelievable. And in that way, I believe that your lived experiences affect the way you enjoy food. Something emerges there. You know, the first oyster that you slurp from the shell, maybe with lemon, maybe with some shallots, ideally by the ocean—under those conditions, you can be moved... an entire world is staged around just one oyster. Whereas when I was in China, I went to an oyster farm because they wanted to show us the pearls, and that didn't awaken any taste memories in me. I saw these huge oysters that they were growing pearls in and I thought they were pretty, although I'm not that interested in pearls. And I also saw the way they were farming the oysters, but I completely didn't associate it with food. I found that fascinating, that I didn't connect this experience to the pleasure of oyster eating. It lost all connection in my psyche. I noticed that my mind didn't stage anything connected to food. Perhaps enjoyment is the moment where our state of mind finally moves in the direction of the object of desire. In the moment where I think, ah, a good Comte, hmm, the aroma, and I immediately imagine myself finely grating it, perhaps over a poached egg and letting it melt just a little. Maybe it's exactly this moment, where I think I know what's waiting for me. And I don't need much of it either, no.

WL   However, what we do need a lot of is time. On the one hand, time to discuss or think about it, like we're doing now, but, on the other, the time that goes into the ingredients, the stories and the techniques to prepare. The best breads take lots of time, the best cheeses too, and so on. Or, certain fermentation processes need an extensive level of engagement and attention.

JRS   So do all of us! We need a certain level of development before we can appreciate certain foods. That's just the way it is. I mean, of course I learned to appreciate a good baguette very early. Over the years I learned to appreciate a certain solidity, a certain sound. And when I came over here and there were no baguettes, just things that were called that [*WL laughs*]—then I came to appreciate it more and more, to this day. Because now I really know the difference. That's also very important: sometimes it is one's own personal development that leads to the ability to enjoy certain things. This is part of the reason why I find enjoyment is such a huge concept. And I would say that we also definitely have enjoyment neurons. I am even convinced that there are people who actually don't have enough food enjoyment receptors. Either that, or theirs are so strictly regulated that they don't have room for enjoyment.

WL   You mean that these stimulation receptors 'go hungry' during certain moments or phases of life?

JRS   Well, sure, to reach satisfaction... for example, with certain types of depression, one's ability to enjoy food is significantly reduced.

WL   What about historically—in eras of fear, persecution or war, for example? Is there a space and time for enjoyment in traumatic times?

JRS   I do think that another space for enjoyment can exist in those times. Because let's say I meet two or three fellow escapees in a cabin or a house, and someone's put a potato in the oven and we savour the smell of it together, then even though this pleasure would have an effect outside of the reality that surrounds me, I would still be able to feel the reality of the pleasure. Many people think back in times of deep hunger to those potatoes that have been boiled and warmed up just so—they really do have a certain aroma. So, there's this memory of food. And I believe that's also an important topic. The fact that food enjoyment is a functional reality allows us to experience it inside of a harsh reality, in a moment of war, like in Ukraine. Despite everything, a few Ukrainians who arrive here, meet up and perhaps cook a certain dish together will, for a short time, feel a moment of contentment through the enjoyment of this shared food. That's another definition of enjoyment, yes.

WL   And that seems to be perhaps exactly the moment where memories find a space. Even with the humblest of means and under the cruellest circumstances, just sharing a simple slice of bread with cheese can create a space for potential memory—and maybe the capacity to remember, too. Perhaps we start sharing certain memories or stories; we remind ourselves while we eat. That idea of 'meal-time' appears here once again, where it's no longer only about what exactly I have on my plate, but about the space that we create with each other by means of this piece of bread, which lets us travel into the realm of memory. People laugh, they cry, emotions are triggered, all from this meagre slice of bread.

JRS   Exactly. And what I find interesting is precisely this sharing. It's true that when this kind of gathering happens, everyone gets emotional. But then everyone is also invited to look into their own memory archives, without anyone else telling them to do so. When I was talking about *Tartarbrot* before, I had no idea that it would release this cascade in you. It happened automatically. And then we just talked about it. Therefore there's a space between stimulus and reaction, and that's what it is all about. It is for that reason that the definition of enjoyment is so complex.

WL   As a farewell and finale to these rich considerations and investigations on the subject of food and food enjoyment, I have a few personal questions for you, and I'd love it if you could quickly take us into your personal history, and/or your Hessen. As a Frenchwoman in Hessen, what role does the region's cuisine play for you? Are there dishes, recipes or techniques in Hessian cuisine that you particularly like, or miss, or does the cuisine of Hessen offer something that can be combined with French techniques? Does the famous Green Sauce (*Grie Soß*) and the Seven Herbs mean anything to you, for example, or have you not been able to warm to it? Is there a concrete recipe or a memory of a recipe that you'd like to share as a final thought?

JRS   Food plays an important role for me personally. When I was very young, my grandmother invited me to 'help' in the kitchen, and I very quickly mutated into her cooking assistant or 'sous-chef'. I was allowed to try everything without restraint. We went shopping together in Les Halles in Paris, and I watched her get inspired. It was definitely the best culinary school of my life.

As far as Hessen is concerned, it is a region that I've basically never really left. So I've been able to learn to appreciate a few specialties. For me, the Green Sauce is like an herby breath of fresh air. Usually we in the region can start buying the 'Seven Herbs' from the middle of April. It's like a cooling aroma on my tongue;

I like to serve fried potatoes with it. What's nice about that is that green sauce has a cooling effect on the hot potatoes. And my trigeminal nerve endings probably register a lot more when I'm eating it. My recipe for Green Sauce has changed over the years. I started out with the recipe from Goethe's mother, Frau Aja. Years later, I learned from an Austrian celebrity chef in Frankfurt, Herr Lohninger, that this sauce also goes wonderfully with a poached egg—with a still-runny yolk, obviously. I do like living in Frankfurt. It is a cosmopolitan city, and it'll only keep changing through integration and immigration. I will continue to let myself be surprised.

WL   Many thanks, *Jocelyne Reich-Soufflet*, for your time and insights.

This talk took place end of March, 2022 in Frankfurt/Main.

*

Thank you, Jimmie and Maria Thereza,
for your debordering inspiration, that always connects us through our stomach-brains.

Thank you, Jocelyne Reich-Soufflet,
for your open-heartedness and trust in realising this text together—a plaisir.

*

BIOGRAPHIES

A writer, editor and researcher based in Berlin, *Wilma Lukatsch* (Dr. phil.) has graduate degrees in Art History, History of Religions and Sociology from the Freie Universität Berlin and the Humboldt-Universität zu Berlin. She has since been working with artists, and is focusing on developing a dialogue-based writing practice in close exchange and collaboration. She wrote her doctoral thesis on the inter-relational practices in the work of Maria Thereza Alves, and has deployed feminist and decolonial methodologies for understanding, addressing and re-imagining artworks and artists' voices.

Jocelyne Reich-Soufflet was born in the Parisian suburbs. After a classical training in dietetics, she studied nutritional psychology in Paris. Since 1977, she has worked as a dietician, nutritional therapist and nutritional psychologist, with an extensive lecture and teaching practice in Germany and elsewhere in Europe (including at nutritional therapy facilities and universities in Frankfurt, Taunus, South Tyrol and Italy). Since 1994, Jocelyne Reich-Soufflet has also had her own practice in Frankfurt am Main and has continued to specialise ever since. For more information see the website: www.reich-soufflet.de

18

This booklet is published on the occasion of documenta
fifteen (Kassel), 18 June – 25 September 2022

It is part of the publication *Jimmie Durham & A Stick
in the Forest by the Side of the Road* with Jimmie Durham
and Bev Koski, Elisa Strinna, Hamza Badran, Iain
Chambers, Joen Vedel, Jone Kvie, Maria Thereza Alves,
Wilma Lukatsch, Giulia Grechi, Alessandra Marino
Al-Mishlab (ISBN 978-3-7533-0260-7, NUR 640)

Text: © Wilma Lukatsch & Jocelyne Reich-Soufflet
Image: © Wilma Lukatsch, *A Mushroom Walk in a Berlin
Forest*, 2018
Editor: Iain Chambers
Translation: Rachel Glassberg
Proofreader: Nicola Gray
Design: Karoline Swiezynski, inspired by Will Holder's
design for *Past Imperfect* by Bik van der Pol, which
shaped the collective solution of this publication

The series HOW TO EAT AVEC PLAISIR is inspired
by and dedicated to Jimmie Durham.

The series will consist of five parts realised with:
Jocelyne Reich-Soufflet (Praxis Reich-Soufflet,
Frankfurt/Main), Katharina Koch (Landfleischerei Koch,
Calden), Susanne Wegerich (Dépa Forschungskantine
– Labor für kulinarische Forschung und nachhaltige
Alltagsernährung, Kassel), Stefan Itter (Biobauernhof
Eiwels, Kirchberg) and Ayami Awazuhara.

Printed and bound in Belgium by Cassochrome with
supervision of ArtLibro Trudy Dorrepaal. Published
in an edition of 500 individual booklets (documenta
fifteen) to be collated in an edition of 1000 books
distributed by Verlag der Buchhandlung Walther und
Franz König, Köln. First published by Verlag der
Buchhandlung Walther und Franz König Ehrenstraße 4,
D-50672 Köln.

Bibliographic information published by the Deutsche
Nationalbibliothek – The Deutsche Nationalbibliothek
lists this publication in the Deutsche National-
bibliografie; detailed bibliographic data is available
at http://dnb.d-nb.de.

Disclaimer: In making *Jimmie Durham & A Stick in the
Forest by the Side of the Road* we have quotes, images
and texts taken from various resources. Information
concerning the original authors and sources have been
credited as detailed as possible. Despite these efforts,
some sources nevertheless could not be identified.
Please contact the author in case of questions
or objections. The ideas and opinions author unless
stated otherwise.

*Jimmie Durham & A Stick in the Forest by the Side
of the Road* has been generously supported by
documenta fifteen.

This publication has been realized in
the framework of documenta fifteen,
June 18 – September 25, 2022

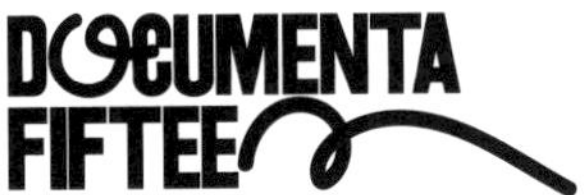

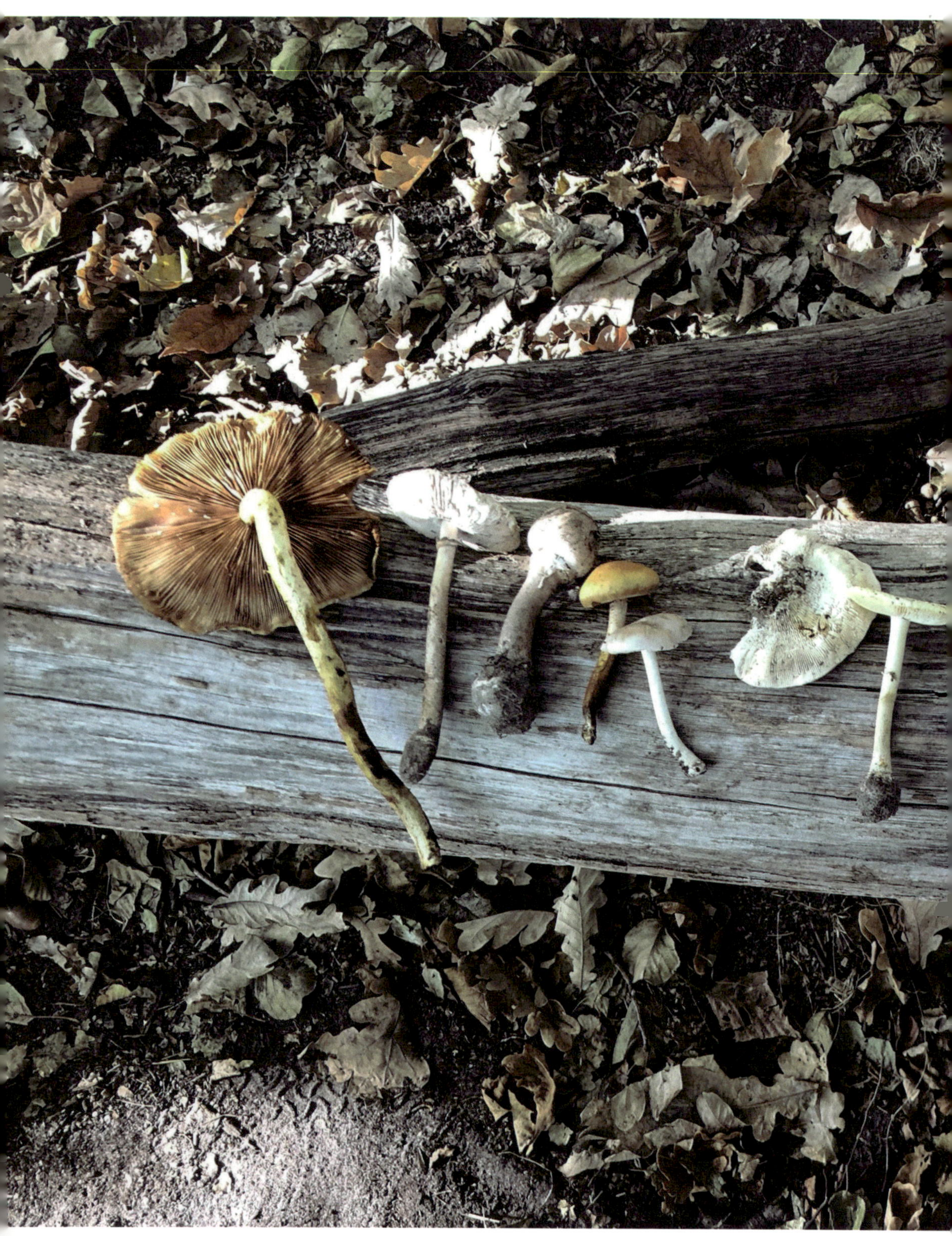

Jimmie Durham & A Stick in the Forest by the Side of the Road

To give us a common place to begin as a collective, Jimmie shortly
before his death, suggested that we go to the woods or even
a parking lot and sit down to spend some time looking precisely
around us where ever we were. It is a comfortable circle of about
160 meters. It is a way to introduce yourself to the place and
to begin to be in the place.

I was in Naples and went to the Capodimonte Woods—the former
grounds of a kingly palace with the landscaped gardens containing
local flora as well as exotics which were being acclimatized in Naples.
These exotics were there as colonial spoils of the Spanish Empire
which Naples was part of at one time. Instead, I chose to go to a local
stand of Oak Trees where Ivy intertwined up its trunk. In this same
stand, I also found the Butia Palm Tree growing. My father is from
the village of Butia in the state of Paraná in Brazil. I never saw one
growing in the village—they had all been cut down. I had once seen
a ornamentalized speciman in the Botanical Gardens of Rio
de Janeiro. But here by the Oak and Ivy they were happily un-land-
scaped. Their palm branches shooting up crazily from the ground
at different angles in between other vegetation. Unfurling a branch
wherever there might be a space and light. Walking a few steps
further, I saw a Poke Plant from Cherokee country. It was a vegetable that Jimmie loved to eat and was not to be found in any store.
The leaves can be harvested in the spring before the dark purple
berries appear on magenta vines which then make the plant a bit
toxic. It is like a spring tonic—making your body alive again to life
beginning. We had seen it growing abundantly in different parts
of Italy. It turns out that it was imported so that the berries could
be used to dye red wine that was not dark enough—now an illegal
practice. And so the plant is no longer much remembered here and
no one knows about its leaves that can be a vegetable.

In the Middle East, carpets traditionally had rich patterns of flora.
They were placed inside spaces, but also transported and placed
outside for meetings—a portable garden, a reminder of complexities
beyond the human. I began to design carpets for my work
in documenta.

And I returned to writing the last stanzas of the poem *Maria*.

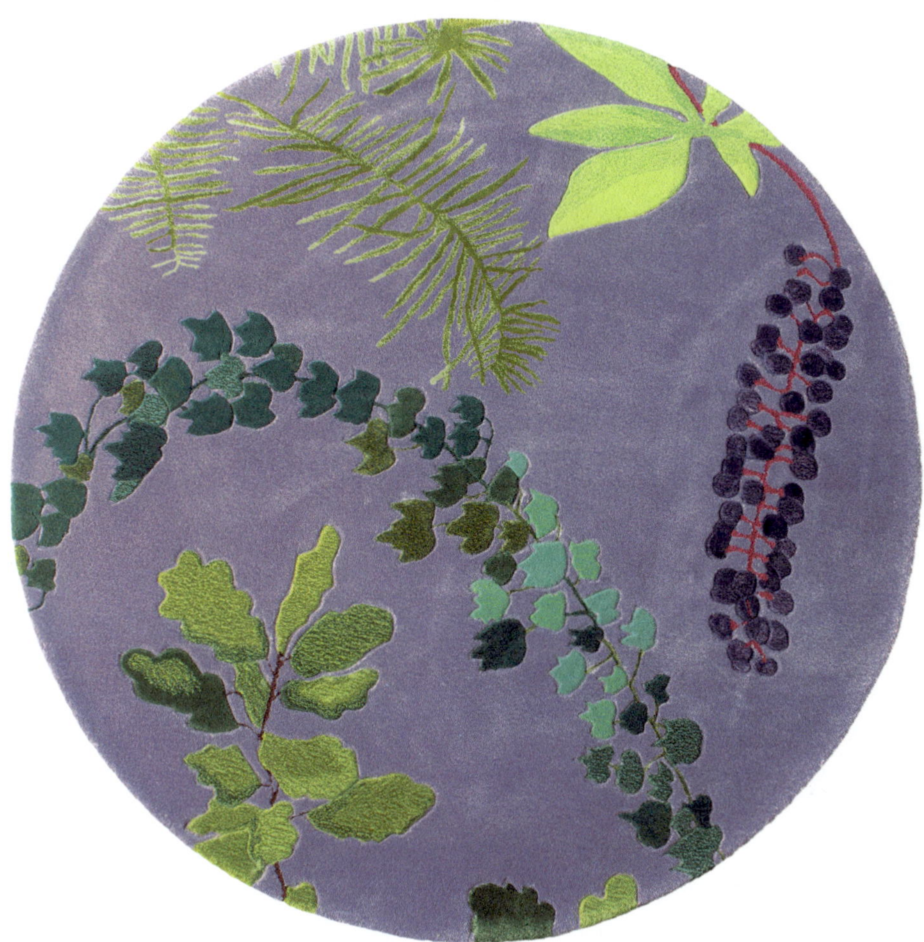

On Responsibilities Acquired while on a Stroll in a Garden in Europe
Maria Thereza Alves, 2022

Oak Tree and Ivy, a Butia Palm Tree and a Poke Plant

Wool and tencel carpet, 160 cm diameter. Produced by CarpetEdition.

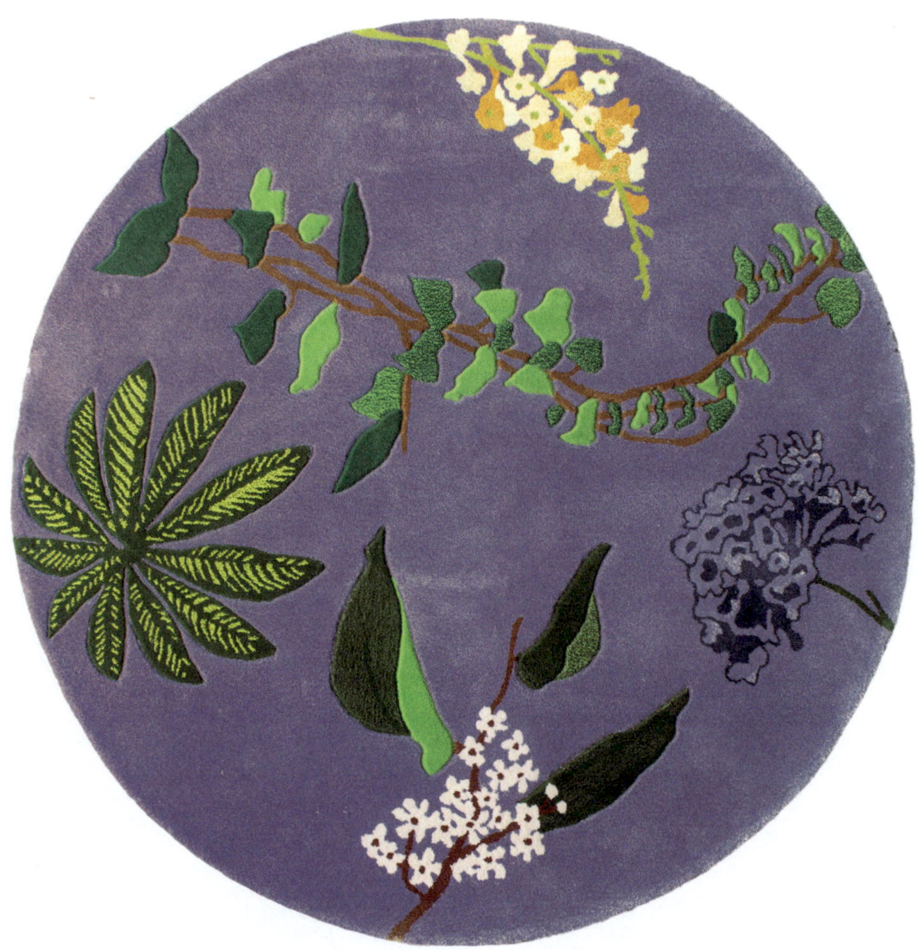

On the Need of Remembering Here before the Onslaught of There Began
Maria Thereza Alves, 2022

Ubatuba is in the Atlantic Forest, of which about 93 percent has been destroyed since colonization, and here is a list of some flora that still exist, at the moment: Jequitiba, Guaparuvu, Ipe Roxo, Embauba, and the vine Ysypo marilombre from which a tea can be made for remembering.

Wool and tencel carpet, 160 cm diameter. Produced by CarpetEdition.

A mariner from the Kassel area went to Brazil in the mid-16th century and got a job as a gunner operating a cannon to kill the Tupinamba Indigenous people. He was captured by them and taken to what was then the village of Ubatuba—where some of my family now live. He was freed and returned home and wrote a book about the "cannibals" of Brazil.

EVIDENCES

Hundreds of years later, this concept is still vivid in the settler imagination. It was reintroduced by elite settler Brazilian intellectuals in 1922 during Modern Art Week, which, at the same time, popularized Modernism.

Now, in 2022, some are celebrating this 100th anniversary and some are not.

The legacy of the mariner's book continues to have repercussions on Indigenous culture, education, health and safety today. The only mention of Indigenous peoples in Ubatuba are plaques that relegate the Indigenous to "cannibals". Ninety percent of the Guaraní Indigenous children in Ubatuba today do not go to school because of bullying.

In 2010, Jimmie Durham and I were in São Paulo to research and make new works for the Bienal. He was making the installation, "Bureau for Research into Brazilian Normality", which was an attack on contemporary colonization in Brazil. As part of his work, Jimmie requested to meet with progressive Brazilian intellectuals in the city. During the meeting, he would say the word "Indian" and we would wait to hear how the Brazilian intellectuals would respond. In every case, eminent progressive intellectuals began with mentioning anthropophagists in their response to the word "Indian".

There is a room in a museum near to Kassel that is dedicated to this mariner. Recently a statue was erected in his honor in the local public square. There is an institute in São Paulo that bears the mariner's name and celebrates him with conferences with invited international speakers. Sometimes conferences are also held in this museum near Kassel to commemorate the mariner and his book. Images of contemporary Indigenous peoples from different regions of Brazil—transformed into generic consumers of human flesh—are used to illustrate the mariner's words in the museum near Kassel.

MARIA

The Butia breathed and their scent floated just beyond the edges of the Araucaria forest.

The Kaingang had helped make this pine forest into a vast being.

Now, a cultural landscape where   Jaguars wandered.

We have evidence,

                                later their skins would decorate living room walls.

Five years before Maria was born, the newspaper advertised:

"request for funds to pay cowboys to beat the forest and chase the forest dwellers away".

                                One cowboy killed over 1000 Indigenous people.
                                He became a celebrated hero.

Maria removed the kerchief around her head.

Her black hair falling below her waist.

Settlers began to come in during the 17ᵗʰ century but the Kaingang resisted fiercely.

A prince in Rio de Janeiro ordered the
                                "suspension of effects of humanity" against the Kaingang.

And still the Kaingang resisted and delayed colonization for another 100 years.

Then came: the Southern Brazil Lumber and Colonization Company.

They laid down railroad tracks.

Maria Thereza Alves

And cut down 15 kilometres of forest

on either side of those tracks.

The forest of coexistence became nothing more than a revenue source.

Fifty million Araucaria trees were felled and shipped to Europe and the USA.

My father said, "This forest was how the Americans got the wood to build their houses."

His brother, an inept gambler, bet and lost all of grandmother's Araucaria trees.

He had left her one but later lost even that one.

The company sold the treeless plots to Germans, Ukrainians and Poles.

"To whiten Brazil", one governor said,
"To purify the national organism of the vices of its origin
And its contact with slavery."

Infrastructure making

A promised land, they were told.

But the rich forest earth had been
a collaboration with trees.
And soon it was unfertile.

Uncle Teco and Uncle Antonio indebted themselves to banks
to buy fertilizer for their tired plots.

In nearby Tres Barras, "Lumber" built the largest sawmill in South America.

The pine monster devoured 150 Araucaria trees a day.

In the War of the Contestados, Indigenous peoples, squatters and the unemployed united against "Lumbe

But they would lose that war.

Today, the Brazilian army's largest training camp is installed there.

Earlier, in the 1850s, began to come *Bugreiros*, Hunters of Indians,

Hired by the government and corporations.

Around the fire late at night they would amuse their neighbors with their killing stories.

They continued to kill Indians legally until 1914 in Paraná, Santa Catarina and Rio Grande do Sul.

Today these are the whitest states in Brazil.

Infrastructure making.

Angelo Kreta from the Mangueirinha Reservation in Paraná who led
the Kaingangs in retaking stolen lands was killed in an ambush on the road
one month before I was to meet him.

Tupa-y, the Guaraní land activist who asked me to continue working on international politics was
assassinated three years later.

Infrastructure making.

Maria, said, "I'm ninety-eight and I don't have one white hair. It's all black. The people here think I'm Italian because of my black hair and fair skin but I am *Bugre*, pure *Bugre*. That's why I don't have white hair."

Bugre means 'booger-man', a racist word to refer to the Indigenous.

Bugre is a word made to make one hate oneself.

Bugre is a word to make one forget one's history and people.

The teaching of German and Italian is mandatory around here.

Yet no Indigenous language is.

Infrastructure making.

Bugreiros were paid upon proof of death—the ears.

Maria was considered the best dancer in the village. Young men chose to dance with her before a date as she was patient with their clumsiness and smoothed out their steps.

Until she was thirty Maria could be hunted and killed with the sanction of the Brazilian state.

Recently I heard there is—now—an Indian killer from the north of Brazil living in New York.

After a meal with friends, he tells his stories of killings I am told.

He used poison on barbecued meat.

In Maria's middle age, the last known massacre was committed against an Indigenous village in this area. The white family who was involved and their descendants still live there.

Infrastructure making.

Where Maria and I met, the forest had long ago been made dead.

I did not ask her if she still held on to the scent of the sweetness of the Butia
as she bit into the pulpy orange flesh.

Since my father had been a young man, he had not seen any Butia Palm Tree that gave
the name to his village.

Infrastructure that is   made forever.

Colonizadora Sinop S.A. is a real estate company in Paraná and Mato Grosso.
Specialising in making appear "out of nowhere, or from certain nothings, identified on the map of Brazil,
environments conducive to the formation of human settlements", a journalist wrote.

And INCRA, the National Institute for Colonization and Land Reform, continues to bring in settlers
and colonize.

Maria's daughter, whose mother and father were Indigenous, does not consider herself one.
Nor do her grandchildren.

There is no romanticism of the Indian here. You are shamed for:

Your wide feet.

Your wrong nose.

Your hair.

Your skin colour and

Your 'ripped' eyes.

Maria Thereza Alves

If you are blond and fair my grandmother said how beautiful you were.
If you were dark like my father, called Rouge (Copper), you were told how ugly you were.
They spoke about my "Japanese" eyes to avoid embarrassing my mother.
Some of us slip into hiding and denial and then loss of oneself—to live.

I came back to visit Maria's family in 2018. We went to the remnant of the forest.

Now private property of a German evangelical pastor.

As we left, he told Maria's grandchild to read, *"Mein Kampf* by Adolf Hitler—a great writer", he said.

Infrastructure making.

When they logged the great Araucaria trees, they came crashing down, breaking all the smaller trees and bushes.

When my grandmother died and they were cleaning out the house there was a photograph of my great-grandmother who was Black. An aunt was asked to take it and refused saying she never had met the woman. In her kitchen, there is a framed picture of the German side of her husband's family. None of these people has she ever met.

It is rather the absences that tell our stories here. The presence is proud white.

This aunt, an unproud descendent of Indigenous and Black women, is making infrastructure for only the white people in her family.

And continues to shame one of her daughters for the colour of her hair and skin, calling her *Preta*—as she explained, "Everything is Black about her." which in this village does not mean Black but *Bugre*—a politeness, it is thought, to avoid referencing the Indian.

Today there are 4.5 million speakers of German and 22,000 speakers of Kaingang in Brazil.

During a conference in Rome, an Italian professor said that those who came to Brazil now were not responsible for the colonization then.

But over 4 million speak Italian in Brazil now.

Infrastructure-making bequeaths inherited privileges.

Making one complicit with genocide and the forever-making colonization.

In 2018, Maria's house was given to me by her daughter. It is a great honor and responsibility.

I went for a walk in the Capodimonte Woods in Naples—the former grounds of a kingly palace with exotic flora that were acclimatized here, a colonial practice. Instead I was studying a humble Oak grove.

On my way out, on top of that hill overlooking Naples, who sent so many immigrants to Brazil, a Butia stood by the side entrance to the palace.

I wonder now what are my responsibilities on this, my second meeting with a Butia.

Maria Thereza Alves
December 17, 2021, Naples

FURTHER EVIDENCES

In 2016, I was in a hotel room in Brazil waiting for an early
morning flight. I turned on the TV and there was a program
on called "The Fashion Squad", where locals contact the station
to request the 'fix up' of a friend. This particular episode was
about Jessica Vitoria, a young law student whose friend had called
up because she did not appreciate that Jessica Vitoria identified
as Indigenous. In Germany, a million Germans go off to the woods
to romantically play at being "Indians" every summer. In Brazil,
where colonialism continues, it is instead a courageous act.
European descendants in Brazil continue to murder Indigenous
activists over land.

At the beginning of the program, Jessica Vitoria said they could
do anything regarding her clothes but that they could not remove
her *terere*, a hair decoration with feathers. Forty minutes later,
Jessica Vitoria's feathered terere is removed.

This program is visual documentation of the quotidian colonial
coercion to remove all that is Indigenous in Brazil and celebrate
the state-imposed "modernizing Brazilianness", which was also
affirmed by those artists who celebrated the introduction
of modernity in 1922 in Brazil.

Fashion Squad

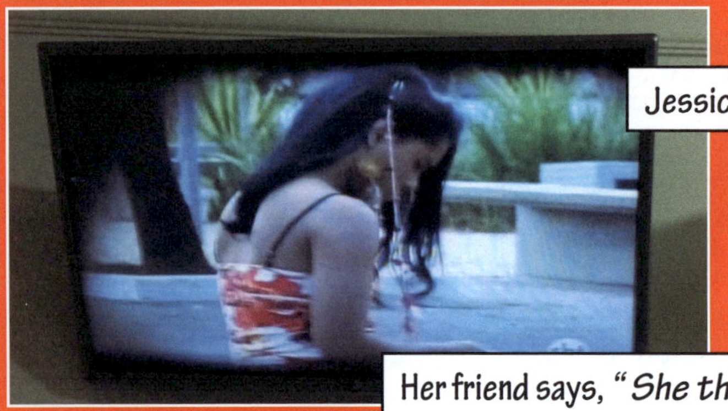

Jessica Vitoria, a law student.

Her friend says, "*She thinks she is Indian, she is not.*" Another friend asks, "*Please take the feather terere from her head.*"

Esquadrão de Moda (Fashion Squad) Arte 1 Television Station:

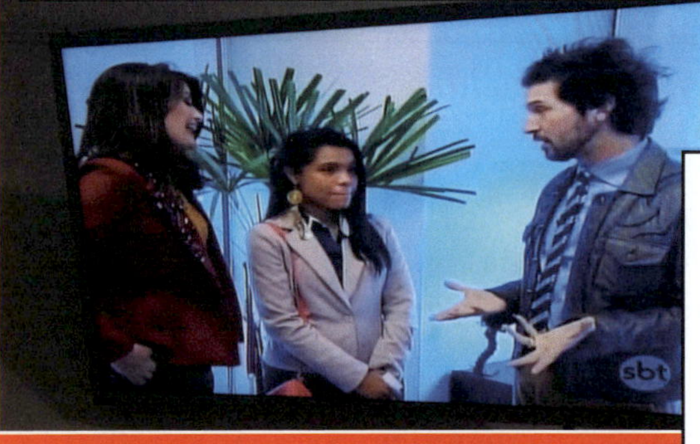

The television hosts create a fake invitation to Jessica Vitoria for a job interview in an important law office in the city. When she arrives, the hosts explain the program and begin to criticise Jessica Vitoria's clothing, particularly her shoes and feather *terere*.

First attempt by one of the hosts to remove the feather *terere*.

Jessica Vitoria replies:

The hosts ask Jessica Vitoria to explain her favourite clothes.

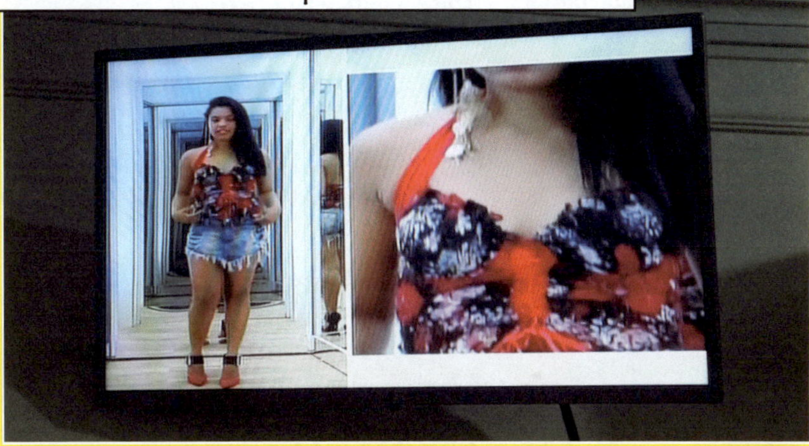

They present an example of 'correct' colours and style.

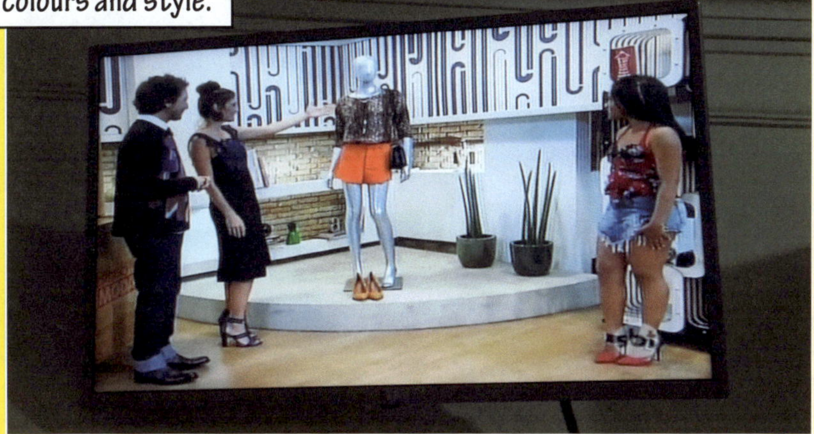

The hosts then begin to dispose of Jessica Vitoria's favourite clothing into a garbage bin.

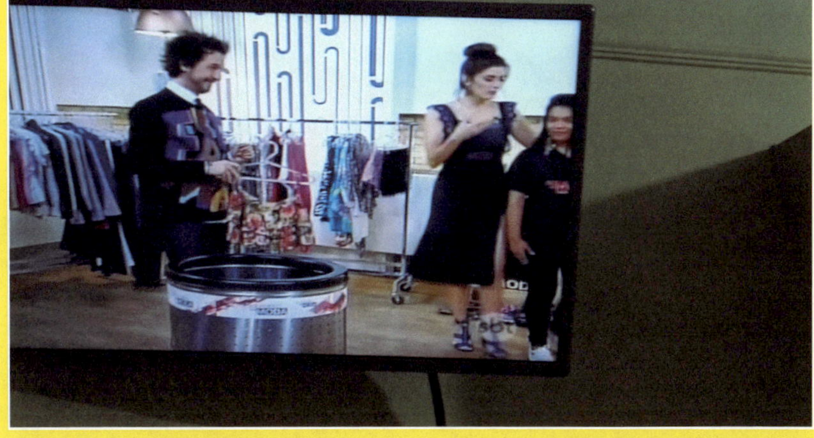

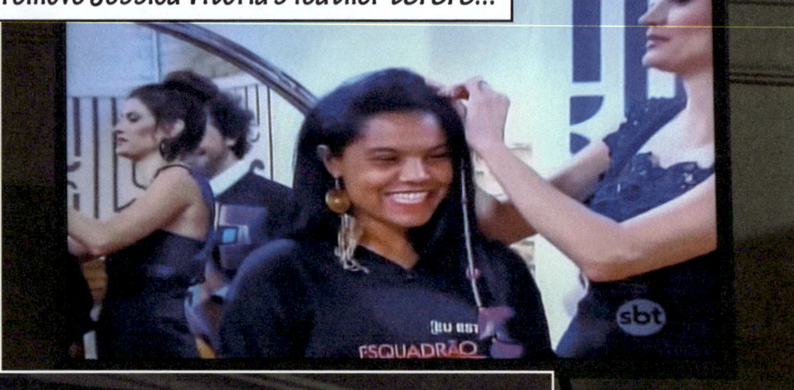

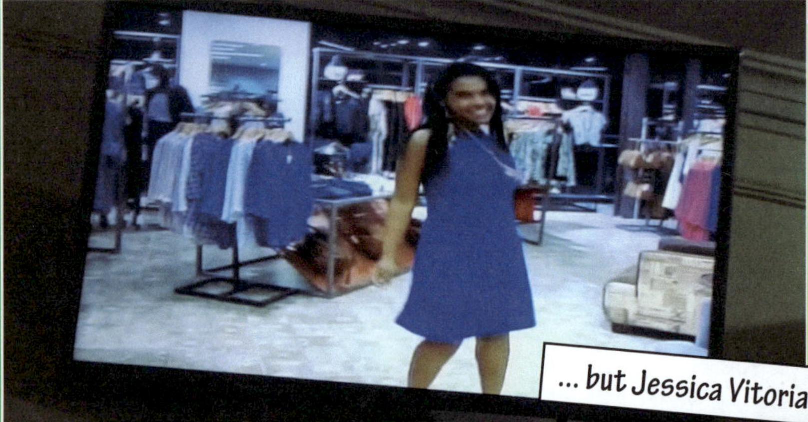

Hairdresser:

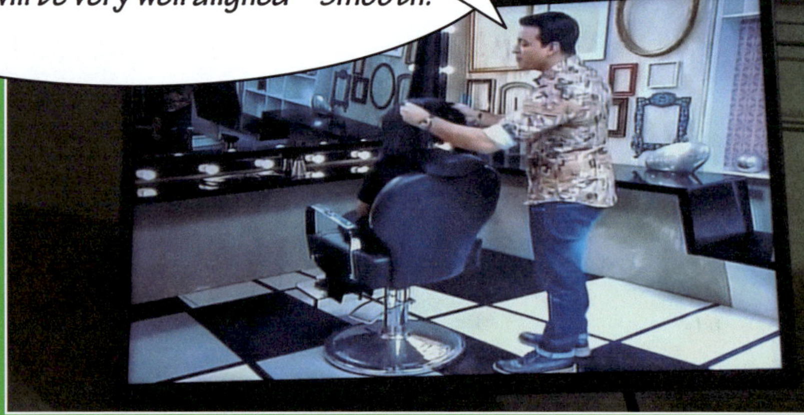

Hairdresser:

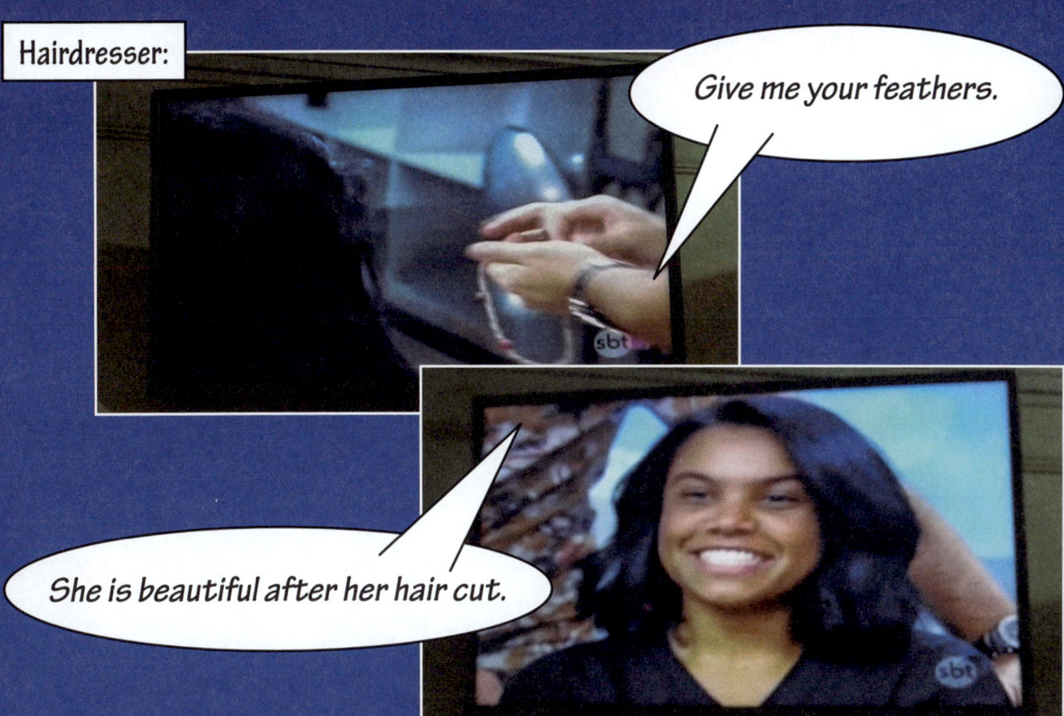

Make-up session. Another attempt to remove the feather *terere*.

The make-up stylist places the feather *terere* on her own head and confronts Jessica Vitoria with it, who is then offered a make-up kit if she gives up her feathers to the stylist.

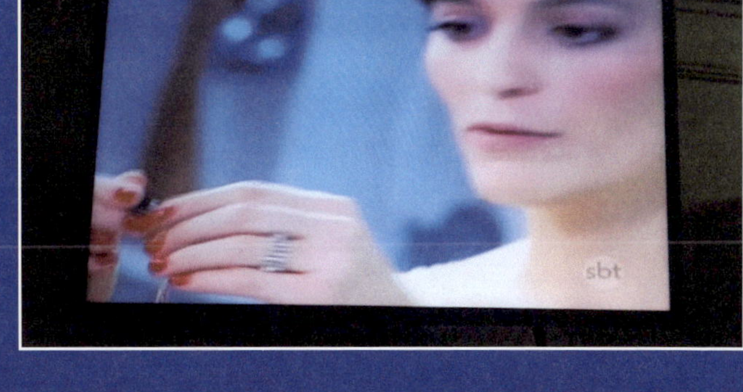

Jessica Vitoria agrees...

Jessica Vitoria:

Female presenter:

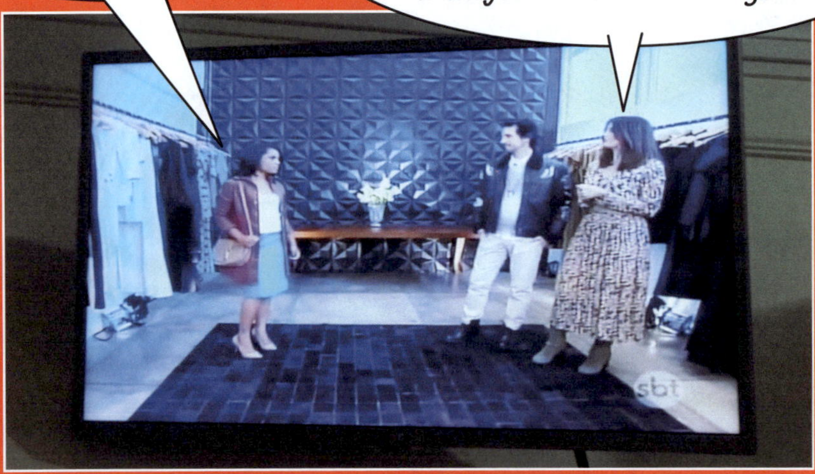

The program ends with this image: a mugshot of the 'before' image of Jessica Vitoria.

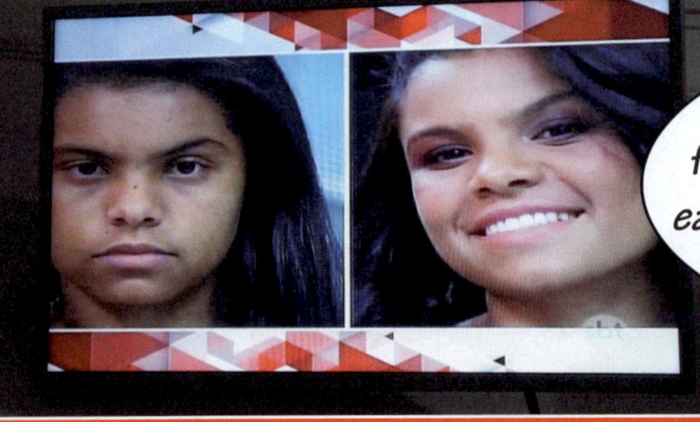

Whereas this is how she smiled at the beginning.

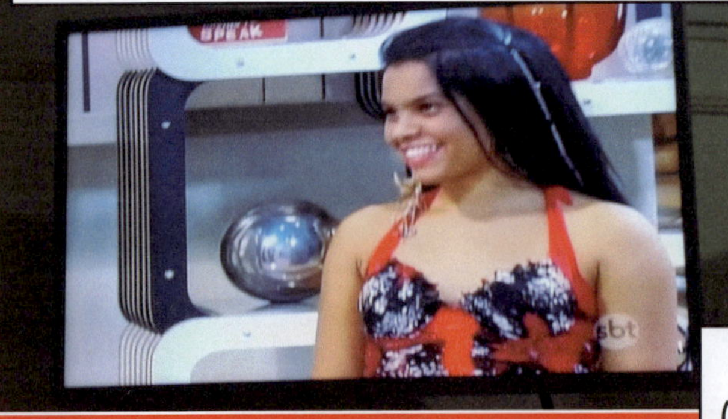

Jessica Vitoria struggled to affirm her indigeneity in the midst of colonial prime time television.

THE END
(of just one battle in an ongoing fight)

This booklet is published on the occasion of documenta
fifteen (Kassel), 18 June – 25 September 2022

It is part of the publication *Jimmie Durham & A Stick
in the Forest by the Side of the Road* with Jimmie Durham
and Bev Koski, Elisa Strinna, Hamza Badran, Iain
Chambers, Joen Vedel, Jone Kvie, Maria Thereza Alves,
Wilma Lukatsch, Giulia Grechi, Alessandra Marino
Al-Mishlab (ISBN 978-3-7533-0260-7, NUR 640)

© 2022 Maria Thereza Alves and Verlag der
Buchhandlung Walther und Franz König, Köln

Text: Maria Thereza Alves
Images: In *Fashion Squad* novella by © Maria Thereza
Alves and images of *On Responsibilities Acquired while
on a Stoll in a Garden in Europe and On the Need of
Remembering Here before the Onslaught of There Began*
are by CarpetEdition
Courtesy: Alfonso Artiaco Gallery, Galleria Jaqueline
Martins, and Galerie Michel Rein
Special thanks: CarpetEdition
Editor: Iain Chambers
Proofreader: Nicola Grey
Design: Karoline Swiezynski, inspired by Will Holder's
design for *Past Imperfect* by Bik van der Pol, which
shaped the collective solution of this publication
Design of *Fashion Squad* novella: Linus Blonduelle

The poem *Maria* was originally commissioned in
conjunction with Alanis Obomsawin's retrospective
exhibit held at Haus der Kulturen der Welt.
hkw.de/AnotherStory, 2022.

Printed and bound in Belgium by Cassochrome with
supervision of ArtLibro Trudy Dorrepaal. Published
in an edition of 500 individual booklets (documenta
fifteen) to be collated in an edition of 1000 books
distributed by Verlag der Buchhandlung Walther
und Franz König, Köln. First published by Verlag der
Buchhandlung Walther und Franz König Ehrenstraße 4,
D-50672 Köln

Bibliographic information published by the Deutsche
Nationalbibliothek – The Deutsche Nationalbibliothek
lists this publication in the Deutsche National-
bibliografie; detailed bibliographic data is available
at http://dnb.d-nb.de.

Disclaimer: In making *Jimmie Durham & A Stick in the
Forest by the Side of the Road* we have quotes, images
and texts taken from various resources. Information
concerning the original authors and sources have been
credited as detailed as possible. Despite these efforts,
some sources nevertheless could not be identified.
Please contact the author in case of questions
or objections. The ideas and opinions author unless
stated otherwise.

*Jimmie Durham & A Stick in the Forest by the Side
of the Road* has been generously supported by
documenta fifteen.

The artist would like to thank Elizabeth Povinelli for
introducing her to the concept of colonial infrastructure
making as inheritance.

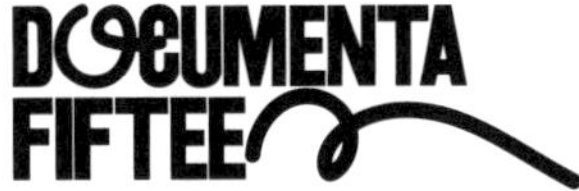

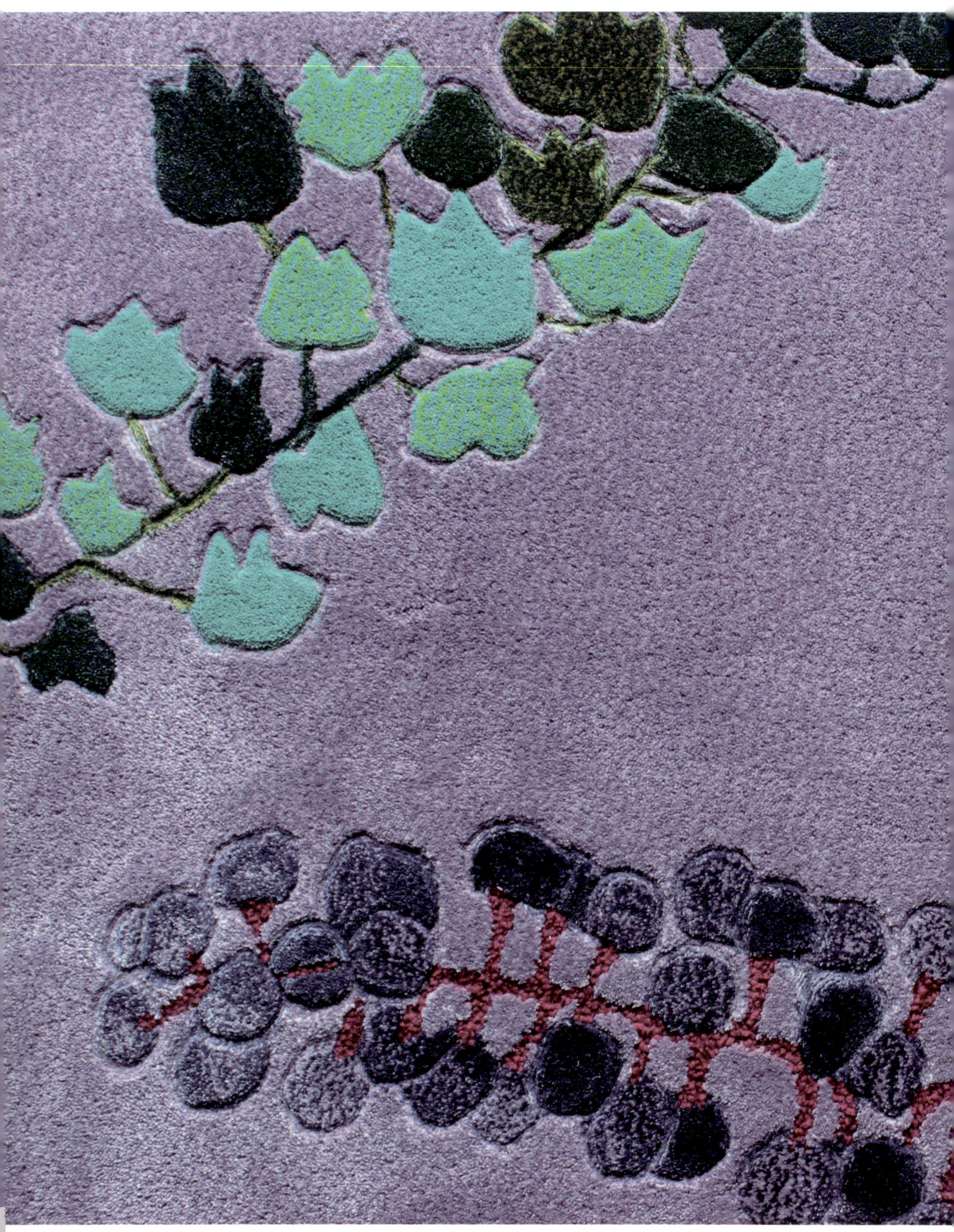

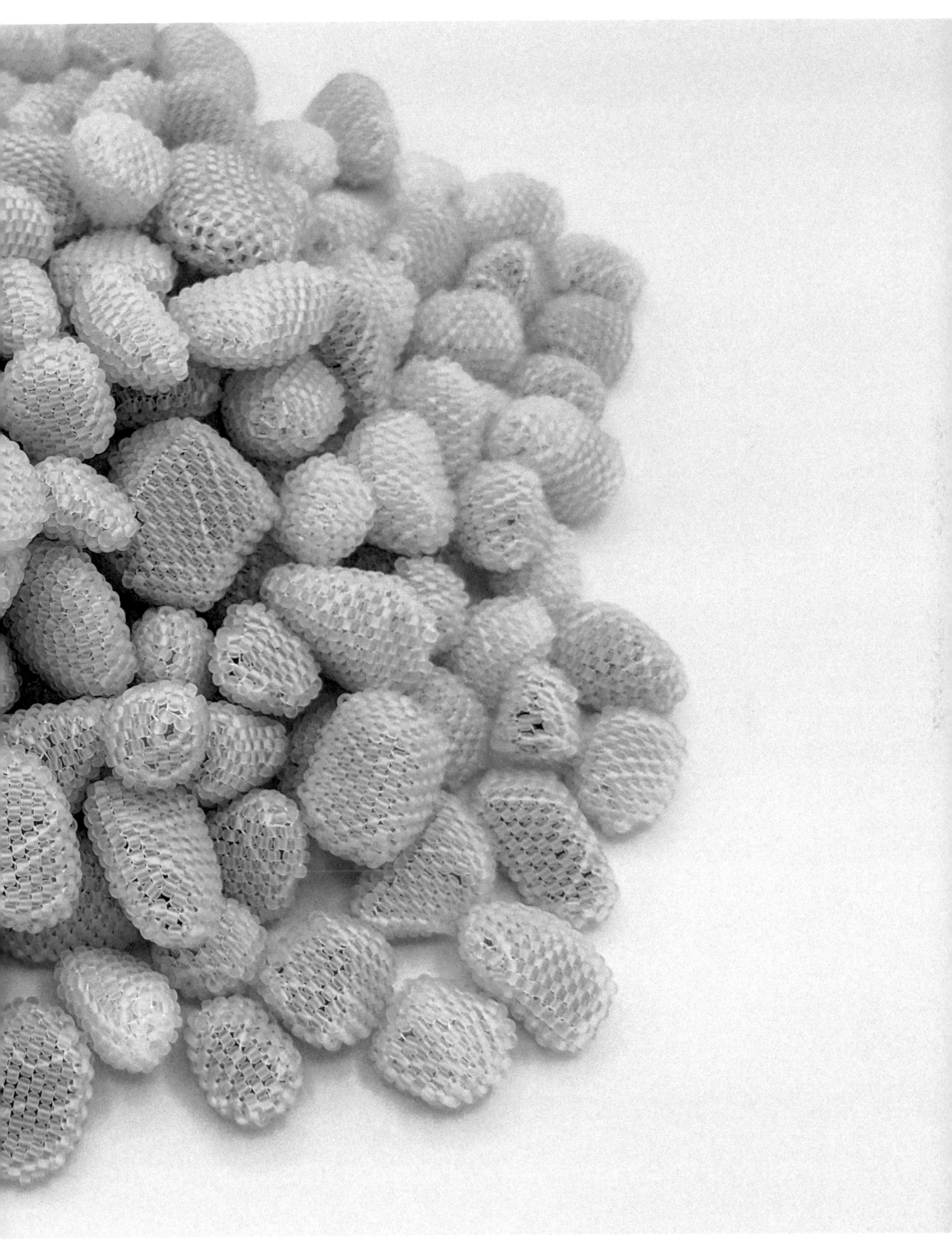

Jimmie Durham & A Stick in the Forest by the Side of the Road

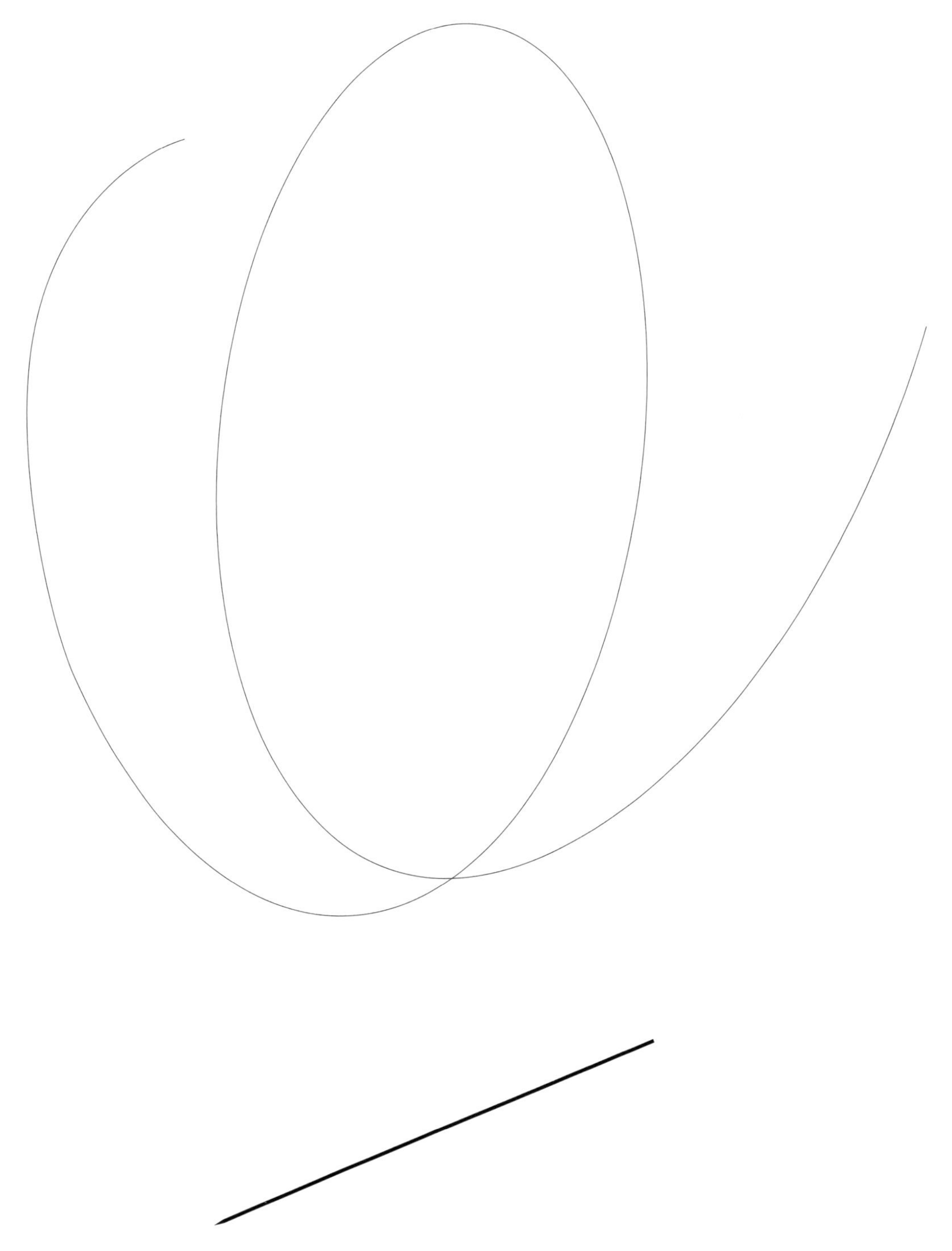

Bev Koski

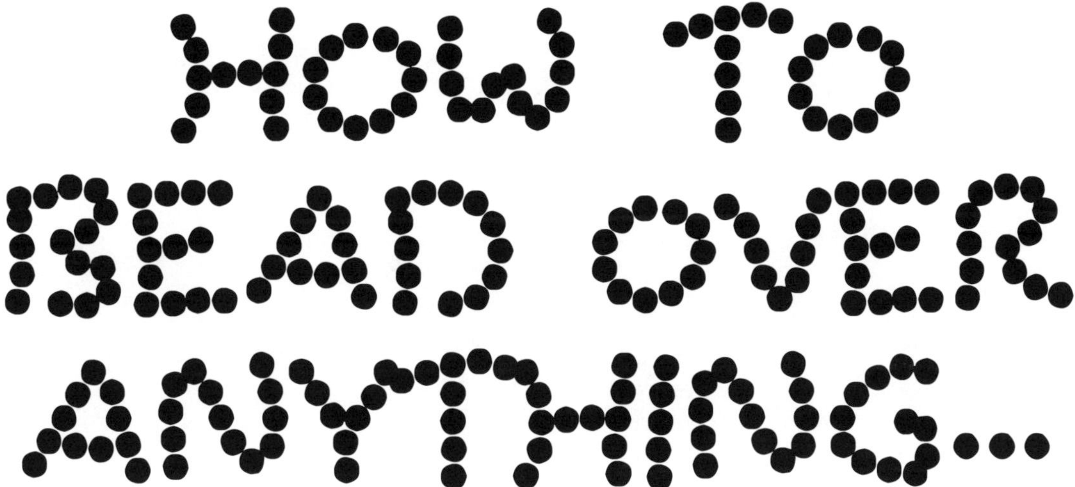

FIND A NEEDLE AND THREAD.

YOU WILL NEED
AN ITEM
OF ANYTHING.

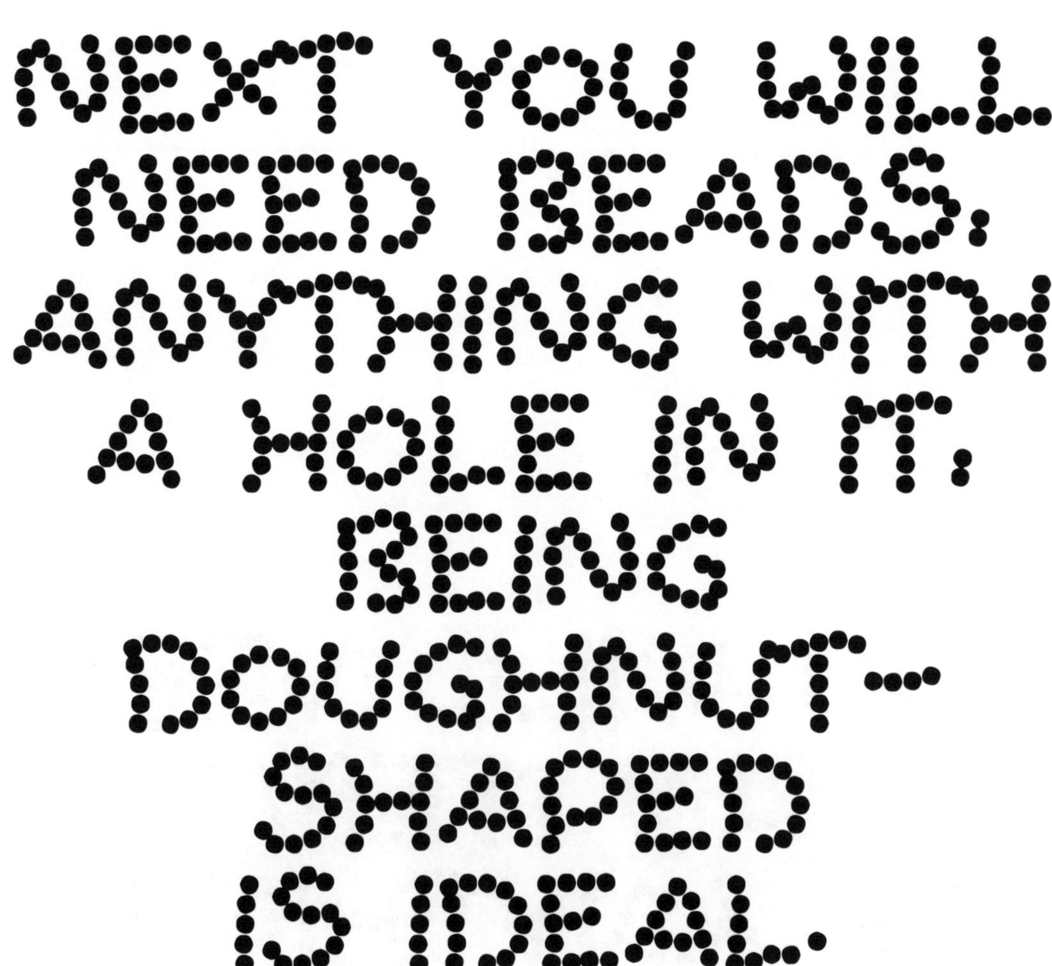
NEXT YOU WILL NEED BEADS, ANYTHING WITH A HOLE IN IT, BEING DOUGHNUT-SHAPED IS IDEAL.

Bev Koski

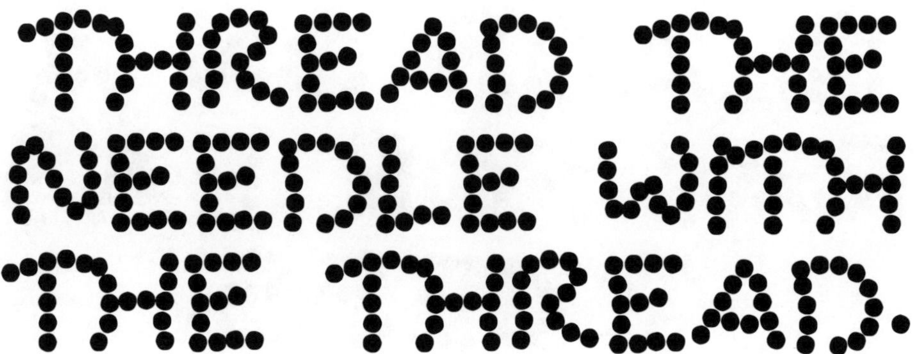
THREAD THE
NEEDLE WITH
THE THREAD.

Bev Koski

THREAD A CE
OF BEADS
THROUGH THE
MAKING A CIR

Bev Koski

THE CIRCLE OF BEADS NEEDS TO BE THE SIZE OF THE WAIST OF THE ITEM.

Bev Koski

PICK UP ONE
BEAD, SKIP
OVER ONE
BEAD AND GO
THROUGH THE
NEXT BEAD.

IF THE ROW OF
BEADS NEEDS
TO BE
SMALLER,
SKIP ADDING
A BEAD.

Bev Koski

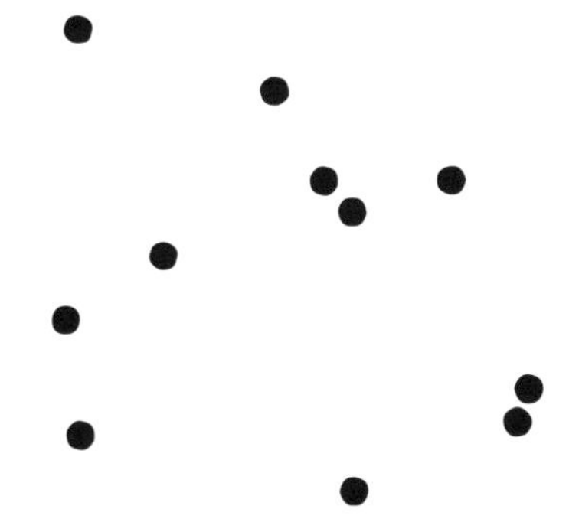

IF THE ROW OF
BEADS NEEDS
TO BE LARGER,
ADD TWO
BEADS INSTEAD
OF ONE.

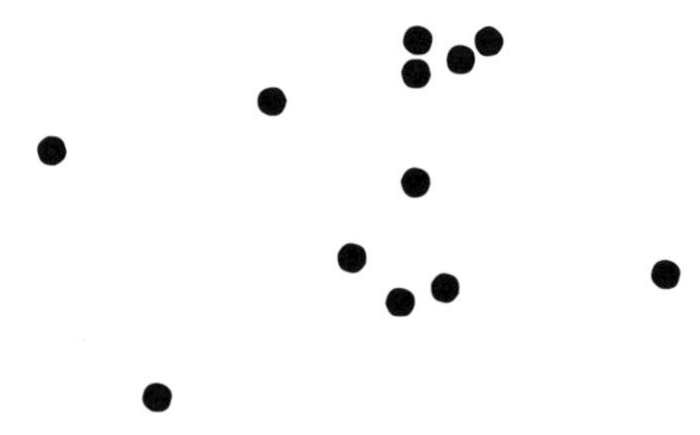

REPEAT UNTIL
ONE END OF
THE ITEM. TURN
OVER THE ITEM
AND REPEAT.

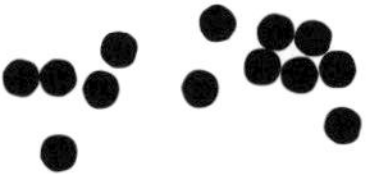

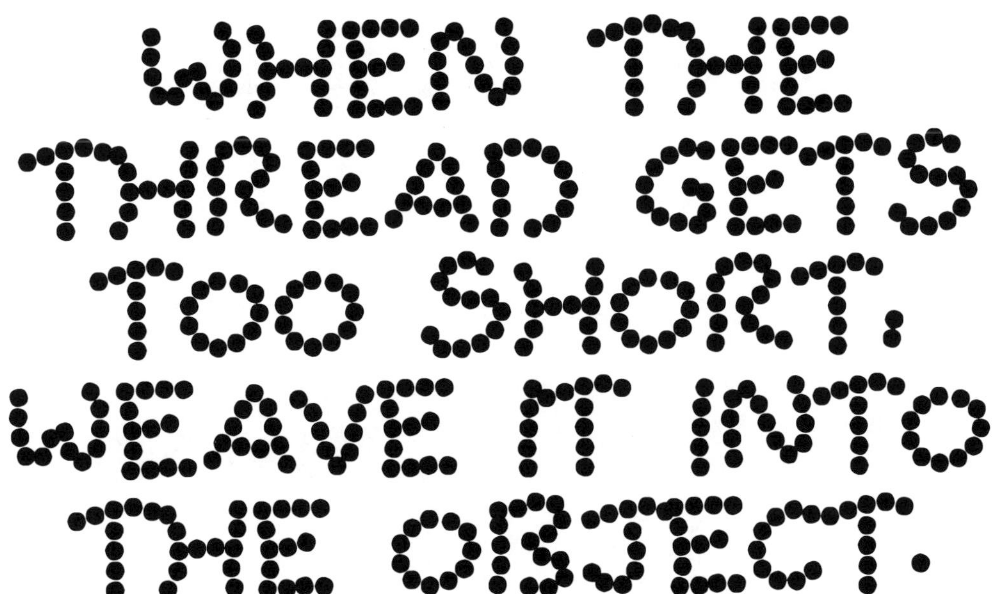
WHEN THE
THREAD GETS
TOO SHORT,
WEAVE IT INTO
THE OBJECT.

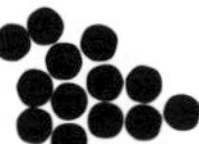

ATTACH
ANOTHER
THREAD BY
WEAVING IT INTO
THE PREVIOUS
ROWS.

This booklet is published on the occasion of documenta
fifteen (Kassel), 18 June – 25 September 2022

It is part of the publication *Jimmie Durham & A Stick
in the Forest by the Side of the Road* with Jimmie Durham
and Bev Koski, Elisa Strinna, Hamza Badran, Iain
Chambers, Joen Vedel, Jone Kvie, Maria Thereza Alves,
Wilma Lukatsch, Giulia Grechi, Alessandra Marino
Al-Mishlab (ISBN 978-3-7533-0260-7, NUR 640)

Text: Bev Koski
Image: © Bev Koski
Editor: Iain Chambers
Proofreader: Nicola Grey
Design: Karoline Swiezynski, inspired by Will Holder's
design for *Past Imperfect* by Bik van der Pol, which
shaped the collective solution of this publication

Printed and bound in Belgium by Cassochrome with
supervision of ArtLibro Trudy Dorrepaal. Published
in an edition of 250 individual booklets (documenta
fifteen) to be collated in an edition of 1000 books
distributed by Verlag der Buchhandlung Walther und
Franz König, Köln. First published by Verlag der
Buchhandlung Walther und Franz König Ehrenstraße 4,
D-50672 Köln.

Bibliographic information published by the Deutsche
Nationalbibliothek – The Deutsche Nationalbibliothek
lists this publication in the Deutsche National-
bibliografie; detailed bibliographic data is available
at http://dnb.d-nb.de.

Disclaimer: In making *Jimmie Durham & A Stick in the
Forest by the Side of the Road* we have quotes, images
and texts taken from various resources. Information
concerning the original authors and sources have been
credited as detailed as possible. Despite these efforts,
some sources nevertheless could not be identified.
Please contact the author in case of questions
or objections. The ideas and opinions author unless
stated otherwise.

Bev Koski's artwork *Beaded Stones #1 – 215* was
generously supported by the Canada Council of Arts.

*Jimmie Durham & A Stick in the Forest by the Side
of the Road* has been generously supported by
documenta fifteen.

This publication has been realized in
the framework of documenta fifteen,
June 18 - September 25, 2022

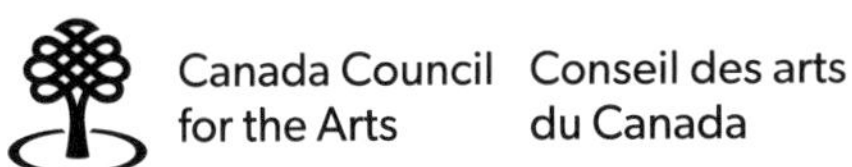

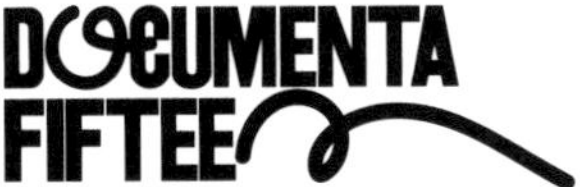

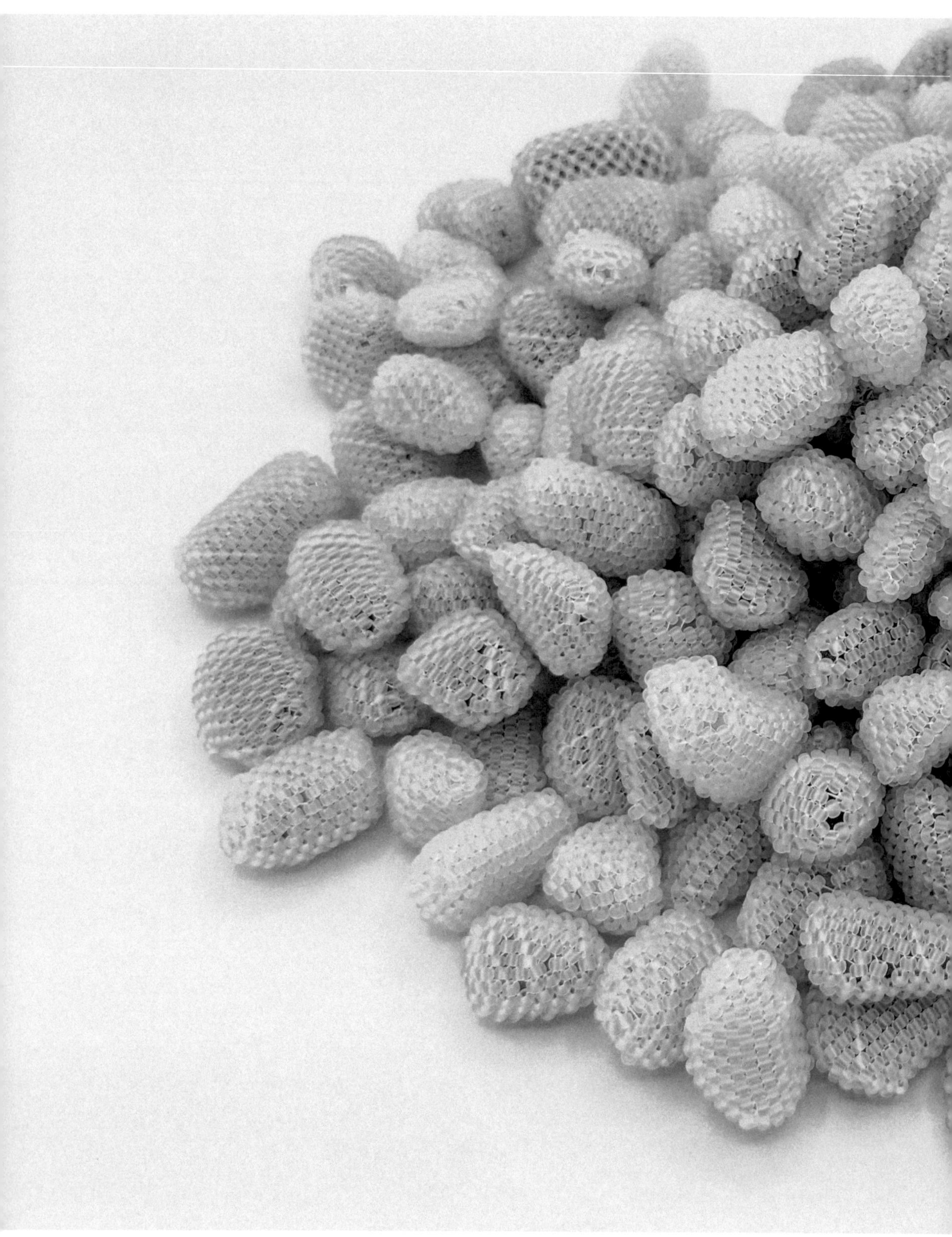

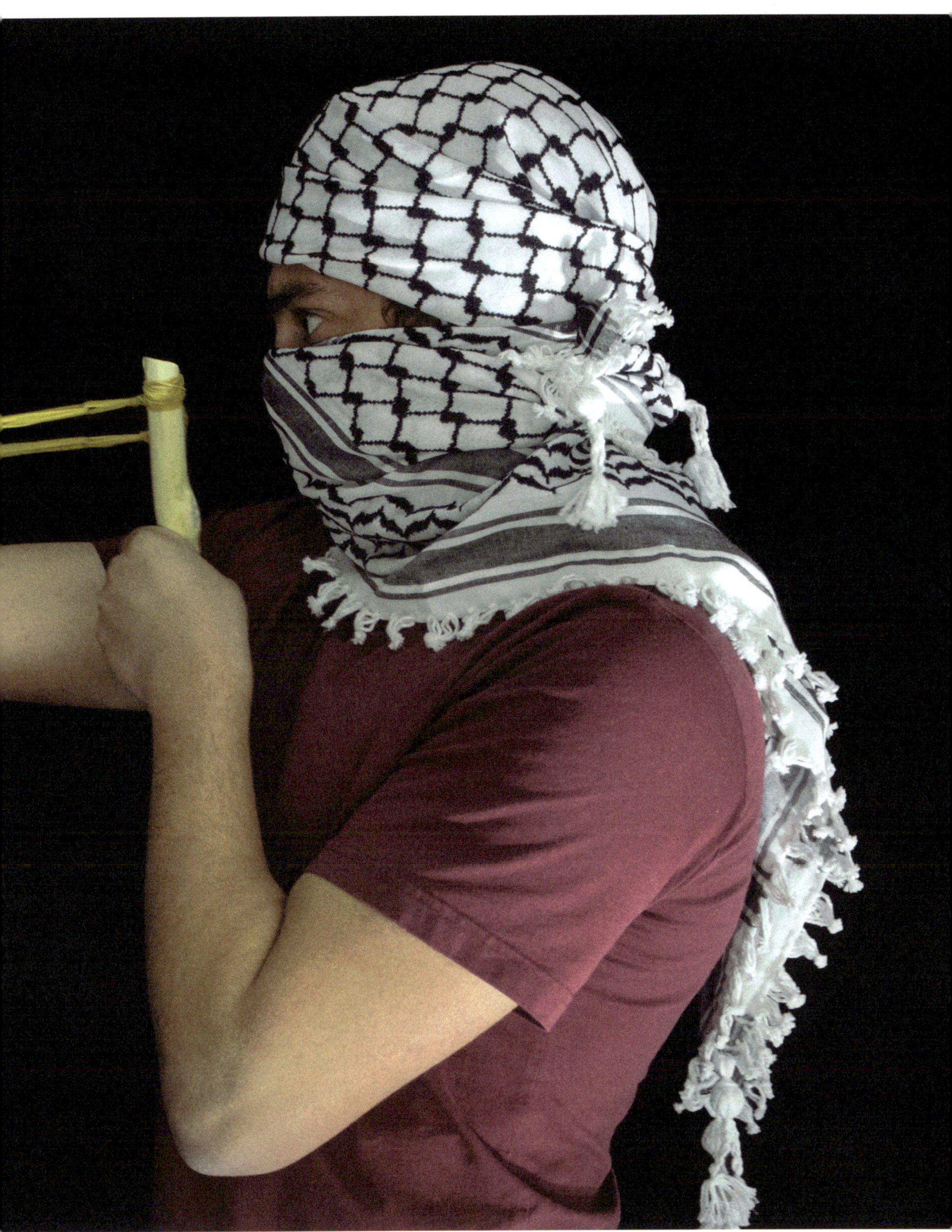

Jimmie Durham & A Stick in the Forest by the Side of the Road

To Jimmie Durham and my grandmother

**"When one's grandmother dies, it is like so much
of the world dies; so much of the past that has given
us courage. But it only means that you must
be on your way to become a grandparent, even if,
like me, you make no children; we are part of the
past and the future."**

Condolences from Jimmie Durham on the death of my grandmother in 2021

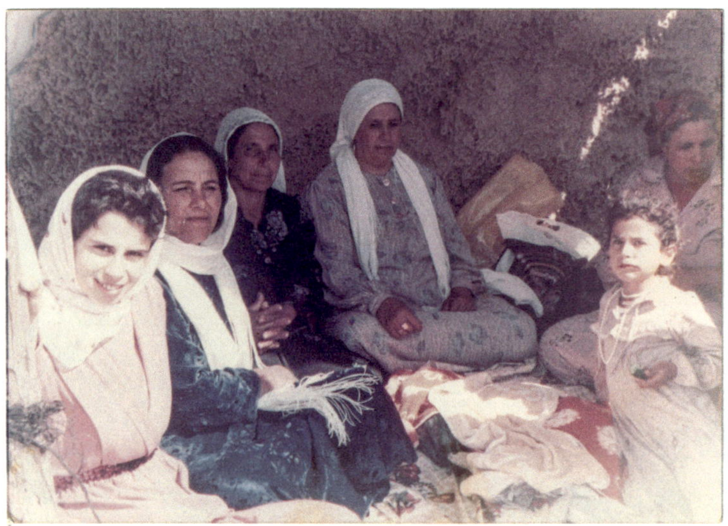

My grandmother, second from left

The Freedom Fighter

"The last night of the night, no way back and no way further, he stopped in the middle of the plane, took the sling shot out of his jeans pocket and shot the pilot in the back of his head with a stone, the stone that was made of a stone. It was too late for the night to see the morning; it was too late for the pilot to see the stone."

Bite the Hand that Feeds You

Bite the Hand that Feeds You is the beginning of a project in which I try to question the role of Western art and the cultural institutions in Palestine. I focus on what Europe expects from Palestinian artists or academics and how funding for the arts and culture in 'conflict-ridden' areas like Palestine is conditioned by Western political and economic agendas. I share here some of my personal stories with art institutions, schools, foundations and associations in Palestine, as well as my experiences with European figures as a Palestinian artist living in Europe. This is just a start.

Did you ever hear of the 'International' Academy of Art Palestine?

I didn't have any idea about contemporary visual arts. I didn't even have that much interest, I was 21 years old at the time, and my only interest was to get high, drink alcohol and rebel against my father's authority. I wanted to do everything he did not want me to do and become all that he didn't want me to become, especially becoming an artist. He sent me to study jewellery making at Dar Al-Kalima University College in Bethlehem in 2012. He thought that after I had learnt working with gold and silver, he would send me to Dubai to work at Damas, a famous jewellery company where a cousin of his worked. He thought I could save him and my family from the poverty we fell into after moving to Ramallah in 2006 from our native village, leaving behind a nice house, land, olive trees and people in order to follow the Palestine state dream that the PLO promoted after the Oslo Accord in 1993. After two years of studying, I was fed up with Dar Al-Kalima University College and the never-ending debates over whether Palestinian Christians are better than Palestinian Muslims, and if Christianity is better than Islam and the other way around. I dropped my studies and went back to Ramallah to study art at the International Art Academy of Palestine. My friend recommended this school to me after he also dropped his studies in Bethlehem. He thought that we would have a lot of fun, travel around the world and smoke a lot of weed and go to many parties if we became artists.

I joined the International Academy of Art Palestine in 2014. The Academy was located in Al-Bireh, next to the Arab Bank in a historical building called Aref al Aref. The Art Academy was very interesting and exciting to me at the beginning; I started to discover that I could be good at it! I was good at drawing and making videos, and very excited at seeing Palestine through different artistic and creative lenses. Some artists and academics from Ramallah used to teach at the Art Academy. Some were famous, or on the way to becoming famous in Europe and the USA. I doubt if any of those artists were known to the Palestinian public, except for some of the elitist Palestinian art and cultural venues, where you only encounter the educated, and the political and rich elites, or people like me, recently arrived in Ramallah from villages and refugee camps who misunderstood their locations in life. The Art Academy was not completely Palestinian, it was a ten-year-long project supported and financed by the Norwegian government and the Oslo National Academy of the Arts. It wasn't even re- cognised by the Palestinian Ministries of Education or Culture, because it did not fit into the public or private universities minis- terial criteria. But this was no big deal to me.

There were many invited professors, philosophers, artists, curators, school directors, researchers and art students, from Norway, Sweden, France, Netherlands and the USA. Once, Slavoj Žižek came to our school. It was really nice to watch him present- ing, even though I couldn't understand anything of what he said, except his German, English and French toilets theories. Most of those who were invited were white Europeans or white Americans; it was extremely rare to see any artists from the Middle East, Africa or Asia, and extremely rare to see an academic or an artist of colour. The atmosphere was very contemporary, or in a Euro- pean sense, 'civilised'. I did not feel I was in Palestine when I was at the Academy. But anyway, I know and understood that it is not easy for a person of colour, especially a Muslim or an Arab, to obtain a visa from Israel to enter Palestine. So, in any case, the visitors in Palestine are predominantly white European and white Americans, because they can enter.

The International Academy of Art Palestine was the first station for me to meet white privilege and accessibility to knowledge and to the world in general. The Palestinian students were also there to directly or indirectly entertain the European visitors and students. We would take them to bars in Ramallah, to parties, to our families, to shisha cafes and even share the intimacy of our lives. We used to think this is how things are supposed to be, we have to present a good image about who we are and how open minded we are. Maybe the Arab hospitality factor some of us believe in played a role in this. We would go to extreme lengths in selling our selves, our time and our thoughts to convince the white arrivals that being liberal is a normal thing in Palestine. As soon as the white students, artists or professors arrived at our Academy, the atmosphere changed completely. All the conflicts between the Palestinian students would disappear. Suddenly, we loved and respected each other. We even spoke nicely to each other. It all seemed a show that made sense to me because each of us was looking for a chance in and from Europe, a chance to get out of the West Bank hell, maybe a chance just to fly. We had to constantly perform to the white visitors how loving, cool, gentle, generous and smart we were in order to get attention and recognition. Our administration office was only waiting for the white professor to say 'this student is good' or 'this student is my favourite', 'we want him\her' in the next exchange programme, or we want them for the next field trip, or we are interested in their work, or he or she could get a Master's degree in a suggested US or EU art school. If we didn't fit these criteria, we were simply not mentioned, invited or noticed at all.

These competitive vibes, and this spectacle we created, wasn't in our favour all of the time. The white students, artists or visitors would sense our striving for recognition, to be valued and be taken seriously. In return, this made the white student or visitor feel superior to us, even though they assumed they did not come to the art school with such intentions. The Academy administration used to empower the white arrivals by insisting on telling us how important this artist is, and how important this visiting school is, and how important it is for us to show that we are grateful and overwhelmed with gratitude and appreciation for their visit and their generous acknowledgments. As soon as the white students arrived, new rules were enforced by the Academy administration, and our freedom to use the art studios became limited and our accessibility to the school facilities changed. For example, a white Norwegian student from the Oslo National Academy of the Arts wanted to practise his performance in our common studio. I knock on the door to enter and do some work as well. He opens the door, and looks me up and down. After checking me out, he shuts the door firmly and locks it. He simply didn't want me in there. As someone programmed not to expect such attitudes, especially from the educated whites, I was shocked. I wanted to complain to the school administration, but then I decided not to. I assumed he would win the case anyway because I was already having a conflict with the student administration office as I wasn't able to pay the fees for that semester, and anyway, he is Norwegian, and the school is Norwegian, so technically he owns the school, and I am sure he would have not shut the door if he didn't believe that he even owns me when I am standing inside a school funded from his nation's money.

On another occasion, I asked a white Norwegian man, who seemed to be a professor visiting our Academy, about a sound piece I was working on. The piece contained sounds from the Academy, from the rain and the streets of Ramallah. The guy only criticised the *adhan* calls to prayer in my piece and called them 'noises'. He recommended that I get rid of them, or try to reference them critically. Another white, French male professor would gaze at me sexually, and even hint at having sex with me almost every time we ended up having a beer in some bar in Ramallah. He once asked me about a young Palestinian woman who had just started working at the Academy. He asked if I thought he had 'a chance' with her. I could not tell if he was serious or joking, and what he meant exactly by 'a chance'. I answered: I don't know what you mean by 'a chance'. He rubbed his thumb and index fingers, gazed at me with one eye and sang, 'money, money is all they want'.

In 2017, the International Academy of Art Palestine came to an end. The Norwegian government decided to close the ten-year-old project, in agreement with the Palestine Association for Contemporary Art. The decision was not communicated to the students until a few months before the Academy's official closing. All the students who were still studying for another year or two were forced to quit, and only students in their last year could continue in another location decided by anonymous individuals. To make the story funnier: a white Norwegian and an American, both male artists, were sent during the Academy closure period to create a miniaturised model of the Academy building and facilities in order to 'honour' the ten-year-old establishment of the

International Academy of Art Palestine. They called their project 'Mini Academy' or 'The Academy Mime'. Of course, most of us were provoked by this puppet idea, especially now that we were in one way or another being forced out of our Academy. We were even forced to help these artists create mini versions of the chairs, the offices, the classrooms, the kitchen, the studios, and many other details. Many of the students refused to work on the 'mini academy' because they found it too ironic and too offensive. Our refusal to work on this piece of so-called 'contemporary art' drove the two 'mini-academy' artists to complain to our Director. They called the students lazy, and not worthy of support. The school's Director insisted publicly that we were the worst group of students ever. As a result, one of the offended 'mini-academy' artists raised his middle finger in a selfie the students took during a celebration at the Art Academy, even though he had not been invited to be in the photo. I contacted him, asking about his behaviour, but he never replied.

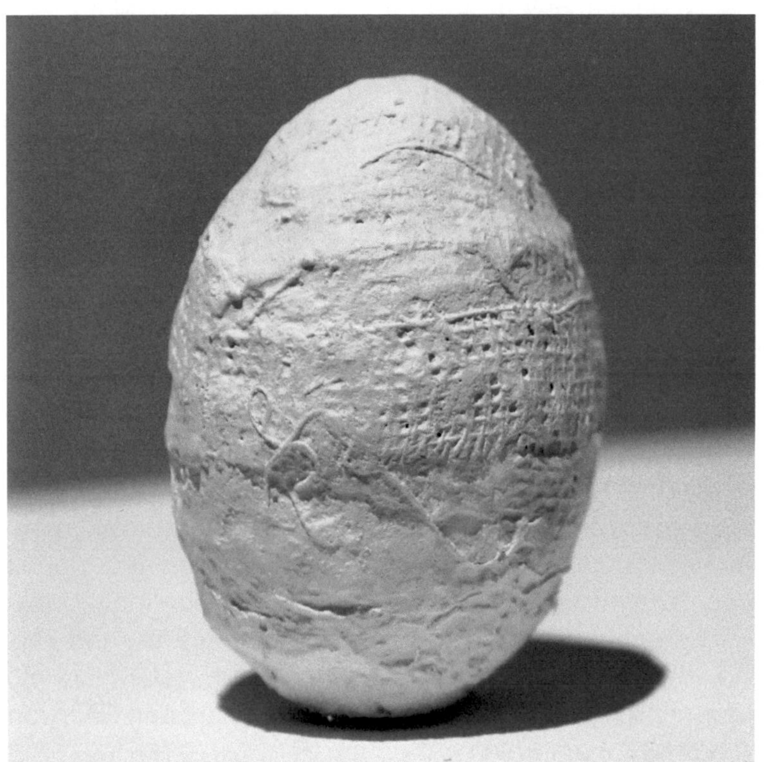

A Chicken Egg, 2019, 4.5 × 6 cm, medical plaster on a chicken's egg

Art School Christmas Party

A few months after arriving in Switzerland to study at Institut Kunst, Basel in 2018, I was invited to the school's Christmas party. The students were staring at me curiously; everywhere I looked I saw curious eyes, gentle smiles and heard gentle voices. The music was familiar, the people were not. I walked up to a friend I had met when I first arrived and whispered to him, do you have any drugs? I think the guy admired my question; he didn't know that even Palestinians could survive a magic mushroom trip. It's actually a very common question in Europe for Palestinians, maybe for Arabs in general: 'Do you have these things in Palestine?' or 'Do you have these things in your country?', referring to drugs and alcohol.

At some point everyone was high or drunk, our teachers left, the lights got dimmer, the drug was strong but good. I wasn't that happy, but I was fine. A white Swiss girl came up to me, curiously; she was dancing next to me, she was also smiling, she spoke in my ear and whispered "Are you the Palestinian guy?" I was too high to process the question, and whether I was for real 'the Palestinian guy'. How did she know I was the Palestinian guy, I asked myself. Maybe she heard that there was a new Palestinian guy in the Master's programme, and then she saw my face at the party and thought it must be me. I don't know. Anyway, the mushroom trip gave me a lot of ideas, and I honestly took a very long time to come up with an answer. She couldn't wait for my reply and whispered directly in my ear, "Do women even have a meaning in your country?"

Giving a Voice for Palestinians

I was invited as a Palestinian artist to present my work at a film festival in Zurich by a Swiss group of people who call themselves 'supporters' of Palestine. They asked me to send a few pictures of my work in advance so they could present them on the big screen. Twenty minutes before the presentation, a Swiss man from the organisers invited me for a coffee at the bar. I asked for a single espresso. The guy was happy to see me, and another Palestinian artist who was invited for the same purpose. I personally felt important, when I believed I was not, or wasn't yet. I thought that what I think and what I know might finally matter to someone. The man spoke, smiling: "Welcome to Switzerland", he said, "we are very happy to host artists from Palestine because we believe that your voices must be heard and we also believe, bla bla bla…" We thanked the guy a lot.

He continued, "What we would like you to present today for the Swiss audience is that Palestine is a great place with great people. We would like them to know that your country has businesses, arts and culture, and that Palestinians are smart and intelligent. It would also be great if you can complement the projects of Bashar Almasri (a Palestinian businessman), especially his newly built city, Rawabi, in the West Bank."

I went downstairs after our discussion to the cinema hall where we were supposed to present 'our' work. I, of course, didn't present any of what I was told to do by the Swiss man. I only presented my work and what I thought of Palestine. After screening two images of my work, I asked for two more screenshots from a film I made about a cat in Greece. The cat was living in the archaeological site of Delphi. This film didn't necessarily have anything to do with Palestine. It was only about a cat running and playing and eating at the 'centre of the world'. The images had not been included in my presentation, as I had requested. I later found out that the Swiss man decided not to include them. I guess he didn't find that my film fitted 'his' Palestine topic, or maybe he didn't find my work 'Palestinian' in the way that he wanted.

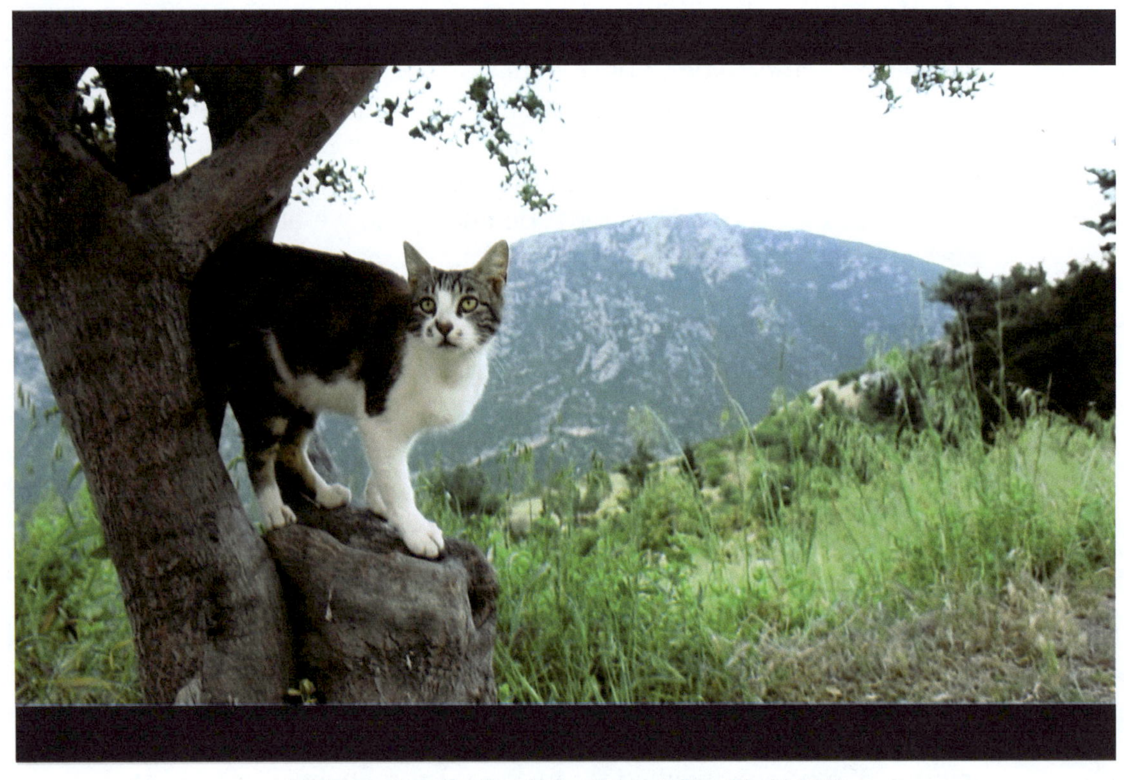

Still image from the film *At the Centre of the World*, 2019

Why Basel?

I had no choice, my English was not good enough at that time
to go to the US and become one of the best artists in the world.
But I was accepted to study in Basel. The city: a beautiful night-
mare. I mean how is a Palestinian supposed to feel walking past
the Stadtcasino or the Hotel Les Trois Rois every day and see the
places where our current misery was decided on?

Many people in Basel do not know that the first Zionist Congress
led by Theodore Herzl was held in Basel. Many do not even know
what or where Palestine is, or what is happening there. All they
know is that 'we' have to stop fighting immediately and become
friends.

I was once asked in a Basel bar by a white Swiss person if
Palestine is in Kosovo!!

Najumoeniesa
49:16 min, 2022

Exhibiting space:
>	Screening in documenta fifteen,
>	KAZimKuBa (Banhof Space), Kassel

Najumoeniesa Damon, a seeker of the silence in our history trauma, present legacy and future transformation graces us with her unique perspective of Cape Town's past, present and future. This film dives into the complexities of the current realities of the most marginalised people in Cape Town. Intertwined in Mrs Damon's voice one can hear the trauma, triumph and concerns of the effects of settler colonialism, development, foreign investment and white privilege that seeks to dominate and strangle the progress of the black body. Ms Damon eloquently details from her perspective the intricacies and delicate entangled realities of what it means to survive and attempt to achieve the "dream" set out in the Freedom Charter and the speeches of many leaders like late president Nelson Mandela.

Text by Rosca Van Rooyen

CREDITS
Directing assistance:
>	Iris Stricker Amleh

Research consultant:
>	Rosca Van Rooyen

Camera:
>	Larry English
>	Hamza Badran

Audio and video editing:
>	Hamza Badran
>	Iris Stricker Amleh

Film by:
>	Hamza Badran

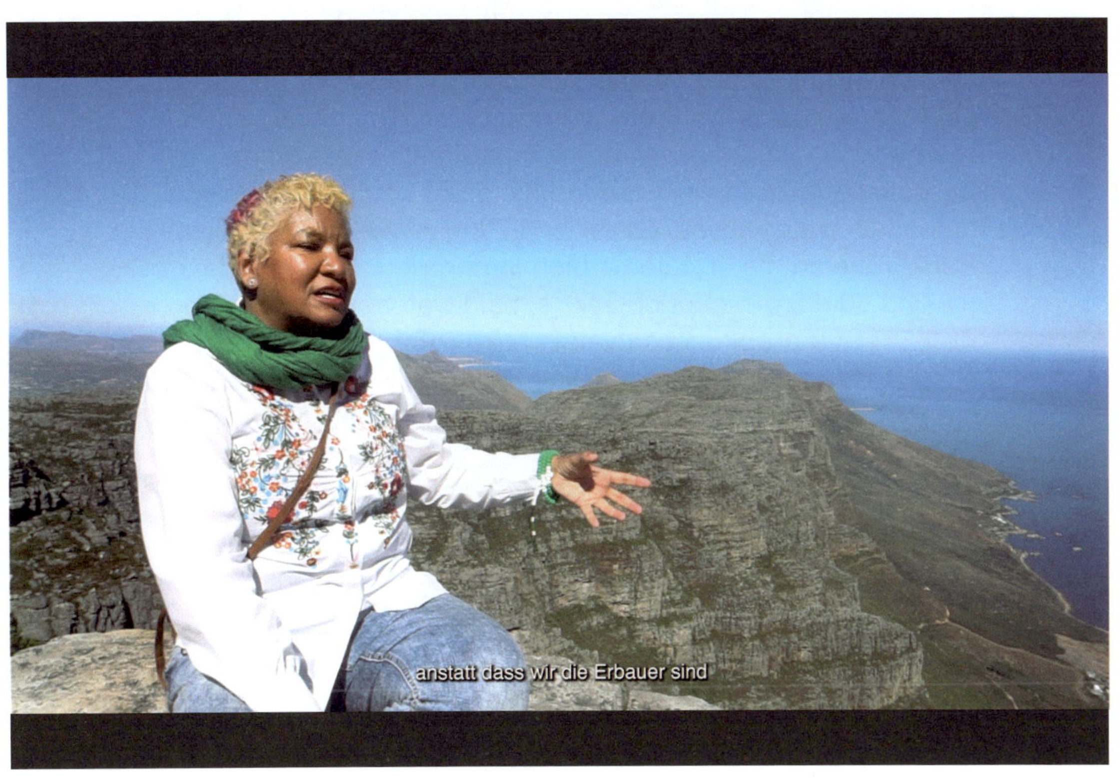

Still image from the film *Najumoeniesa*, 2022

Hose in Hose
19:00 min, 2016

Exhibiting space:
Screening in documenta fifteen,
Lumbung cinema, Gloria Kino, Kassel

This video documents an attempt to provide the Gaza Strip-Palestine with portable water through collecting the largest number of small water hoses from the inhabitants' houses in the West Bank-Palestine, then to connect the water hoses to each other and pump the water into Gaza. The video contains recorded conversations with the inhabitants taken when my colleague and I went around the West Bank asking them to lend us water hoses. Gaza is 93.2 km away from the West Bank. (The aquifer's water is high in nitrogen and chloride, making 90–95 per cent of Gaza's main water supply unfit for drinking and problematic even in terms of agricultural use).

CREDITS
Camera, editing, interviews:
Hamza Badran
Noora Said
Assistance:
Waseem Makhlof

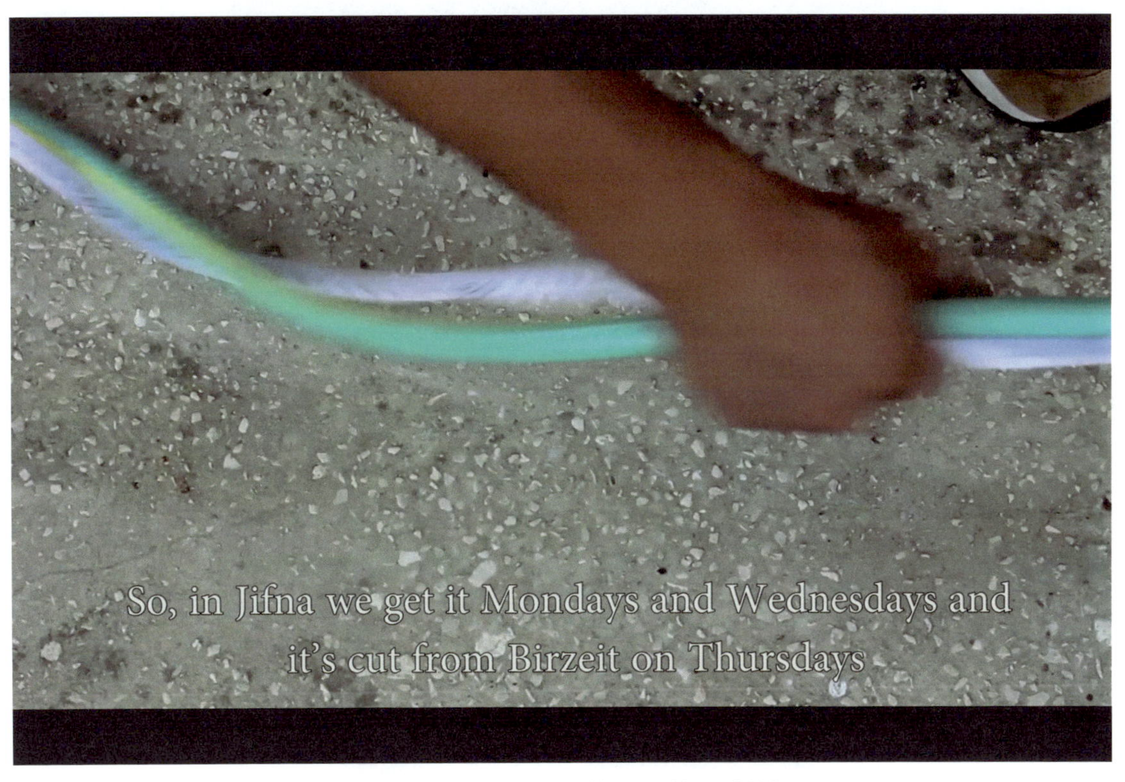

Still image from the film *Hose in Hose*, 2016

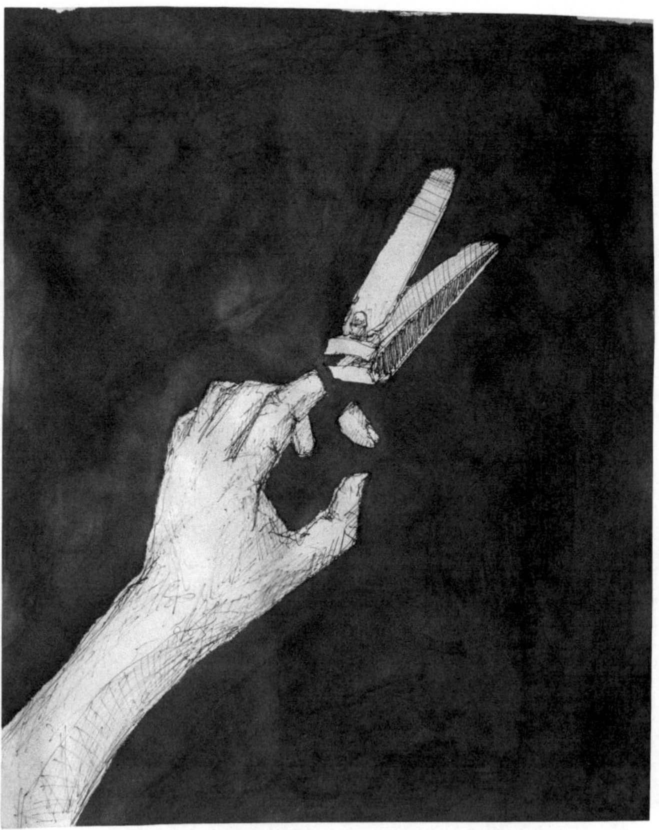

The Nail Clippers, ink on paper, 2019

This booklet is published on the occasion of documenta
fifteen (Kassel), 18 June – 25 September 2022

It is part of the publication *Jimmie Durham & A Stick
in the Forest by the Side of the Road* with Jimmie Durham
and Bev Koski, Elisa Strinna, Hamza Badran, Iain
Chambers, Joen Vedel, Jone Kvie, Maria Thereza Alves,
Wilma Lukatsch, Giulia Grechi, Alessandra Marino
Al-Mishlab (ISBN 978-3-7533-0260-7, NUR 640)

© 2022 Hamza Badran and Verlag der Buchhandlung
Walther und Franz König, Köln

Text: Hamza Badran
Images: © Hamza Badran; Cover image: Hamza Badran,
Freedom Fighter (Self-Portrait), 2019
Editor: Iain Chambers
Proofreader: Nicola Grey
Design: Karoline Swiezynski, inspired by Will Holder's
design for *Past Imperfect* by Bik van der Pol, which
shaped the collective solution of this publication
Thanks to: Iris Stricker Amleh, Rosca Van Rooyen,
Saad Amira

Printed and bound in Belgium by Cassochrome with
supervision of ArtLibro Trudy Dorrepaal. Published
in an edition of 250 individual booklets (documenta
fifteen) to be collated in an edition of 1000 books
distributed by Verlag der Buchhandlung Walther und
Franz König, Köln. First published by Verlag der
Buchhandlung Walther und Franz König Ehrenstraße 4,
D-50672 Köln.

Bibliographic information published by the Deutsche
Nationalbibliothek – The Deutsche Nationalbibliothek
lists this publication in the Deutsche National-
bibliografie; detailed bibliographic data is available
at http://dnb.d-nb.de.

Disclaimer: In making *Jimmie Durham & A Stick in the
Forest by the Side of the Road* we have quotes, images
and texts taken from various resources. Information
concerning the original authors and sources have been
credited as detailed as possible. Despite these efforts,
some sources nevertheless could not be identified.
Please contact the author in case of questions or objections. The ideas and opinions author unless
stated otherwise.

*Jimmie Durham & A Stick in the Forest by the Side
of the Road* has been generously supported by
documenta fifteen.

This publication has been realized in
the framework of documenta fifteen,
June 18 – September 25, 2022

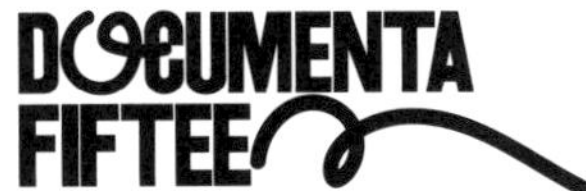

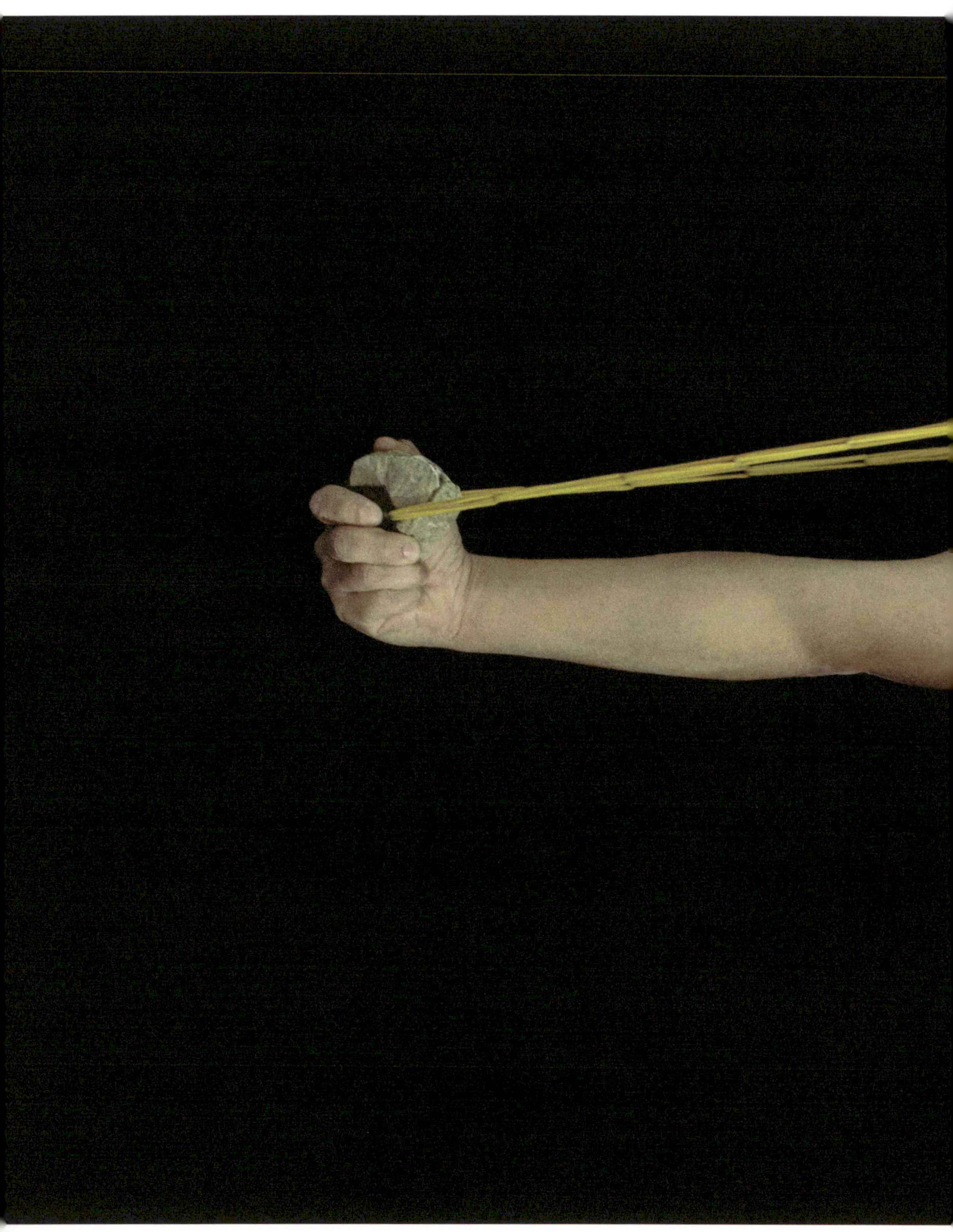

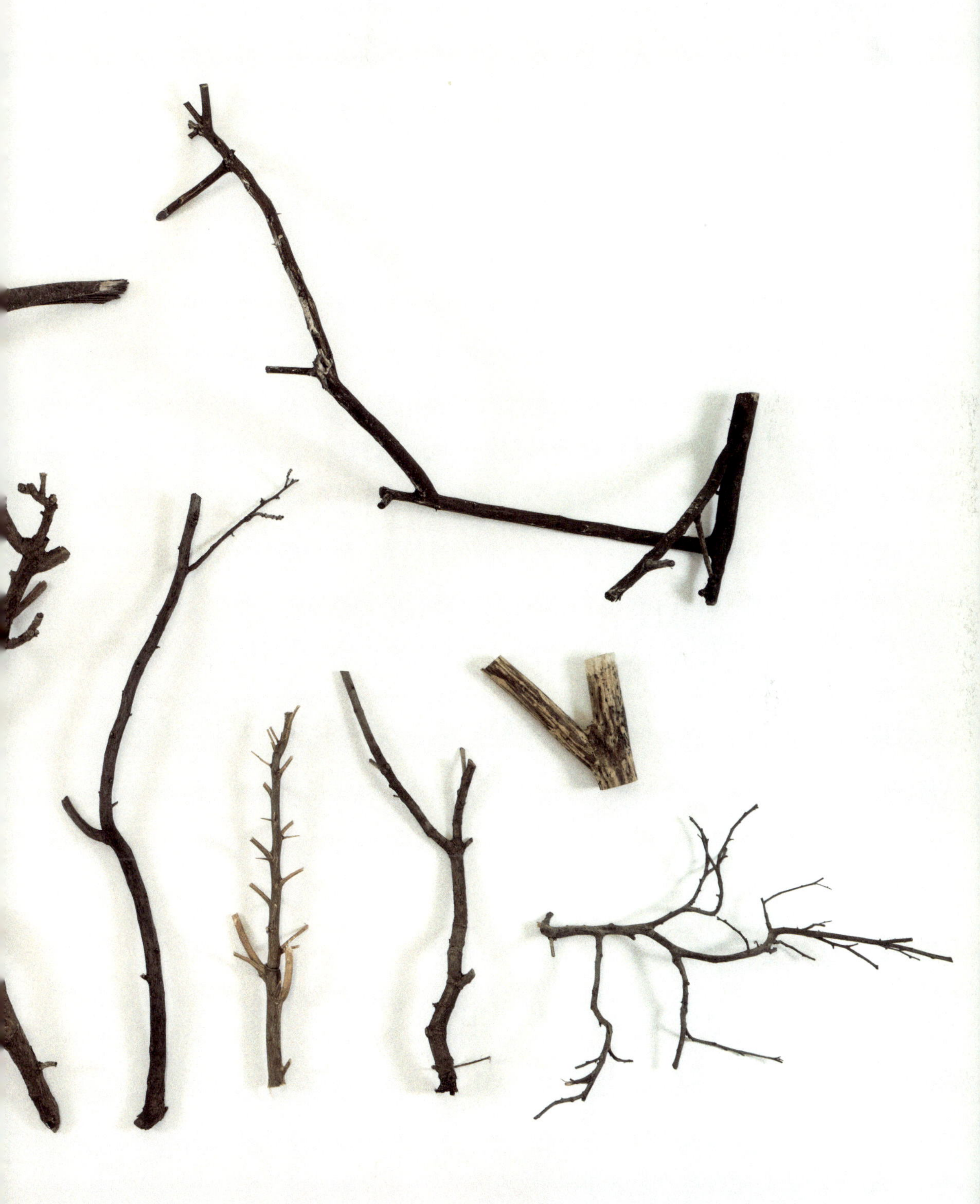

Jimmie Durham & A Stick in the Forest by the Side of the Road

"I often describe myself as
a theoretical biologist—
which is not like a theoretical physicist,
but almost the same.
I like to think about biology
and make up theories about biology."

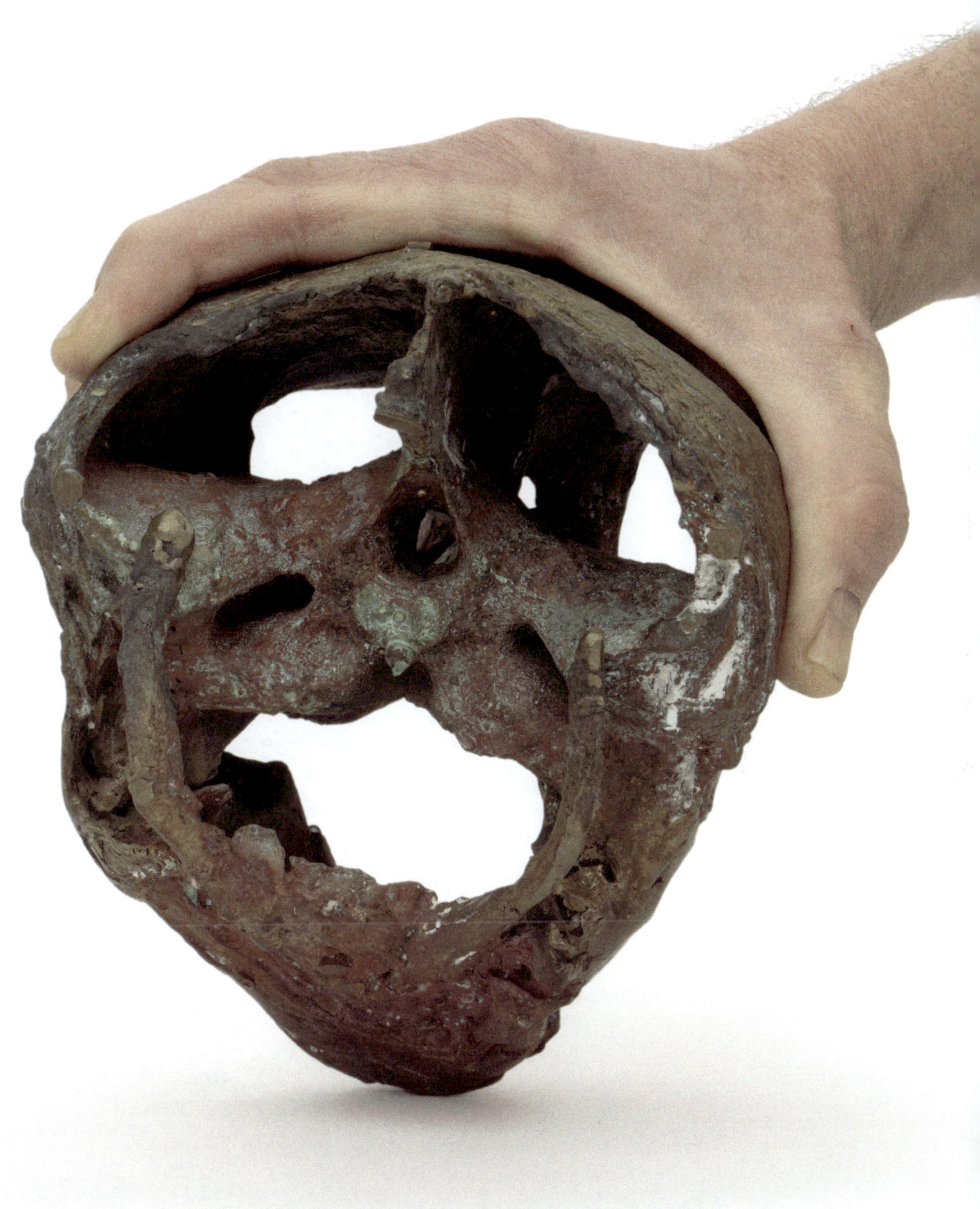

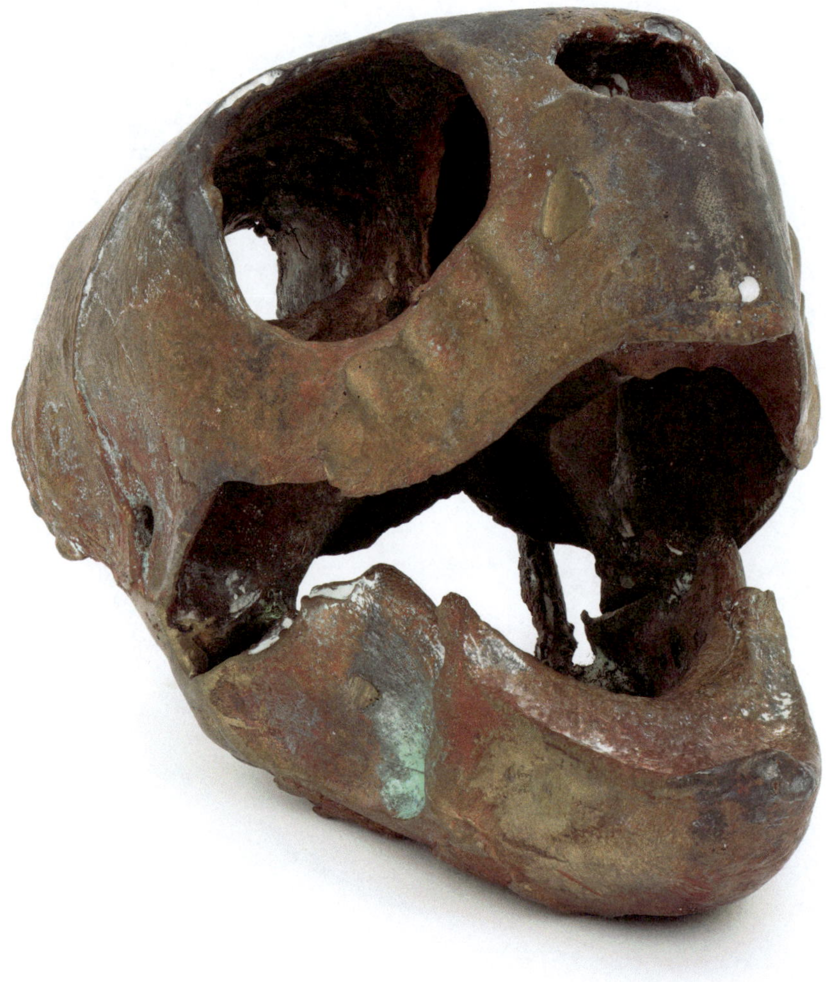

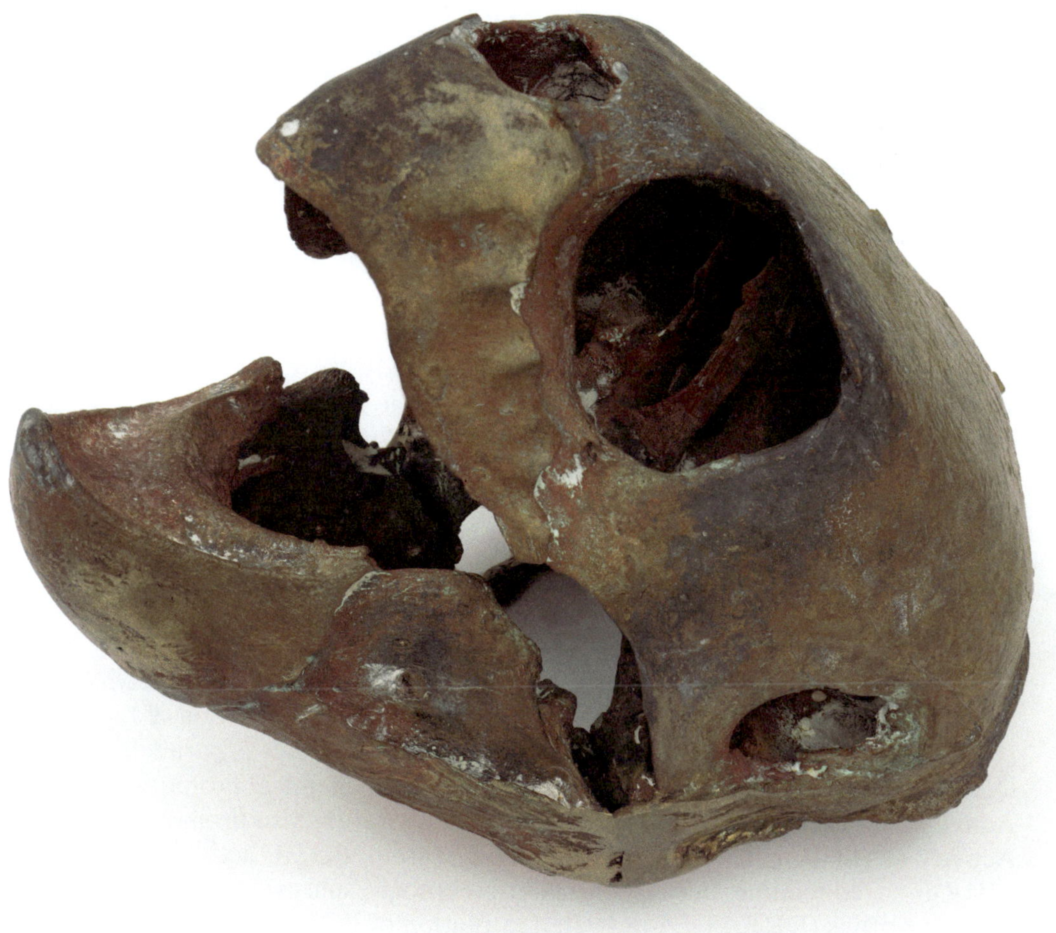

APOCALYPSIS,
or
THE DRAGON IN HER CAVE

Calypso is the leading technology platform for cross asset trading,
Accounting, processing and enterprise risk management.

Key words:
> Cross asset
> Enterprise
> Accounting
> Trading
> Technology
> Risk
> Management

Certainly
> Verbosity

Necessarily hopeful verbosity.

Marco Koch, Luis Varela, Jae Geun Kim, Jung Dae Kim, Francisco
Hernández-Nuño, Stephanie Simonds, Carlos Castorena, Claudia Vianna,
Joel Elmquist, Yury Morozov, Pasko Rakic, Ingo Bechmann, Michael
Cowley, Klara Szigeti-Buck, Marcelo Dietrich, Xiao-Bing Gao, Sabrina
Diano & Tamas Horvath

Published an article in which they wrote that,

"Hypothalamic pro-opiomelanocortin (POMC) neurons promote satiety.
Cannabinoid receptor 1 (CB1R) is critical for the central regulation of food intake.
Here we test whether CB1R-controlled feeding in sated mice is paralleled by
Decreased activity of POMC neurons. We show that chemical promotion of CB1R
Activity increases feeding, and notably, CB1R activation also promotes neuronal
Activity of POMC cells. This paradoxical increase in POMC activity was crucial for
CB1R-induced feeding, because designer-receptors-exclusively-activated-by-
Designer-drugs (DREADD)-mediated inhibition of POMC neurons diminishes,
Whereas DREADD-mediated activation of POMC neurons enhances CB1R-driven
Feeding. The Pomc gene encodes both the anorexigenic peptide α-melanocyte-
Stimulating hormone, and the opioid peptide β-endorphin. CB1R activation
Selectively increases β-endorphin but not α-melanocyte-stimulating hormone
Release in the hypothalamus, and systemic or hypothalamic administration of the

Opioid receptor antagonist naloxone blocks acute CB1R-induced feeding. These
Processes involve mitochondrial adaptations that, when blocked, abolish CB1R-
Induced cellular responses and feeding. Together, these results uncover a
Previously unsuspected role of POMC neurons in the promotion of feeding by
Cannabinoids."

Key words:
          Article
          Satiety

Another guy wrote that,
"Seasonal variation in box-office revenue is a statistical illusion:
If you release blockbusters in July and dogs in January,"

'Box-office' is almost certainly a key word there.
It surely may not refer to an office of boxes,
Or an office for boxes.

My feelings are indescribable.
Many of my feelings are indescribable.
The physiotherapist asked me to describe my pain on a scale of one to ten,
And if it was sharp, dull or pulsing.

It seems there may be no way
Of moaning eloquently
Yet many man-made musical instruments
Are capable
In the right hands.

Almost everything in the world is light-years away
From us.
But heavy,
Weightlessly insupportably heavy are the years
Passed and many splinters stay too near.

Every grain of sand
Find its way to our salad bowls.

Berlin, 2015

News in focus

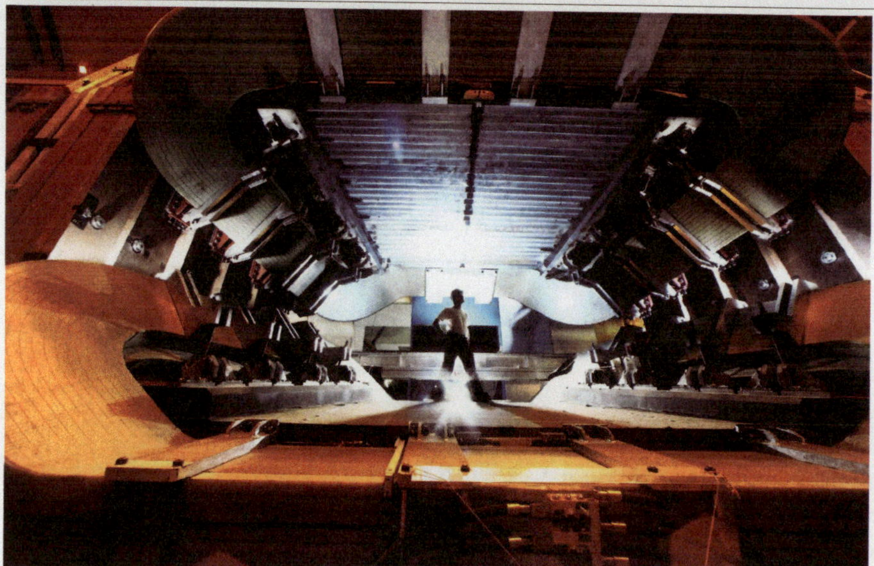

PETER GINTER/CERN

The Large Hadron Collider's LHCb detector, pictured, reported anomalies in the behaviour of muons.

MUON RESULTS THROW PHYSICS THEORIES INTO CONFUSION

Surprising particle behaviour has physicists trying to concoct new explanations.

By Davide Castelvecchi

Physicists should be ecstatic right now. Taken at face value, the surprisingly strong magnetism of elementary particles called muons, revealed by an experiment last month, suggests that the established theory of fundamental particles is incomplete. If the discrepancy pans out, it would be the first time that the theory has failed to account for observations since its inception five decades ago — and there is nothing physicists love more than proving a theory wrong.

But the result — announced on 7 April[1] by the Muon $g-2$ experiment near Chicago, Illinois — poses a riddle. It seems maddeningly hard to explain it in a way that is compatible with everything else physicists know about elementary particles. And further anomalies

in the muon's behaviour, reported in March[2] by a collider experiment, only make that task harder.

Take supersymmetry, or SUSY, a theory that many physicists once thought was the most promising for extending the current paradigm, the standard model of particle physics. Supersymmetry comes in many variants, but, in general, it posits that every particle in the standard model has a yet-to-be-discovered heavier counterpart, called a superpartner. Superpartners could be among the 'virtual particles' that constantly pop in and out of the empty space surrounding the muon, a quantum effect that would help to explain why this particle's magnetic field is stronger than expected.

These particles could solve two mysteries at once: muon magnetism and dark matter, the unseen stuff that, through its gravitational pull, seems to keep galaxies from flying apart.

Until ten years ago, various lines of evidence had suggested that a superpartner weighing as much as a few hundred protons could constitute dark matter. Many expected that the collisions at the Large Hadron Collider (LHC) outside Geneva, Switzerland, would produce a plethora of these new particles, but so far none have materialized. The data that the LHC has produced so far suggest that typical superpartners, if they exist, cannot weigh less than 1,000 protons.

"Many people would say supersymmetry is almost dead," says Dominik Stöckinger, a theoretical physicist at the Dresden University of Technology in Germany, who is a member of the Muon $g-2$ collaboration. But he still sees it as a plausible way to explain the experiment's findings. "If you look at it in comparison to any other ideas, it's not worse," he says.

There is one way in which Muon $g-2$ could resurrect supersymmetry and also provide evidence for dark matter, Stöckinger says. There could be not one superpartner, but two appearing in LHC collisions, both of roughly similar masses — say, around 550 and 500 protons. Collisions would create the more massive one, which would then rapidly decay into two particles: the lighter superpartner plus a run-of-the-mill, standard-model particle carrying away the 50 protons' worth of mass difference.

The LHC detectors are well-equipped to reveal this kind of decay as long as the ordinary particle – the one that carries away the mass difference between the two superpartners – is large enough. But a very light particle could escape unobserved.

The trouble is that models that include two superpartners with similar masses also tend to predict that the Universe should contain a much larger amount of dark matter than astronomers observe. So an extra mechanism would be needed – one that can reduce the amount of predicted dark matter. This adds complexity to the theory.

Meanwhile, physicists have uncovered more hints that muons behave oddly. An experiment at the LHC, called LHCb, has found tentative evidence that muons occur significantly less often than electrons as the breakdown products of certain heavier particles called B mesons[2]. According to the standard model, muons are supposed to be identical to electrons in every way except for their mass, which is 207 times larger. As a consequence, B mesons should produce electrons and muons at nearly equal rates.

Other options

The task of explaining Muon $g-2$'s results becomes even harder when researchers try to concoct a theory that fits both those findings and the LHCb results. In particular, the supersymmetry model that explains Muon $g-2$ and dark matter would do nothing for LHCb.

Some solutions that could fit both do exist. One is the leptoquark – a hypothetical particle that could have the ability to transform a quark into either a muon or an electron (which are both examples of a lepton). Leptoquarks could resurrect an attempt made by physicists in the 1970s to achieve a 'grand unification' of particle physics, showing that its three fundamental forces – strong, weak and electromagnetic – are all aspects of the same force.

Most of the grand-unification schemes of that era failed experimental tests, and the surviving leptoquark models have become more complicated – but they still have their fans. "Leptoquarks could solve another big mystery: why different families of particles have such different masses," says Gino Isidori, a theoretician at the University of Zurich in Switzerland.

There is one other major contender that might reconcile both the LHCb and Muon $g-2$ discrepancies. It is a particle called the Z' boson, because of its similarity to the Z boson, which carries the 'weak force' responsible for nuclear decay. Both leptoquarks and the Z' boson have an advantage, says Ben Allanach, a theorist at the University of Cambridge, UK: they have not been completely ruled out by the LHC.

The LHC is currently undergoing an upgrade, but it will start to smash protons together again in April 2022. The coming data could strengthen the muon anomalies and perhaps provide hints of long-sought new particles. Meanwhile, beginning next year, Muon $g-2$ will release further measurements. Once it's known more precisely, the size of the discrepancy between muon magnetism and theory could itself rule out some explanations and point to others.

Unless, that is, the discrepancies disappear and the standard model wins again. A recent recalculation of the standard model's prediction for muon magnetism[3] gave a value much closer to the experimental result. So far, those who have bet against the standard model have always lost, which makes physicists cautious. "We are – maybe – at the beginning of a new era," Stöckinger says.

1. Abi, B. et al. Phys. Rev. Lett. **126**, 141801 (2021).
2. LHCb Collaboration et al. Preprint at https://arxiv.org/abs/2103.11769 (2021).
3. Borsanyi, Sz. et al. Nature **593**, 51–55 (2021).

(Not the Point)

In the beginning, or perhaps
Close to when something began,
There were probably only
Three or four or five
Things.

Possibly two or three or four of
Those were only words,
But words too heavy to remain in
Place.

We don't know
Who said what
First

+>^^)!!!:(?)=///<</?

(Is the world watching)

"I think there is no division
between art and science.
Art and science are the same thing.
There are differences, in the way
that there are different kinds of art
and different kinds of science.
The problem of why we think there is
a difference is an interesting one.
It relates to what we think science is
and what we think art is."

LISE MEITNER
(After Primo Levi)

Supernova nucleosynthesis
May be why so much gold
Is in earth's surface.

Even so, gold will dissolve in mercury
Or in nitro-hydrochloric acid.
That last is part of the acid test, of course.

Mercury makes the painters' tint vermilion
And the mineral cinnabar which even
Finely ground is not good to eat.

Urbain called hafnium celtium,
Denied also the heuristics of zirconium.
O, mercury is often used for sphygmomanometers.

Hafnium is more common than gold
But often spontaneously ignites (a Latin word meaning
To catch on fire) if left on the table in its pure form.

The atomic number of hafnium is seventy-two.
As I write I am seventy-five and
The number of gold is seventy-nine
So maybe it will all work out.

Remember, hafnium is a tetravalent transition metal.

THE ESSAYS LISTED IN THE LETTERS SECTION OF THE
TABLE OF CONTENTS OF THE SEPTEMBER, 2015 ISSUE
OF NATURE MATERIALS MAGAZINE

Spatially resolved ultrafast magnetic dynamics
Initiated at a complex oxide heterointerface

Resonant internal quantum transitions
And femtosecond radiative decay of excitons
In monolayer WSe2

Potential-dependent dynamic fracture
Of nanoporous gold

In situ study of the initiation of hydrogen bubbles
At the aluminium metal/oxide interface

Enhancement of low-energy electron emission
In 2D radioactive films

Brownian diffusion of a partially wetted colloid

Subnanometre ligand-shell asymmetry leads
To Janus-like nanoparticle membranes

Directing cell migration and organization
Via nanocrater-patterned cell-repellent interfaces

Berlin, 2015

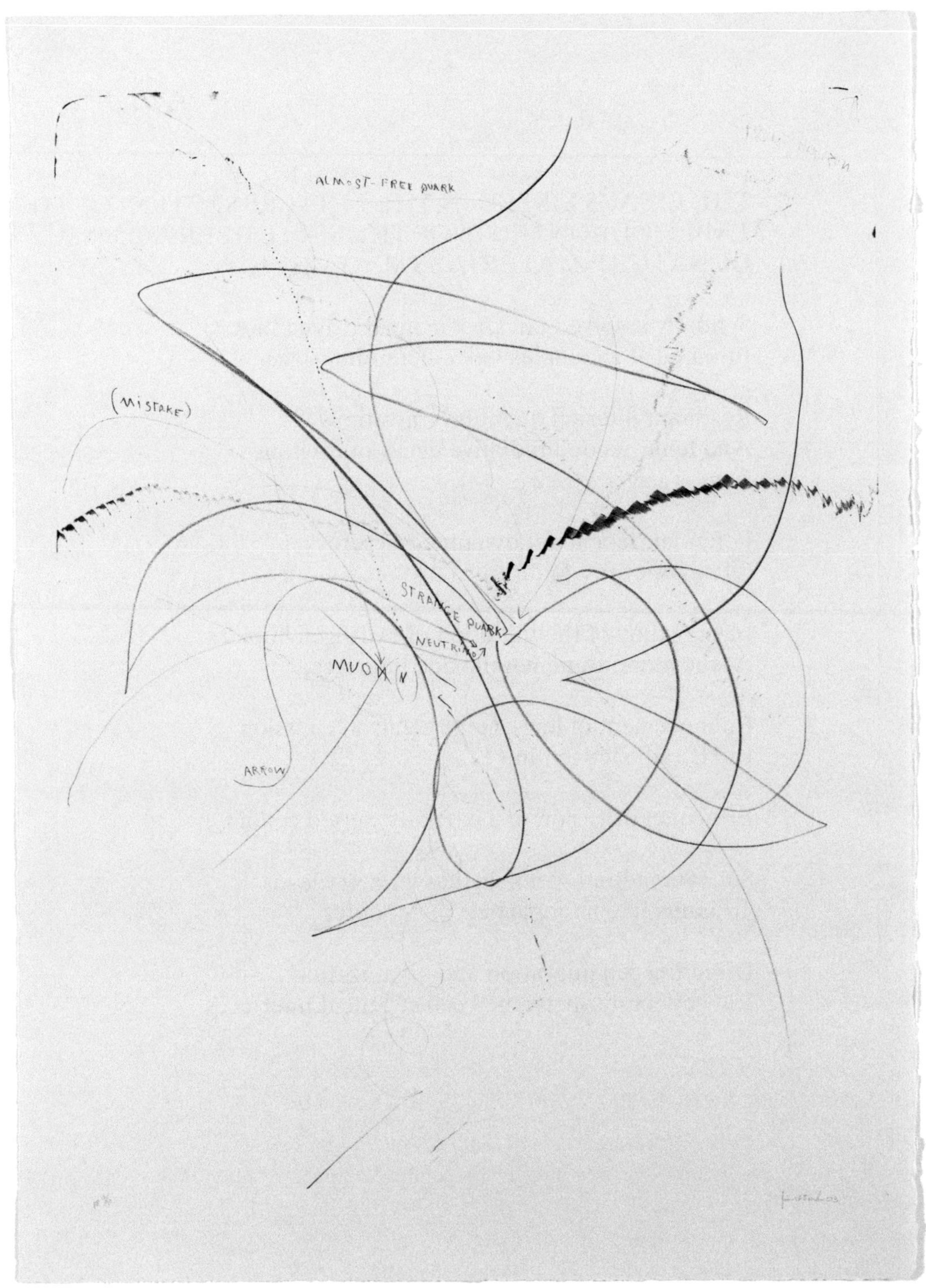
ALMOST-FREE QUARK
(MISTAKE)
STRANGE QUARK
NEUTRINO
MUON
ARROW

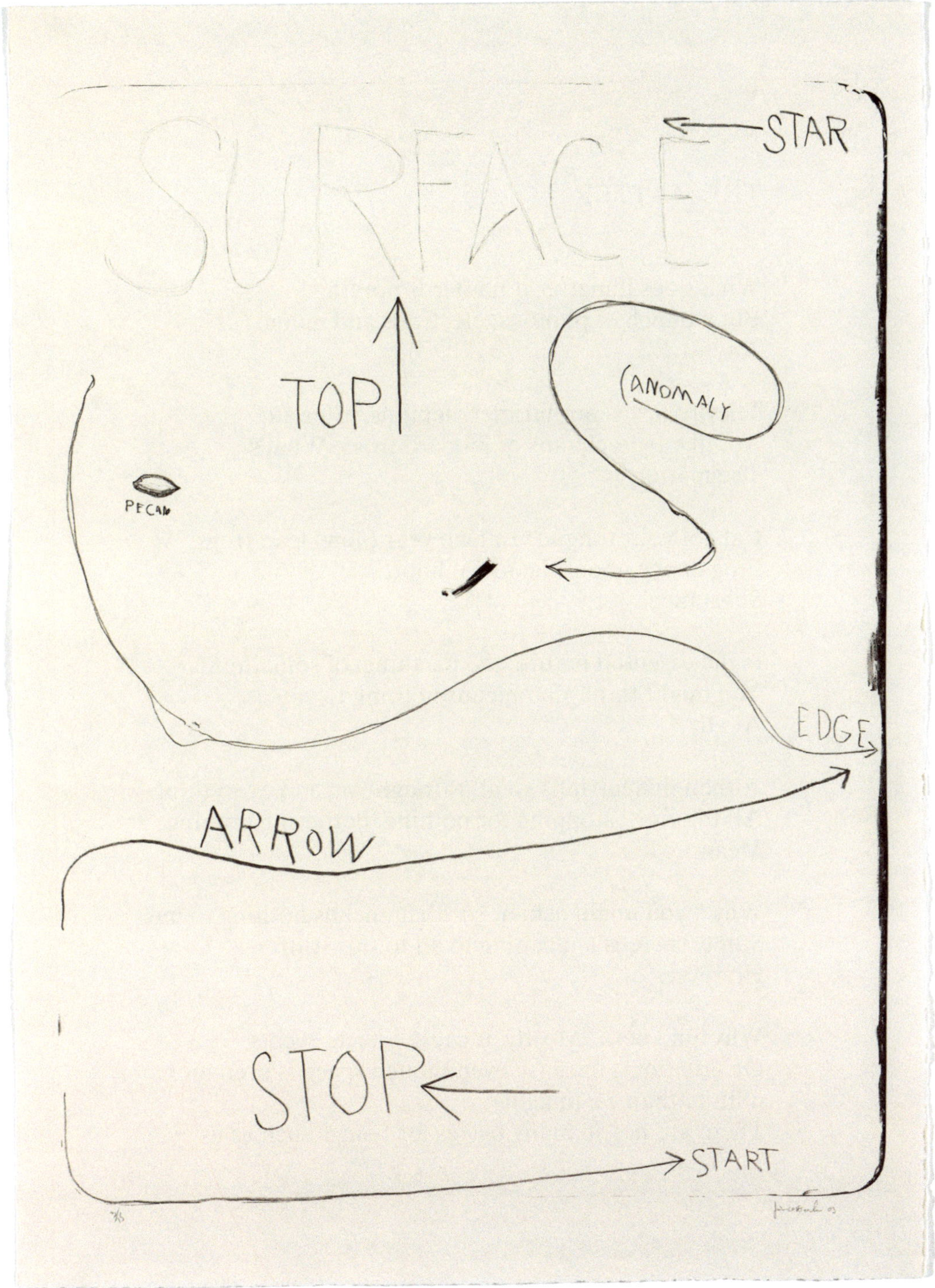
SURFACE
STAR
TOP
ANOMALY
PECAN
EDGE
ARROW
STOP
START

THE MATTER

What does it matter if matter is nothing
But a bunch of photons, electrons and muons
Anyway?

They're just semi-harmless leptons, after all.
Not like leprechauns or leopard frogs. What's
The matter,

Cat got your tongue? In leap year (now) leap frogs
Frog dance about the forest floor.
Substance

Is the essential nature, the meaning, of something.
You might think that means nothing to you
At all,

Although neutrinos go all through you and everything
All the time, stopping for nothing, bothering nothing,
Meaning less.

Why?, you might ask, or so what; means nothing to me.
Surely there is a meaning to all to this stuff
However.

Why am i here? Mostly, if cause effects events
Or situations, because even though space is even more
infinite than we imagine,
There are not so many places for beings such as us.

Napoli, 2020

CRYSTAL SKIPPER
OF THE NORTH AMERICAN FAMILY OF HESPERIIDAE

In this large family a new member has been discovered
In the Barrier Islands of the Carolinas;
The Crystal Skipper.

In an attempt at context here are some other
Members of the family: Cryptic Skipper
Confused Cloudywing Skipper
Dreamy Duskywing Skipper

Celia's Roadside Skipper
Coyote Cloudywing Skipper
Funereal Duskywing Skipper
Redundant Skipper

Julia's Skipper Elissa Roadside Skipper
Malicious Skipper
Fantastic Skipper
Delicate Skipper

Mary's Giant Skipper
Green-backed Ruby-eye Skipper
Glowing Skipper Dull Firetip Skipper
Pallid Scarlet-eye Skipper

Frosty Flasher Skipper
Mournful Duskywing Skipper
Mercurial Skipper
Red-studded Skipper
Whirlabout

Berlin, 2019

"I want to think of interruption,
not like a definition of identity,
but like the good part of identity.
I want to think of my own identity
—and identity in general—
as something completely
contingent on relationships.
When I try to make art,
I don't want to be in a studio and think
about a piece of art I want to make,
I want to be with a group of people
not knowing what I might make.
I want a discourse, not an invention."

This booklet is published on the occasion of documenta fifteen (Kassel), 18 June – 25 September 2022

It is part of the publication *Jimmie Durham & A Stick in the Forest by the Side of the Road* with Jimmie Durham and Bev Koski, Elisa Strinna, Hamza Badran, Iain Chambers, Joen Vedel, Jone Kvie, Maria Thereza Alves, Wilma Lukatsch, Giulia Grechi, Alessandra Marino Al-Mishlab (ISBN 978-3-7533-0260-7, NUR 640)

Editor: Iain Chambers
Photos: Nick Ash
Proofreader: Nicola Gray
Design: Karoline Swiezynski, inspired by Will Holder's design for *Past Imperfect* by Bik van der Pol, which shaped the collective solution of this publication
Special thanks: Kai-Morten Vollmer

Poems on pages 6-7, 12, 13, 17, from *Particle/Word Theory*, Wiens Verlag, Berlin und Edition Hansjörg Mayer, London, 2020
Poem on page 10 from *Poems That Do Not Go Together*, Wiens Verlag, Berlin und Edition Hansjörg Mayer, London, 2012
Poem on page 16 was originally commissioned by *Pompeii Commitment. Archaeological Matters* (https://pompeiicommitment.org) and was published 07.01.2021. Courtesy of the artist and Pompeii Archaeological Park.
The quotes on pages 2, 11 and 18 are all from the book *Jimmie Durham: Waiting to be Interrupted. Selected Writings 1993–2012*, Milan, Mousse Publishing, Antwerp, M HKA, 2014. p.2 and 11 are quoted from p.111, p.18 from p.104–5.

Printed and bound in Belgium by Cassochrome with supervision of ArtLibro Trudy Dorrepaal. Published in an edition of 500 individual booklets (documenta fifteen) to be collated in an edition of 1000 books distributed by Verlag der Buchhandlung Walther und Franz König, Köln. First published by Verlag der Buchhandlung Walther und Franz König Ehrenstraße 4, D-50672 Köln

Bibliographic information published by the Deutsche Nationalbibliothek – The Deutsche Nationalbibliothek lists this publication in the Deutsche National-bibliografie; detailed bibliographic data is available at http://dnb.d-nb.de.

Disclaimer: In making *Jimmie Durham & A Stick in the Forest by the Side of the Road* we have quotes, images and texts taken from various resources. Information concerning the original authors and sources have been credited as detailed as possible. Despite these efforts, some sources nevertheless could not be identified. Please contact the author in case of questions or objections. The ideas and opinions author unless stated otherwise.

Jimmie Durham & A Stick in the Forest by the Side of the Road has been generously supported by documenta fifteen.

This publication in connection with documenta fifteen attributed to Jimmie Durham as author is a selection edited posthumously by us, the collective *Jimmie Durham & A Stick in the Forest by the Side of the Road*, and tries to bring to life the thoughts, processes, ideas and interests of Jimmie in his last months.

On his worktable, there was the bronze skull of a turtle that had died on a beach which a friend found and gave to him. While cleaning the original skull, he discovered that the inside of the turtle skull had a bone partition. He wondered if this meant it had two brains or what was going on. He intended to do research on this and to eventually make a sculpture honoring this turtle for some future exhibit.

This publication has been realized in the framework of documenta fifteen, June 18 - September 25, 2022

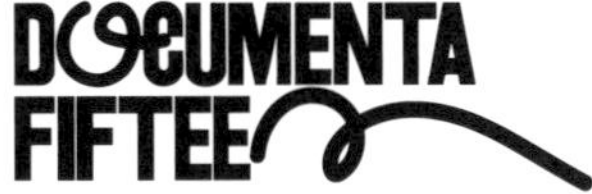

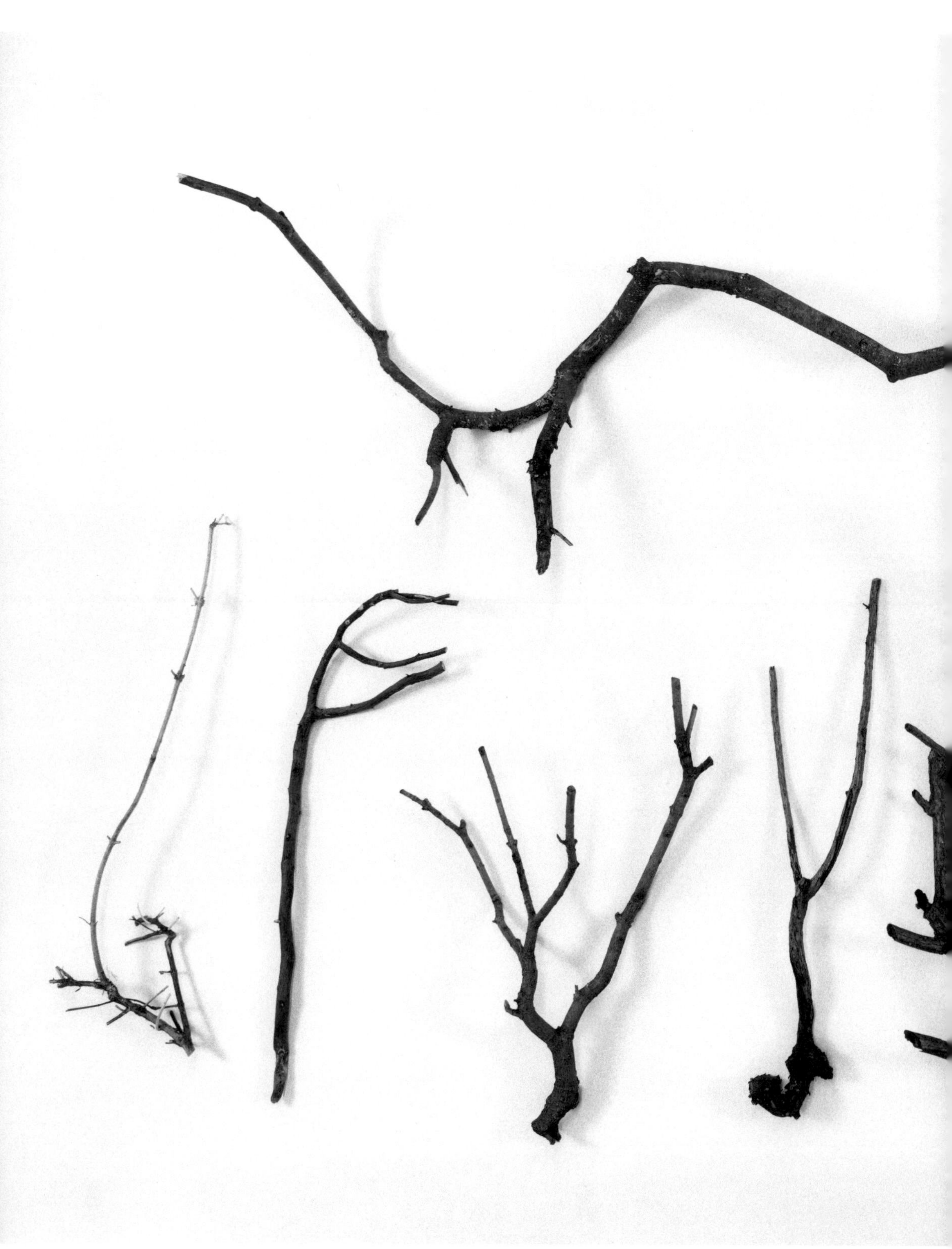

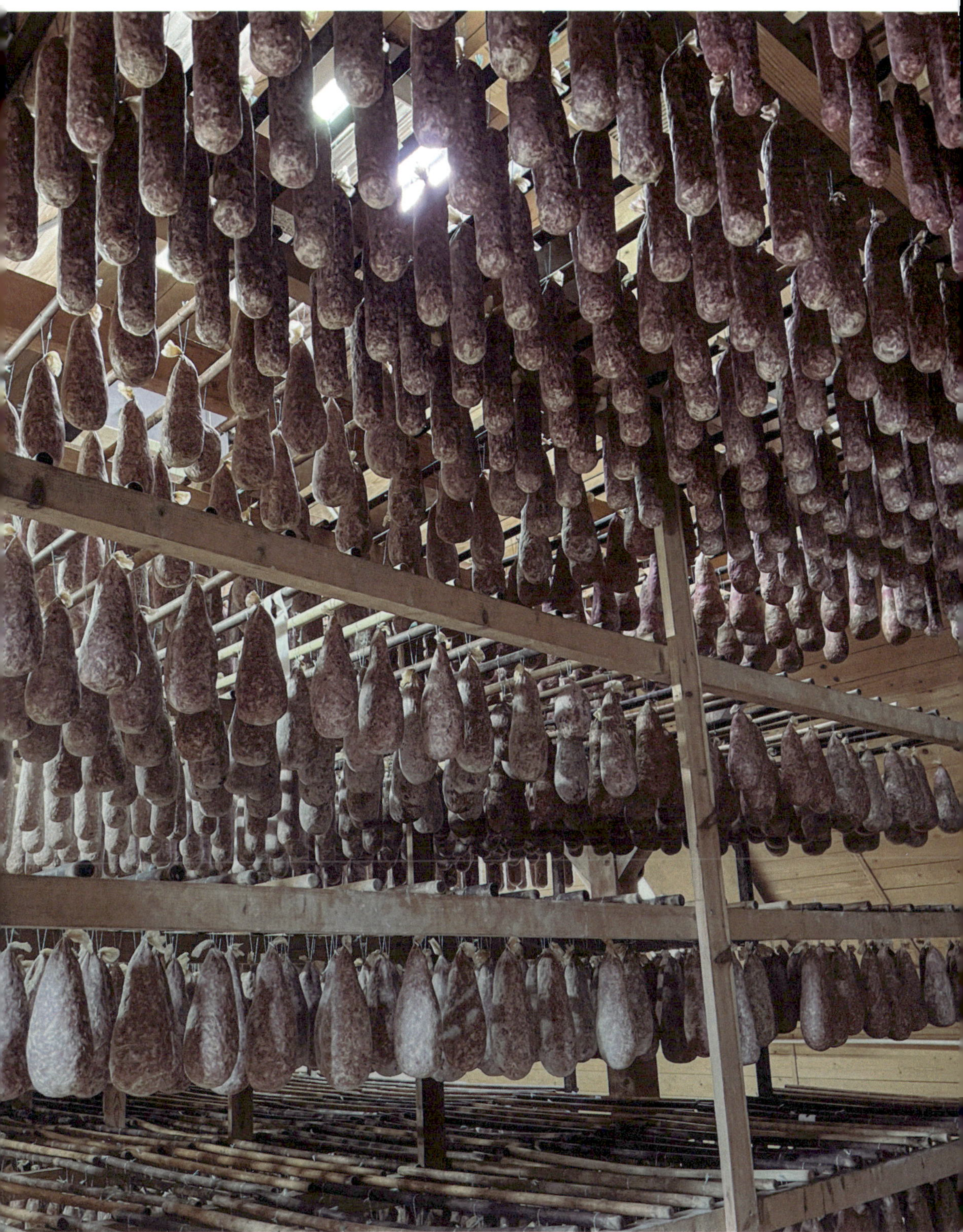

Jimmie Durham & A Stick in the Forest by the Side of the Road

A SHORT INTRODUCTION TO THE PROJECT

As my project within the collective *Jimmie Durham & A Stick in the Forest by the Side of the Road* is wandering around the many ways to memorise and honour Jimmie Durham, I decided to centre it around the joy and pleasures of spending time together whilst sharing some bites, sips and life. And after all, it was through Jimmie that I learned that working and cooking in parallel, always and everywhere, is just the way to make things work out, as well as make them as tasty as possible at the same time. Sitting and being surrounded by pleasant smells and nicely prepared food, people start to share time and times. Histories, memories, recipes, and all other sorts of stuff are on the table.

Isn't it true that space and time and their histories are shaped through food, and through processing what we experience whilst sitting together? Even (or especially?) the lack of food or of ingredients can bring our histories closer together, and possibly open up potential spaces for recognising the common ground.

I understand food and time as taking pleasure in what nourishes us; *plaisir* as an ingredient that we give to ourselves and to the language which connects each other. It is all about the HOW TO EAT AVEC PLAISIR.

In the conversations that I had with various actors in the food world in the context of *documenta fifteen*, I focus on expanding our gastrosophical understanding, our imaginations and our specific way of dealing with recipes as formulations, with traditions and their (re-)interpretations, with taste as a carrier of memories, with ingredients as inspiration for positive change. To what extent could examining food and the memories coming with it also make historical trauma tangible and allow for possibilities of non-Western constellations to know?

Knowledges and ways to know each other are colonised, when acted upon each other to divide and re-establish colonial differences. Knowing structures flatten out plurality, multiplicity and the joy of variety and cornucopia, just as, alongside, the human microbiome and digestion system is dying for the same reasons and logic at work. By seeing both as connected and intertwined, we could recognise food and eating habits as more than biological duties but as methods of memorisation through digestion—a social, historical and possibly decolonial methodology of responding.

It is through the richness of ingredients, the unfolding of their stories, that we can experience other ways to sense and enjoy recipes, to celebrate tastes and textures, to give complex life/meaning to preparation time. Eating and food histories can enable us to experience and enrich our connectedness as our microbiome, and through that can destabilise Western ways of reducing complexity and producing tasteless and indigestible stuff. By taking time for understanding food stories, we might change the vision of telling histories past and ahead. So, listening, and a good portion of sticking around, are the main ingredients for both tasty, delicious and just food as well as rich and just history.

This talk with Katharina Koch, owner of *Landfleischerei Koch & Wurstehimmel* in Calden, near Kassel, goes off into the world of *Ahle Worscht*, the famous sausage of North Hesse. What role does the history of this region play when we are in this heaven of *Ahle Wurst (Wurstehimmel)*, and which processes make the fine difference when it comes to the manifold tastes of the sausages and their textures. How much taste is added by a specific place and care for the history of a local tradition? And how much specifics and knowledge of regional food, its history and its preparation methods are layered when we eat onto *Ahle Wurst* and become part of the same microbacterial climate?

HOW TO EAT AVEC PLAISIR

The Wild Life of Taste in Sausage Heaven

A conversation between
Katharina Koch and Wilma Lukatsch about place-specific taste,
the beauty of diversity and savouring imperfection

Wilma Lukatsch (WL) I'm happy I could visit you here at your business, *Landfleischerei Koch* in Calden/North Hesse. It was important to me that we have the conversation right in your slaughterhouse and butchery. It often happens that the most decisive impressions, questions and ideas only arise at a place and not through emails or internet research.

Katharina Koch (KK) I think it's great that you came out.

WL The first thing that strikes me is that you are quite a young person, who has taken over this old family business. One can already see in the layout of the butchery that there is a different spirit here from what one is used to at a butcher's. Tradition appears in an unfamiliar layout.

KK Yes, exactly, it is being cast in a fresh way. That is the concept, while still paying attention to and respecting the old ways. We are a traditional business, after all. The butchery has been around for over 140 years, since 1877, and we have kept many of the old recipes and production methods. But we are always developing them further, so as to keep up with current trends and the *zeitgeist*. The good thing is that there has been a kind of return to many of these old techniques, from which you can learn an incredible amount. For us, this trend is great, because the supply chain is being completely overstretched in many respects. You can see that in both meat production and food production in general. But if you go back to working the same way your ancestors did, from 100 years ago, or before, then you notice that it holds many solutions for today. Many of the different ways of preparing meat arose from shortages or household needs. Meat was something valuable, and you had to figure out how to use the whole animal if possible. These topics are back in vogue now.

WL Yes, and more and more people are looking at and appreciating the whole animal and its many parts. They are no longer differentiating between the 'gourmet' and the 'trash' cuts.

KK Yes, exactly. Before that, it had become a totally weird culture.

WL In which, for example, fat was completely frowned upon, and still is today, no?

KK Yes, precisely. At some point fat was demonised, and so were a lot of other things. It got to the point where there were many animal parts that people no longer wanted to eat or regarded as totally worthless. But that's nonsense. I mean, an animal doesn't die just so that you can use the filet and the ham and throw away the rest. That's just scandalous, especially in this day and age and from a sustainability point of view. It is also important that we conserve resources and waste less. Our ancestors did that completely naturally, because they had no other choice. They *had* to do things that way. At some point we started having this prosperity and luxury where everything is constantly available in huge quantities, where you can get every type of food at any time of year or day. Now, thankfully, it is going the other way, where we're saying: Okay, a certain product—like the naturally aged sausage we make here—is gone when we have used it all up. That's the way it is, and the customer has to deal with it.

WL That is also the case with wine, and it is completely normal.

KK Yes, when a certain vintage sells out, it's gone. It's not something that can just be conjured up. This also creates a different appreciation for it, a different understanding of the entire process that is taking place. That's lovely, and that's why I'm so happy to have been able to take over this kind of business, and to have a great product that fits so well into our current times.

WL Was taking over the business an obvious choice for you?

KK Absolutely not. I mean, I studied political science at the Free University in Berlin. I have two older brothers, and, classically, the way it goes in this trade is that it is the men and the elder siblings who are supposed to take over. But my brothers both decided to do something else. One even tattooed 'Go Veggie' on his arm. So I returned, because my father asked me if I could possibly imagine moving back home and doing this. That was already eight years ago.

WL Was it a difficult decision? I mean, you probably grew up here, with the family stories, the recipes and everything.

KK Yes, I did.

WL I would also be interested in hearing more about that. Does anything about your grandparents or great-grandparents stick out for you in particular? Were there memories that helped you make your decision? After all, this isn't something you just decide to do for a year—it's a tough decision.

KK Yes, exactly, you really have to consider it carefully. I also knew from growing up here that it is a lot of work and you have to have a lot of dedication, a lot of commitment. You can't do it on the side or for one or two years. This kind of decision is a responsibility. I mean, we have twenty employees here. You can't just stand up and tell them, 'Well, bye, I changed my mind'. I thought about it very carefully, and I honestly haven't regretted it for a single day. For me, it was like coming home. You never let go of those childhood memories. Growing up here, we were so closely connected to food and food production, and with many of my customers it was the same. They always tell me, because *Ahle Worscht* is such a typical homemade product, everyone in this region used to make it with pigs they slaughtered themselves. They used to be very self-sufficient here; they tell me, 'Ach, Frau Koch, it's so nice that you're making this sausage, because it tastes exactly like what I had as a child'. Taste and food are something that is associated with an incredible amount of emotion. It can trigger so much in us. I also always took this sausage with me no matter where I went in the world—or I had some sent to me. It is a product bound up with loads of memories and emotion. It is still the case now that when I walk into these rooms and smell it, I just feel at home. The world is so complex, fast-moving and crazy that it is especially nice to have that. I think that is also an important moment, and one reason why many people value good food so much these days. It is a thing that somehow gives you I don't want to say security but a kind of consistency. Thinking back to the old stuff, to what you used to eat at your grandma's house, for example, has become important because the times are so turbulent right now.

WL I also think the aspect of time is significant. It is an ingredient in itself, which in a way contains within it a love for people and things, animals and stories—one's own memories, but also of those who made the product I have on my plate.

KK Yes. Absolutely.

WL I find it important that we realise and understand that there is a chain of time and attention involved in things and food. And it seems to me that this aspect is currently being viewed more strongly, because it is experienced as a part of savouring one's food and taking time for one's meal. But the question exists nonetheless: what is enjoyment, and what does it mean in our everyday lives? In other words, what is everyday pleasure, and what does it take to attain it?

KK Yes, exactly, that is the challenge. It is a very decisive point.

WL Of course, there is a lot at play there, and it is a very complex topic. But in relation to your sausage production, you're also concerned with how to present your love for the product and how to convey the process of production, aren't you?

KK Yes, the process of production is incredibly long. People need to learn to understand it again, or else at some point there won't be anyone alive who knows how to do it. There is such effort behind it. It starts with the farmers: they build the stables, clean the stables, raise the animals—every day. It's a huge task, to have to take care of all this and do everything every single day. It is such a long process. Then when the animal comes here, it is slaughtered, cut up and processed. The sausage is made, and each one is cleaned every day. It all takes a long time and there are so many things to do. So much time and effort go into it that the product can't simply cost €1.99 in the end. People just have to appreciate that. Otherwise, it would be an insult to all the work and strenuous effort of the people who made it. Rather, it is better not to eat it every day, and reserve the joy of eating it for really special occasions. But it is definitely an important question for the future: How do we want people to be fed? You need to eat every day, after all, and how do we want to provide people with good, tasty and healthy food. How do we want to manage that? Every single day! It is a huge achievement that has to be done collectively. On the one hand, there is the trend that people are thinking more about their food, or cooking at home more; on the other, everything is moving faster and faster. Most people can't cook every day, that's just how it is. It is not the case anymore that women are at home taking care of the household and the kids while the men are at work, the way it was before. Back then the women would go shopping in the morning and spend half the day cooking or whatever. That is not happening anymore. Most women are working, so whatever you eat has to be fast, but also good. Honestly, there should be more healthy fast food. That is definitely a challenge for the future.

WL *Landfleischerei Koch* has been here in Calden since 1877, and the recipes for the products that have been developed and sold have surely changed over the years in relation to current times and realities?

KK What is nice is that we still have many farmers who keep and feed their pigs like in the old days. We only work with businesses that haven't switched to mass farming or liquid manure or anything like that, and keep their animals on straw and feed them with fodder they grow themselves. Everything's good in that regard. But with the production and the recipes, we have had to watch out a little that we don't use as much fat as in the past. Sausage used to be incredibly fatty. But you've got to remember that people ate a lot less of it back then. Papa always says that in those days, people ate a piece of bread that was this thick [*holds her thumb and pointer finger several centimetres apart*] with a piece of meat that was this thin [*narrows the distance to a few millimetres*]. Today it's the other way around, because we are simply a more prosperous society. In addition to that, people used to do a lot more physical labour. Today you've got to go to the gym to burn your calories after a day at the office. But back then, if a worker came home after a day of physically demanding work, it was fine if he ate a piece of bacon, it would be burned off anyway. People today don't want to eat so much fat, from a health perspective or otherwise. Earlier, meat products were much fattier—and much tastier because of it. Fat is, of course, a well-known flavour carrier. That's why I'm happy that it's also started coming back a little. For example, a partner restaurant of ours in Kassel is currently making a dish with pork chin. That is basically all fat, and it is a part of the animal that was never used before. But it tastes great.

WL   That sounds amazing. I've never heard of that.

KK   Yes, I didn't know about it either. The chef is from Bavaria, where they use all kinds of pig parts, including chin. At first, I thought: What do you mean by chin? On a pig, the chin is the snout. But the part called 'chin' is actually underneath it. It's great that these kinds of parts of animals are being rediscovered and given new value. That is very important, but you also always have to go with the *zeitgeist*. We're putting less salt in the sausage, for example. In the old days, salt was used primarily as a preservation aid. Before salt was a seasoning, it was a preservation aid. You used it to preserve things like sausage because you wanted to make sure the sausage wouldn't spoil. But you can also lower the amount, and we are driving that down to its absolute lowest limit right now. People don't want their sausage to be as salty anymore because, like I was saying, they are eating it on its own or with a smaller amount of bread, and we are supposed to reduce our salt consumption anyway. I mean, in the end people are driving themselves absolutely crazy over this. Sure, it's good to pay attention to these things, and for us it is also very good that people are eating more consciously and thinking more about where their food comes from, how it's produced and what's in it. But on the other hand, it's also being stretched to its limit and people are driving themselves crazy. Our body actually tells us what it needs and what it wants; if you just listen to your natural urges a little bit, it makes sense. What is important, simply put, is that we eat a balanced and varied diet. You don't have to eat meat every day, but avoiding meat entirely also doesn't make sense to me. Your body needs a varied, balanced diet and you shouldn't go to extremes. Theoretically, you can eat or drink anything as long as it is not an extreme amount. Take coffee: if I drink ten litres of coffee a day, that is definitely not good. But if I drink two or three cups, surely that's okay. [*both laugh*] It is the same with alcohol, or any of these things. Your body copes with it pretty well, I think.

WL   But that means you've always got to keep an eye on what is currently in demand and what your customers are asking for. When people say, 'No, not this wurst, it's too fatty for me', then you have to react.

KK Exactly, you have to make concessions to the *zeitgeist*, and you always have to be thinking from the customers' point of view. That is a challenge. On the one hand, I find it our responsibility as food producers to make customers an offer and say, hey, buy something good for a change, but, on the other, we can't afford to do that all the time. Because in the end, it is the customer who decides. I can offer lots of things in a given direction, but if nobody wants them, it doesn't work. You can't force customers to do anything, after all. You can give them guidance to inform them better, which we, as a specialty store, can do well. But it is a long process. Of course, we're also constantly working on product innovation. We're looking at current trends and making our sausage in many different varieties. That is one trend that we are seeing: the customer wants variety, to always have something new. So, we're making our *Stracke* with fennel here, walnuts there, et cetera.

WL For me, my documenta fifteen project HOW TO EAT AVEC PLAISIR is about learning about the many worlds of food and the origins of our groceries, and about the subject of enjoyment and preparation techniques. If you're saying that it is always a question of changing and adapting recipes to fit the time, then a sort of family tree of different recipes can be created in this way. Is there something from your childhood or from your grandparents' or great-grandparents' time that was in demand then, or something that has disappeared or reappeared? Are there ingredients or experiences that set loose memories in you and spark your imagination today? For example, I saw *Stracke* with a chilli coating down there in the shop. But first of all, I would love to better understand what a *Stracke* is.

KK I will show you that later, up in sausage heaven [*Wurstehimmel*]. But I agree with what you're saying, and that is also a nice thing about this job. You can really try out a lot of things, create lots of new things and immediately see what kind of product comes out of it. You also get direct feedback from the customers; that is incredibly concrete. When I tell people I studied political science, the question sometimes follows: So why did you switch to manual labour? The fascinating thing about it is really the concrete results, the absolutely tangible product. In politics, the processes are very lengthy. You can't properly see what you've done. In the evening, after a three-hour committee meeting, you have the feeling have we even changed anything? Did we make the world better, or did I contribute anything today? And here in the shop, it is amazingly concrete. You know what you've done, you see it, and you can even accomplish something new every day. I also earned my *Meisterbrief* [master craftsman's certificate], and that was a great experience for me. You have to break down a leg of beef, for example, and for that you need proper skills. You have to be able to turn one thing into another, and that was a super-cool feeling. It is the same with new products. There are old products that people know from the past that you can certainly revive. My father does that sometimes, where he says: Ach, you know, your grandfather or my grandfather used to make such and such, let's give it a try again. Many things from back then were developed out of necessity. One example I remember well is that there used to be bratwurst made with potatoes or carrots. You did it to stretch out the meat supply, because there wasn't very much of it and that way there would be enough for everyone. Now it is totally trendy again, because it has less fat and less meat—things that people are paying heightened attention to these days.

WL That's practically a meal in and of itself.

KK Yes, exactly, a full meal in one sausage. [*both laugh*] Or the *Weckewerk*—that was also that kind of typical product. We're making that as a second documenta product, next to the *Stracke*. The *Stracke* is a typical northern Hessian product, and documenta want to serve that to its guests coming from other countries or regions. It is, I believe, one of the top five things one associates with Kassel. The *Ahle Worscht* and the *Stracke* belong on that list next to documenta, with the Hercules monument, the Brothers Grimm and raccoons, and I don't know what else. But in my eyes, the *Stracke* is one of the top five things associated with the region. It is a food with incredibly deep roots in the region, a sausage with a real cult status. It's like Schwarzwald ham, or other things in other regions. Unfortunately, it doesn't have that status yet, but we definitely have to work on getting more people from the rest of Germany to associate it with the region. Here in the region, it is obviously famous already; everyone knows what it is. But outside of it, or in other countries, that's not necessarily the case. You see this more and more often. We North Hessians started working on it far too late, I believe, when you look at how famous Parma ham is around the world. As a product, *Ahle Worscht* isn't any worse or any weaker. It truly can match a Parma ham in terms of complexity, as well as quality.

WL So why is that sausage so typical for this region—historically, I mean?

KK Exactly; there is a historical context for it. On the one hand, this is due to the fact that people in this region used to live self-sufficiently. North Hesse always had weak infrastructure. The people were poor, and they had to provide for themselves. So almost every household kept a pig; a pig because it was easy to keep, easier than a cow or any other kind of animal. You could feed it your leftovers or whatever, and you could make sausage out of it. It surely took a little trial-and-error before they figured out how to preserve it. Of course, they boiled it, cured it, et cetera. Then they found out that preservation by air-drying also works. Oftentimes a family only had one pig, weighing 150 or 200 kilos. It was slaughtered in January, and during the slaughter week they ate an incredible amount of it. But you didn't want to use it all right away, of course. So, they filled various casings with it, aged it for varying amounts of time. In the thin casings, the sausage was ready after a few weeks; in the thicker ones, it took a lot longer, up to a year. Through the long aging process of these annual sausages, a new aroma emerged, whereby the cold, damp winters in North Hesse allowed for a slower aging process and ultimately a still-creamy bite. In this way, you could eat one pig over an entire year. That was the foundational idea, to preserve the meat somehow. Then they realised that, in addition, it also tastes great. And that was the origin of the *Ahle Worscht*—combined, of course, with climatic conditions that were suitable for air-drying. It is very typical for North Hesse to be five degrees colder than everywhere else.

WL I already noticed that after spending a day in Frankfurt at the end of March to visit Jocelyne Reich-Soufflet there. [*both laugh*]

KK Yes, it's always that way. The climate here is due to the special location. It is a little like the Parma region in Italy, which actually feels like it would be too warm but is not. My best example was in Spain, in Salamanca, where they make Iberico ham. I was there once in June visiting ham businesses, and I only brought a sweater because I thought, I'm going to Spain in the summer and it's totally going to be warm. But the reason they make such good ham there is because it is located high up on a mountain. They have the ideal climate conditions. You'll see the same thing in our sausage aging room, where we've got something similar up in the attic. It is like in Parma or Salamaca; we open and close the hatches. It is so cold at night here that you can let the cold air in and then close it up for the rest of the day. That way, the sausage can hang unrefrigerated even in summer. The special climate here has to do with the low mountain range. We have exactly the right temperature and humidity that are ideal for sausage making. It happens that we also have the ideal building for it, the North Hessian half-timbered house. The building material used for it is from the region. In the past, they used it out of necessity because the material insulates well and keeps the humidity and tempera- ture constant. And those are also ideal aging conditions for this kind of sausage. That is a rough outline of the historical context.

WL   And *Ahle* means what?

KK   Old.

WL   That is what I thought, but I wasn't quite sure.

KK   Yes, it is an incredibly bad marketing term, 'old sausage'. Old is always a term with negative connotations. But that is what it is, an aged sausage. *Ahle* is 'old' in northern Hessian dialect. *Stracke* is perhaps better as a word?

WL   That's also how they call it in a lot of other regions in Germany.

KK   Yes, true. *Stracke* is simply the form. And each region has developed its own prepara- tion method and ripening process. So, it is really a piece of culture, and I think the diversity is great.

WL   That's why it might be best to stick with the name it has here, *Ahle Worscht*, instead of trying to come up with something new that ends up not working.

KK   Yes, you're right. Nothing would come out of that. It is the name, after all, and we've got to live with it. *Ahl* is old, and the people here say '*minne Ahle*', my old lady.

WL   And when you're coming up with new *Ahle Worscht* creations, how do you find out whether an idea will function as a sausage?

KK   We always make a test batch first, in order to see if a new product works or how it is received. You have to taste it beforehand to make sure the ingredient proportions are right. Especially with a product that has to mature for so long.

WL   Yes, totally. How long is the sausage actually aged for?

KK   Different lengths of time. The thinnest ones are ready after six or eight weeks. We always use the thinnest casings when we are making test batches, so that we can find out how it tastes as quickly as possible and adapt the recipe, especially when we are experi- menting with new ingredients. The biggest sausages are aged for up to a year. Like I said, that is how people would feed themselves the whole year long. The sausage from January would be sliced at Christmas.

WL In terms of the shape of *Ahle Wurst*: sometimes they are straight, sometimes it resembles an ear, sometimes they are thicker towards the bottom and so on. Are these all called *Ahle Wurst*?

KK *Ahle Worscht* is the general term, and then there are subcategories. There is *Dürre Runde, Stracke, Feldkieker,* but it is all *Ahle Worscht. Ahle Worscht* just means a sausage that is aged naturally for a long time, whether air-dried or smoked. That exists too; it varies locally.

WL You also call the smoked version *Ahle Wurst*?

KK Yes. Well, opinions are divided. There are arguments over it, which is also why there is no protected geographical indication of origin for it yet. There are so many little differences between localities alone, whether north of Kassel or south of Kassel or wherever. The result is that people are not unified on it. But I think we have just got to find a basic common denominator, and then everyone can say, ah look, we do things this way, or ours is special because... But fundamentally, the product has to have the protected geographical indication first. We are still working on that. The process has started, but it will take a while.

WL In terms of the seasoning, what has been the most exciting or surprising ingredient you have tried so far? Or did anything just plain not work?

KK I always find completely new ingredients exciting. We made a gin *Stracke*, for example, with juniper berries and such. When these kinds of new food trends come long, I find it very fascinating. We also worked for a long time on an *Ahle Worscht* with Hütt beer, the *Bier-Stracke*. That was fun, because there you have additional fermentation involved in the ripening process. There are definitely times where you say: No, that won't work. With the *Bier-Stracke* we had to think about whether we should use hops or whatever, and then we found a way. We had to do two or three test batches before it was really nice and everything came together. But the strangest one was possibly the one with honey. Many people find it unusual, but it has been very well received. Luckily you can do a lot of things with *Ahle Worscht*. It's like salami—although you're not supposed to say that, *Ahle Worscht* is not salami! All of North Hesse agrees on that. But theoretically, in principle, it is an aged raw sausage, and you can do a lot with it. You know it from the salami field, where they season it with all kinds of different herbs.

WL Is there a definitive difference between salami and *Ahle Wurst*?

KK Yes, there is indeed. The production process itself is different. *Ahle Worscht* actually has more in common with *Mettwurst* than salami. It is more similar to *Mettwurst,* and the decisive difference is that it is made from warm meat. This is something very out-of-the-ordinary. In fact, you won't find it in almost any other sausage or in virtually any other region. It comes from the pig being slaughtered at home. The meat was still fresh from the slaughter, so it was body temperature as it was being worked on and stuffed into the casing. When it is that temperature, the microbiological processes involved in aging the sausage go somewhat differently. You have got to imagine that before rigor mortis sets in, the meat contains other substances, phosphates and such, which get broken down as the meat cools. But those substances are still there during the preparation of *Ahle Worscht*. That is why it binds together so incredibly well and gets this special consistency. And that makes it so *Mettwurst*-like, not hard and rubbery like a salami but always tender, always creamy somehow. It is only because of the meat being prepared while it is still warm from slaughter, and it's very special. Salami, on the other hand, is made with very cold meat, almost frozen. Salami is also much more finely minced, while *Ahle Worscht* is very coarsely ground. They are different methods.

WL Could you say, then, that as far as the timing of the production process is concerned, one of the things that is special about *Ahle Wurst* is that right from the moment of slaughter you know you start the process of making the sausage, whereas with salami you can process and freeze the meat and make the sausage whenever you want?

KK Yes, exactly.

WL That's interesting, because the awareness of the temporal processes in the production is different, as it must be. In this case, the sausage production already begins with the slaughter.

KK Yes, exactly, and that is a very clear difference. There aren't many businesses that still make the sausage right after slaughter, because these days meat production is very compartmentalised: there's a slaughterhouse, a meat processing plant, and then there is a sausage producer. That's how it has become organised in the industry. It is all divided and alienated. With us, everything is happening in one place at almost the same time, so everything has also got to move fast. We slaughter animals two days a week, Mondays and Thursdays. We always start very early, at 4 or 5am, and then the sausage is produced immediately afterwards. That also has to happen during these hours. You can't say: Ach, we will do it tomorrow, we are short of time today. That is not an option. In order for the natural aging process to really function, the meat has to still be warm. Today, as with all these things, there are people who do it with starter cultures or whatever kinds of additives. But what I find beautiful about the *Ahle Worscht* is how *clean* a product it is and can be. This also fits with our current times. It doesn't have any additives, because they didn't have them back in the day either. The preservation happens through salt, and the rest, the aging process, happens naturally because of the slaughter-fresh meat. People use the same methods for other products today, they have been rediscovered. We use the methods a lot in our organic line. When we make organic *Brühwurst* or bratwurst or wieners and such, we don't have to use any phosphates if we start with meat that is still warm from slaughter. Because of the body heat, the meat still has a lot of its own phosphates, and then it binds together through the protein alone. If you are used to working with freshly slaughtered meat, you can produce that way.

WL Shall we go upstairs?

KK Yes, good idea. Let's go to sausage heaven. [*They ride the elevator to the attic where the sausages ripen*]

WL Was your family using the name 'sausage heaven' before you took over the business?

KK Yes, my dad actually called it that. And then after I took over, we decided to turn it into a brand name. He liked the idea, too; he wanted to use it. He was always saying to me, 'You have to create a brand'.

WL Did your father ever cook any of his own butchery's products at home?

KK Not so often. It used to be really quite classic here for the men to work and the women to cook. Papa was never the best chef. My mother did the cooking. That is how it was really.

WL But did you often have meat on your plates when growing up? Because it does not automatically mean that having a butchery business goes hand in hand with consuming meat a lot or going into a creative frenzy when it comes to cooking it.

KK We had meat fairly often. But, you know, there is that saying, 'The shoemaker's own lasts are often the worst.' But it really was important in my family that we never ate fast food, for example. My friends laughed at me because at the age of 18 I had never eaten at McDonald's or tried a döner. But I simply didn't know that stuff. We never had it at home. My parents refused. There was simply no fast food at home in any form. The same went for drinks. To this day I only drink juice and water, because I never got used to Cola or anything like that. We didn't have it. Anyhow, here in *Wurstehimmel* you see that each sausage constantly has to be rinsed off, because it grows natural mould on its surface as part of the aging process. This is washed off, and then the sausage looks like this again. These rings here are the youngest. They'll be ready in four, six, eight weeks, and then they can be sold, depending on how firm or soft you like them. And these here are the historical clay chambers. They are still exactly how they used to be, with clay plaster. The walls of the chambers are half-timbered and lined with clay bricks, or it is ancient wickerwork with clay sealing. The clay is mixed with straw and develops a special climatic effect as far as humidity is concerned. It works like a regulator: extra moisture is removed from the air and given back as needed. This regulatory property directly benefits the quality of our sausages. They don't shrink abruptly, but contract slowly and continuously. The sausages mature in this climate, and on the labels, you can see when the respective batches started. They also say whether we have tried something differently in the recipe. And here are those hatches I was talking about, that we are always opening and closing. When the air is cold, we let it blow through, and if it starts getting warmer, we close it up. Then there are these ventilators for extra dehumidification or humidification, as needed. It is all manual work and takes a lot of effort. Everything constantly has to be hung up and moved and washed off. It is an incredible amount of work.

WL Are we now in the attic of the same house that we were just sitting in down there?

KK Yes, exactly. You've got to imagine, and this was very classic back in the day, the timber-frame house took up the whole street. Farming, butchery and restaurant at the same time was a natural coming together of business. It all belongs so well together; everything complemented everything else. At some point it started going in the other direction, because people started specialising in one thing. Agriculture was usually the first to go, because it was often too much. Today, you can hardly afford to do all that, although we might also soon be going back to the point where people say, 'We should probably start keeping our own pigs again, because nobody's farming them anymore.'

WL What really stands out in these rooms is, indeed, the climate. It feels like there is a lot of humidity.

KK Yes, that is as it should be, because the sausage should dry slowly. A humidity level of between 70 and 80 percent would be best.

WL The way everything is hanging from the ceiling in this geometric way really reminds me of some artworks. It's insanely beautiful, an artwork on its own.

KK Yes, I love it too. It's nice that you also see it that way. I can't get enough of looking at it. We are just about to fill all the rooms up again, because as the traditional saying goes, *Ahle Worscht* is only produced in the R-months. That is determined by the climatic conditions of the place and this region here. It is a little like mussels. And because we only age our sausages naturally, we usually stop in May and start again in September, depending on how mild the autumn is.

WL I also know the R-rule with pantyhose. Children are supposed to wear pantyhose in the R-months so as not to get sick.

KK Ah, I didn't know that one. That is nice. [*both laugh*] I only know the saying with mussels and *Ahle Worscht*, that you only produce it in the R-months. It is an old farmers' rule, because May to August is, indeed, quite warm. You don't make the thick sausages at all then, because it is just too hot. It was more extreme way back when; you couldn't cool anything down at all. You only slaughtered the pigs in winter, because you really can't slaughter a pig when it is 25 or 30 degrees outside. It would go bad immediately. That is why the slaughtering was in winter, because it was naturally cold then. It is the same with us. We are currently still in the main production months, which run through the end of April. We produce the thinner kinds all year long, though. You've got to do that, because customers want availability. But the really big ones, the 'year sausages', they're only available in autumn and winter. They are produced in autumn and winter, and then they mature for a year until the next autumn/winter. And when we are out of them, they're gone.

WL And how do they hold up beyond that?

KK You've got to keep them cold. That is why we keep the humidity so high here, so as not to age them too fast. When they age too quickly, they shrivel up in an extreme way. It is a science in itself. It has all got to be done very slowly and carefully, and you've always got to check: How is the humidity? How is the weather? If it's very humid outside, then the moulding process speeds up. It is a genuinely natural product, after all. It is the same as with wine. There are always vintages that people say are better than others. Just yesterday, we drank a white wine from 2018, and we remembered that it was so great because 2018 was an exceptionally hot summer. The grapes got lots of sun. It is similar with sausage. It is dependent on the weather: Was the winter especially humid or dry or particularly cold? That all has an effect on the sausage. You've also got to realise that every pig is a little different.

WL And certain cultures, in turn, are also embedded in the material and air conditions here in the attic. If you were to go away for a year and not do anything, that would affect the whole microbacterial climate of these rooms, wouldn't it? I mean, these rooms have a very specific microbacterial composition.

KK Yes, totally. The mould is a part of the location. The mould bacteria are here for a very long time.

WL Yes, they're here, and they also need to be taken care of, so as not to tip the balance of the composition, right? Because in the end, everything depends on the concreteness of the place and the treating of it.

KK Yes, they have to be cared for. They can't go into the negative. Because this white mould that you see here, that is the good kind of mould; it's ripening mould. Black and green mould can't be allowed, though. It's not good, and therefore you have to keep an eye on it. That is why you've always got to keep the room sufficiently ventilated. You also can't just say: Ach, we need more sausage, let's just put some in the house next door and let them age there. It doesn't work, because the cultures aren't there. I have had colleagues tell me they renovated their buildings and everything was new, but then there weren't enough microorganisms anymore.

WL It is basically the same as how other products are inoculated. I suddenly just thought of the miso barrels in Japan. The ancient materials have the climate that the new approach requires in order to create a certain quality of miso again.

KK Yes, exactly. It is the same with balsamic vinegar.

WL Or whisky, or ultimately anything that's aged or fermented.

KK Yes, the ripening cultures have to be there, and they are definitely here in these chambers. The sausages are impregnated by the microbiological climate of their immediate surroundings. It is the place-specific principle of each location, as with making wine or cheese. The place and its specificity provide for the unmistakeable taste. That also means that when you bring new, fresh sausage in, you can't put in too much at once or keep adding new ones all the time. There always has to be enough of the old stock to infect the new. You can't just decide out of nowhere to hang sausages somewhere in your flat or in any old room and expect it to be fine. Or maybe it will, somehow, if you have the other factors under control. But there is a special aroma that has to do with the place. It is also something totally crazy: We could butcher a pig now and one butcher could take one half and we take the other half—so, two halves of the same pig. We could both grind them and season them with the same spice mix, and then he would hang his in his sausage room and we would do the same in our sausage heaven. And the sausage would taste different. It is really funny. There are many factors that play together.

WL And I believe or hope that there is more and more understanding of and joy in the diversity and richness that can be found in such products, whether the *Ahle Wurst* or a good piece of bread, as well as joy in thinking about these processes and connections.

KK Yes, I think that too. It is coming back.

WL This might also have an impact on how we deal with things that might not have worked out perfectly in our own kitchens at home. That one is not thinking, well, next time it will be better, but that one takes pleasure in thinking about the possible connections: Why did it turn out so differently? What was different from last time, etc? In fact, that could also mean that we learn to understand recipes not as something fixed or set in stone, but as historical formulas that can, and sometimes must, be changed over and over depending on circumstances and necessity.

KK Yes, exactly. I think that is an important topic in food as well as products. They are something totally natural and living and because of that, like in life or with us people, there is no such thing as perfection. It is not something that you can finalise, standardise and package, which is nonetheless often what happens these days. We live in such a regulated world; everything has to have a standard—especially in Germany. But it is also the case with food, that it is alive and not perfect. That is the beauty of it. It is like that with people, and that could certainly be why we have such a special connection to it.

WL Are the sausages mostly made from pork, or do you have some with other kinds of meat?

KK We have a few beef ones hanging over there—we're making some with beef and sometimes also with game, wild boar. But pork sausage is the classic.

WL Yes, you were saying before that that also has to do with the region and the tradition of home slaughter.

KK Yes, exactly. These here are the giant *Stracken*, they mature for a year. They are being produced now for the end of this year. And these ones are old classics, which we just starting to produce again. It goes back to when they used to stuff sausage in colons. Nobody's been doing that for a long time, because people think sausage in a rectum is disgusting. The sphincter muscle's even in there, which led to disgust in the new, modern world where everything is supposed to be perfect. There, these sausages were unwanted. These here are all in natural casings, but they are so-called glued pig intestines. That means the intestine is heated up and turns into a sticky mass of protein. This is then poured into a cast, and the sausages come out like this. It is important for the ripening process, because the intestine fuses with the meat and can shrink along with it. The *Stracken* are practically bulging when they are very fresh, but a half-year later they are only almost half as thick, because they lose water and dry out. This production method wasn't used for a long time because it can't be standardised. Every sausage is different, almost a unique work of art, and it's beautiful. [*both laugh*] Yes, we're coming back to that a lot more nowadays, and that is why I think the current development is good. I see things developing in a positive direction—I would not have taken over this business if I didn't believe it had a future. I believe very strongly that there are people who will deal with these topics even more intensively in the future. Not everyone, of course. But there are lots of people who commit to it and take genuine pleasure in doing so, and who are also ready to take a longer route or spend more money for the sake of it.

WL   Yes, I am seeing the same thing. One can definitely notice it in Berlin. There, it is sometimes even drifting in the direction of 'the more expensive the better', without asking where the products or ingredients come from. Expensive is the category, so to speak. But on the bright side, I am also noticing that the joy people take in a place's specificity and its typical culinary characteristics is growing, and becoming more and more valued and supported. At this point, one more thing comes to mind: I met with Stefan Itter yesterday at his organic farm in Kirchberg. And as we were driving to his farm, I was struck by the beauty of the hilly landscape. It is a great deal of *plaisir* for me to get to know all these aspects and people as part of HOW TO EAT AVEC PLAISIR, and to see how much richness there is here in the area. It is so diverse and the landscape is exciting, especially in contrast to how barren everyone always says it is.

KK   [*ironically*] Yes, there is nothing here, as we always say to ourselves. But it is an incredibly beautiful landscape and it is totally underrated, along with a lot more that the region has to offer. I don't know, it is really down to the northern Hessians and their mentality that they don't sell themselves. If only they would sell themselves as the Bavarians or Swabians do, who stand up with total self-confidence for their landscape, their cities and even their products. But the North Hessians aren't like that; they're more like: Hmm, well, yeah, this place is okay. One really has to draw people in, and then they do also become enthusiastic. It is starting to change, but in principle North Hesse would rather stay hidden. But yes, the landscape is wonderful here, and I only rediscovered that after being away for almost ten years. I had never perceived it that way before. I only realised it when coming back after having seen a lot of elsewheres.

WL   Yes, and ultimately that is probably the case with every region.

KK   Exactly, every region has its own idiosyncrasies, and they should remain. Diversity should remain. That is important to me.

WL   So, one last thing concerning the sheer plentifulness of the different sausages here: Is what we see in sausage heaven your entire production?

KK   Yes. We have up to 50,000 sausages hanging here. Every single one is filled by hand, clipped and hung up. It's a crazy amount of work, but it's good work.

WL   Thanks so much, *Katharina*, for your time and for the possibility to think about how processing meat and the taste of a place are connected with each other and how we can enjoy this complex entanglement and history.

This talk took place in March and May 2022 in Calden, near Kassel

*

Thank you, Jimmie and Maria Thereza,
for your debordering inspiration, that always connects us through our stomach-brains.

Thank you, Katharina,
for your trust and openness in realising this text with me. Your generosity is nurturing.

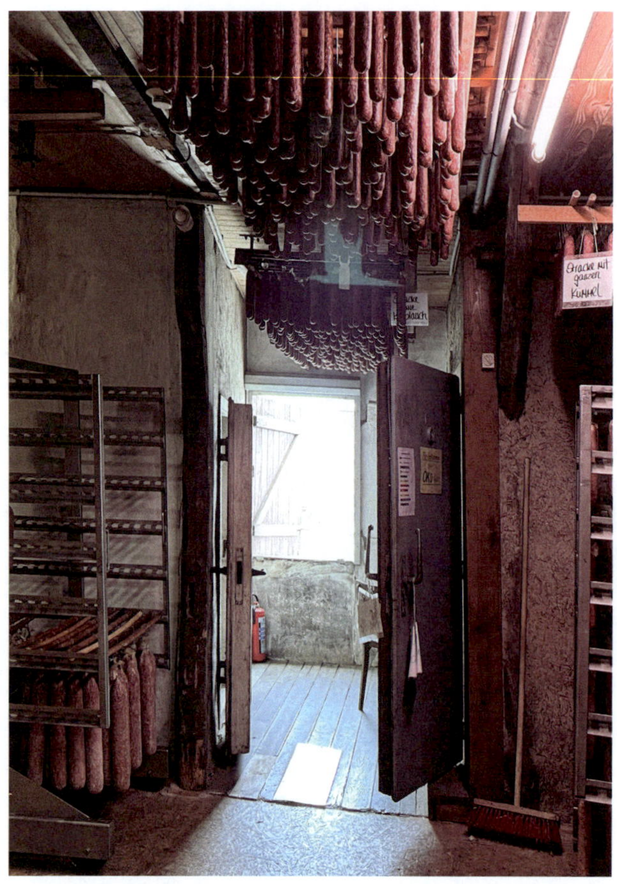

BIOGRAPHIES

A writer, editor and researcher based in Berlin, *Wilma Lukatsch* (Dr. phil.) has graduate degrees in Art History, History of Religions and Sociology from the Freie Universität Berlin and the Humboldt-Universität zu Berlin. She has since been working with artists and archives, and is focusing on developing a dialogue-based writing practice in close exchange and collaboration. She wrote her doctoral thesis on the inter-relational practices in the work of Maria Thereza Alves, and has asked for feminist and decolonial methodologies for understanding, addressing and re-imagining artworks, archives and artists' voices. For many years she has been engaged in writing and publishing books that connect art and histories to voices and space, in order to shift research and narrations to a praxis of being entangled.

Katharina Koch was born in Kassel in 1986, and studied journalism and political science in Berlin and Paris. After working in the German Bundestag and at the United Nations in New York, she returned to her home in northern Hesse to take over her parents' butcher's shop. Since 2018, the master butcher has been the fifth generation to run the business, which has been in operation since 1877. Koch is involved in giving voice to the butcher's trade and the North Hessian *Ahle Wurst*. For more information, see the website: www.landfleischerei-koch.de

This booklet is published on the occasion of documenta fifteen (Kassel), 18 June – 25 September 2022

It is part of the publication *Jimmie Durham & A Stick in the Forest by the Side of the Road* with Jimmie Durham and Bev Koski, Elisa Strinna, Hamza Badran, Iain Chambers, Joen Vedel, Jone Kvie, Maria Thereza Alves, Wilma Lukatsch, Giulia Grechi, Alessandra Marino Al-Mishlab (ISBN 978-3-7533-0260-7, NUR 640)

Text: © Wilma Lukatsch & Katharina Koch
Images: © Wilma Lukatsch, *Zu Besuch bei Katharina Koch im Wurstehimmel in Calden*, 2022
Editor: Iain Chambers
Translation: Rachel Glassberg
Proofreader: Nicola Gray
Design: Karoline Swiezynski, inspired by Will Holder's design for *Past Imperfect* by Bik van der Pol, which shaped the collective solution of this publication

The series HOW TO EAT AVEC PLAISIR is inspired by and dedicated to Jimmie Durham.

The series will consist of five parts realised with: Jocelyne Reich-Soufflet (Praxis Reich-Soufflet, Frankfurt/Main), Katharina Koch (Landfleischerei Koch, Calden), Susanne Wegerich (Dépa Forschungskantine – Labor für kulinarische Forschung und nachhaltige Alltagsernährung, Kassel), Stefan Itter (Biobauernhof Eiwels, Kirchberg) and Ayami Awazuhara.

Printed and bound in Belgium by Cassochrome with supervision of ArtLibro Trudy Dorrepaal. Published in an edition of 500 individual booklets (documenta fifteen) to be collated in an edition of 1000 books distributed by Verlag der Buchhandlung Walther und Franz König, Köln. First published by Verlag der Buchhandlung Walther und Franz König Ehrenstraße 4, D-50672 Köln.

Bibliographic information published by the Deutsche Nationalbibliothek – The Deutsche Nationalbibliothek lists this publication in the Deutsche National-bibliografie; detailed bibliographic data is available at http://dnb.d-nb.de.

Disclaimer: In making *Jimmie Durham & A Stick in the Forest by the Side of the Road* we have quotes, images and texts taken from various resources. Information concerning the original authors and sources have been credited as detailed as possible. Despite these efforts, some sources nevertheless could not be identified. Please contact the author in case of questions or objections. The ideas and opinions author unless stated otherwise.

Jimmie Durham & A Stick in the Forest by the Side of the Road has been generously supported by documenta fifteen.

This publication has been realized in the framework of documenta fifteen, June 18 - September 25, 2022

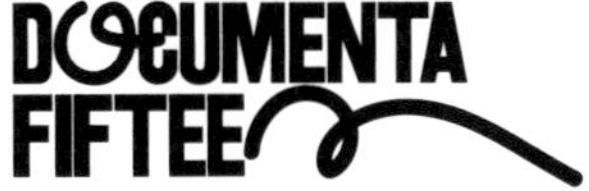

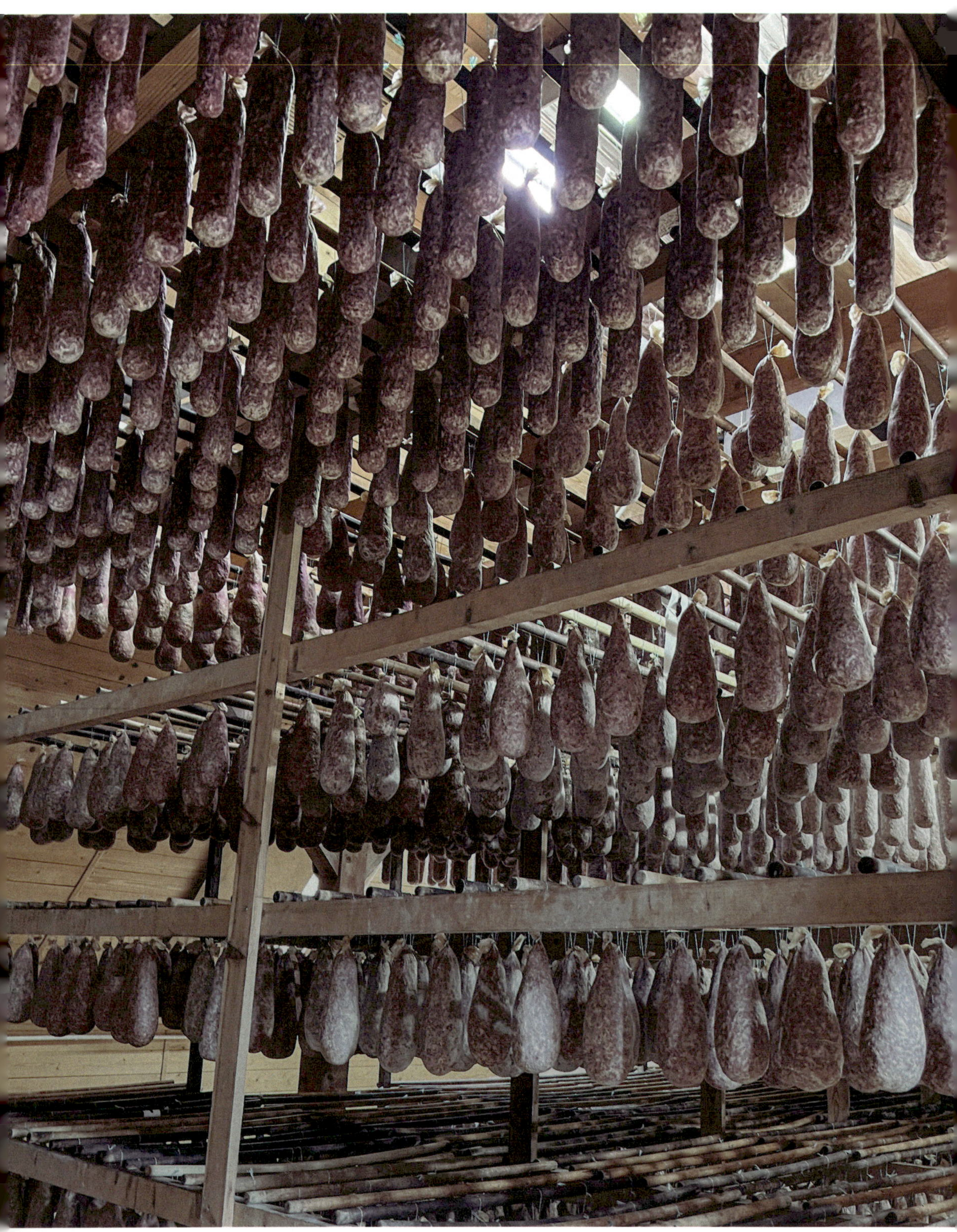

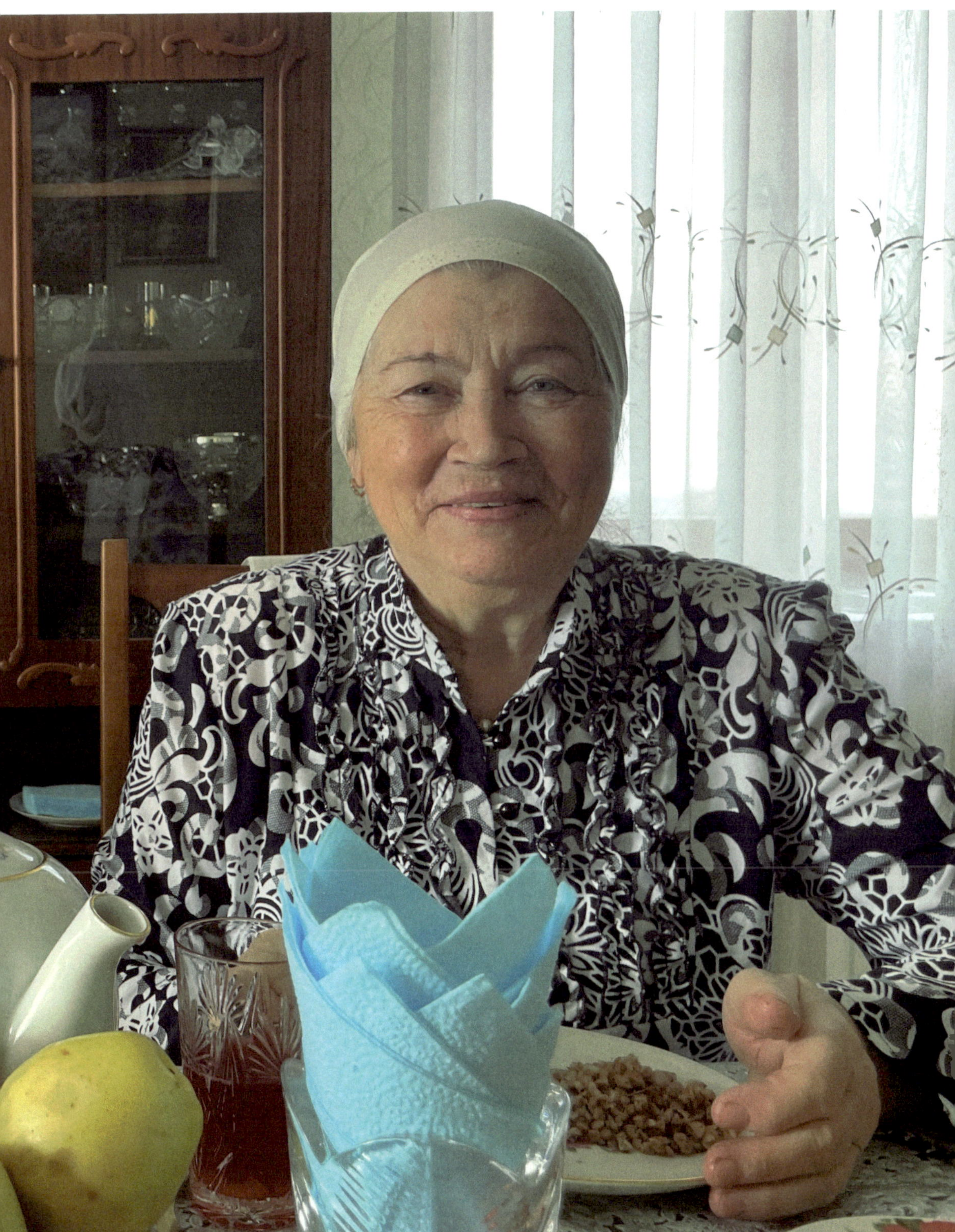

Jimmie Durham & A Stick in the Forest by the Side of the Road

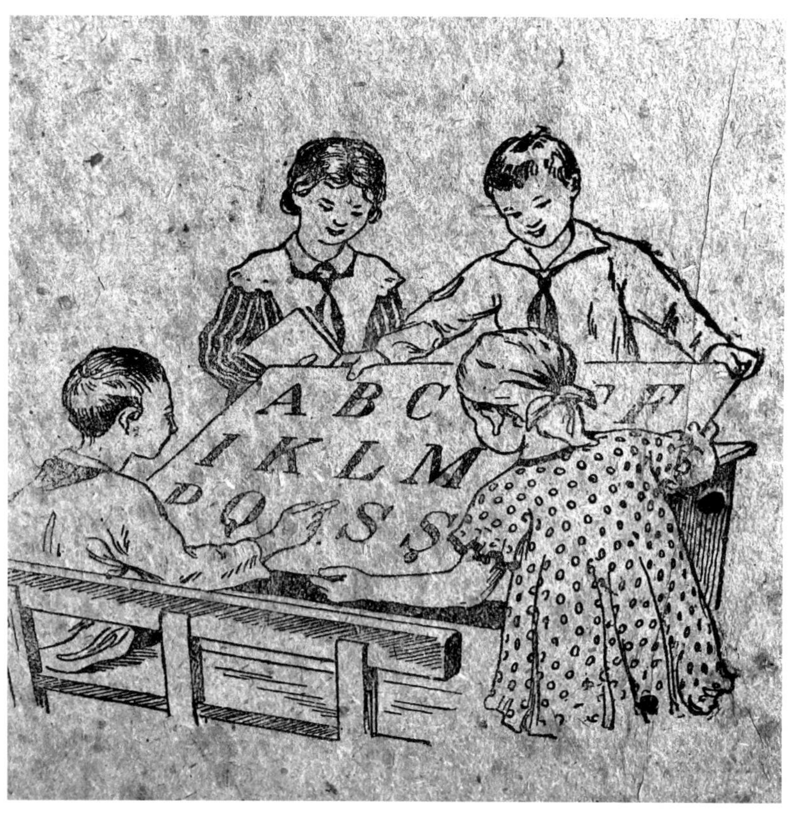

Joen Vedel and Yana Mikhalina

The Struggle Starts with the Struggle of the Tongue:

An Affective Dictionary of Tatar

Kereş süz [Introduction] Jimmie Durham taught me a lot over the years. Among many other things he taught me not to take language too seriously. And to take language deadly seriously. When Jimmie invited me to take part in documenta fifteen, I immediately thought of this context as a place for learning, rather than a place for exhibiting.

As part of my contribution to documenta fifteen, I have collaborated with my partner, the artist Yana Mikhalina, and invited the audience into my own process of learning the language of Tatar, which is Yana's mother-tongue and the language spoken by her family in Tatarstan. Every day over the 100 days of the exhibition, I have been learning and practising a new phrase in Tatar with Yana's grandmother and aunt over the phone. All phrases have been chosen for their everyday usefulness, poetic qualities, political relevance, and particularities to Tatar culture. These language classes were recorded and up-loaded to the speaker system located in an empty hall in the Kulturbahnhof in Kassel, changing daily along-side the official announcements of trains departing and arriving. The title of the sound-installation is *Tiñla alaysa, añlamasañ* (If you don't understand, listen).

This booklet is a compilation of the 100 Tatar words and phrases that I have learned over the 100 days of the exhibition. Situated between a syllabus, a glossary, and the documentation of a process, it aims at tracing Tatar in different co-existing logics peculiar to the language: from the acoustic images in the words to particular grammatical forms, and from personal anecdotes to folk wisdom. We call it 'an affective dictionary', as it deals first and foremost with relationships and uses love as a methodology. Unlike most other dictionaries, the affective dictionary doesn't stem from the desire for an objective and comprehensive list of words and phrases; rather, it highlights language as something beyond a mere tool for communication and the production of meaning. It speaks to the ongoing process of unlearning and undoing of the knowledge structures that prevail; language not as something human beings have but something human beings are.

As a small gesture of resistance to the ongoing Russian imperialism and as an act of solidarity with the decolonial movement inside Tatarstan, we have adapted the Latin script for the Tatar phrases in this booklet. Although the Arabic script has been used as the graphic base for centuries, with some letters borrowed from the Persian alphabet, the later Tatar independence movement chose Latin as their preferred script. Needless to say, language plays a crucial role within any settler-colonial state and any decolonial form of resistance. In 1938 Joseph Stalin forced the Cyrillization of Tatar, although it doesn't represent the sounds of the Tatar language. And in 2002, Vladimir Putin signed a law prohibiting the writing of indigenous' languages in non-Cyrillic script. The measure stated that Tatarstan's adoption of Latin was 'a threat to Russian national security' and banned other constituents of the Russian Federation from using Latin script to print Tatar.

We invite all readers and listeners to join the struggle —the struggle starts with the struggle of the tongue: **Maqsatıbız bäysezleq!**

Ahır zaman zhitte [The end of the world is here] *Ahır zaman* literally means "the end of time", a very popular phrase nowadays.

Aña künelle balada, bala künelle dalada [The mother's soul is in the child, the child's soul is in the steppe] Tatar folk wisdom.

Aşağan belmi, turağan belä [The one who shares knows, not the one who eats] This idiom became famous in 2016 after the president of Tatarstan said it to the Russian minister of finance in the polemics about the centralised redistribution of regional budgets. The idiom itself originates from Tatar peasant society, where families typically had many children and the scarcity of food meant it had to be shared equitably.

Aulaq öygä rähim itegez [Welcome to the *aulaq öy*] *Aulaq öy* literally means "secret house" and refers to a social and educational gathering that young women used to organise in their homes when their parents were away. After the October Revolution these practices slowly disappeared as the Bolsheviks forcefully introduced the more "progressive" institution in the form of the houses of culture. Today, *Aulaq öygä rähim itegez* can be heard in the opening line of a TV programme on Tatar TV.

Avıznı ülçäp aç! [Think before you speak!] The literal meaning is "Weigh, when opening your mouth".

Awılım, sin da qartaydıñ [My village, you also grew old] A line from a poem by an unknown Tatar female poet, one of many.

Ayak-kullarıñ sızlausız bulsın [Never let your arms and legs feel sick] This expression is used for craftspeople who make things with their hands.

Ayu munça saldırğan, munçasında yöri-yöri, tübetäem qaldırğan [A bear has sold the sauna, he walks and walks in the sauna, he left his *tyubetäi* (a religious skull-cap) there] A children's nursery rhyme popular in Tatar villages in the 1960s. The bear is an important animal in Tatar folklore, and *munça*, "sauna", has been a part of Tatar culture since the 13th century.

Azatlıq/hörriyat/irekleq [Freedom] *Azatlıq* is used for both "freedom" and "will". *Hörriyat* is used for "national freedom" and the fight for political rights, a very important notion for Tatars living under colonial regimes for centuries. *Irekleq* is the most depoliticised of the terms and is used for a "freedom of choice" when translating from the Russian *svoboda*.

Ähirät duslar ber-bersen yaqlarğa tieş [Girlfriends should support each other] *Ähirät dustim* literally means "an intimate female friend". At the same time, *ähirät dön'ya* (literally "the world of the girlfriend") means "the other world".

Ämänätkä hıyanät itmägez [Do not give up a parting wish] *Ämänät* means the parting word of a dead person, a non-material wish that is to be remembered after death. *Hıyanät* also means "a treason", which in this context is considered to be an ethical injunction to remember.

Aydä örek belän çäy eçäbez! [Let us have tea with dried apricots] *Örek* is an "apricot", but most commonly it is referred to as a dried apricot, which is an integral part of Tatar cuisine, used in desserts and just by itself, with tea.

Balaçaknıñ ber könenä äylänep qaytsañ ide [If only one could return to childhood for a day] A line from a poem by an unknown Tatar female poet.

Batır ber ülär, qurqaq meñ ülär [A brave person dies once, a coward dies a thousand times] *Batır* is a Turkic name for a hero. *Batır quyan* ("brave hare") means "pretentiously brave".

Batır bulsan – yöräktän, köçle bulsan – teläktän [Courage comes from the heart, strength comes from the elbow] *Yöräk* is "heart". Apart from referring to the body organ, in the Tatar linguistic worldview the heart relates to bravery (see the difference between *yöräk, küñel´* and *moñ* in the relevant dictionary entries).

Baqa tuye yasamağız! [Stop talking nonsense!] *Baqa tuye* literally means "the frog's wedding" and means a clueless conversation in which no one hears and everyone interrupts each other. *Yasamağız* means "don't make", which points to the materiality of the act of speaking for Tatars.

Bähil bulığız [Sorry for everything] There are many ways to say "I am sorry" in Tatar, depending on the situation. *Bähil bulığız* means "sorry for everything" and is usually used before a person dies or goes on a lengthy journey.

Ber adım da artqa çigenmibez [We will not fall back even one step] *Adım* means both "a step" and "an independent, decisive deed".

Ber şırpıdan ut bulmıy [One match will not start a fire] *Ut* is a common word for "fire", with minor variations in Tatar, Yakut, Turkmen, Chuvash and Mongolian.

Bergä-bergä yaşiyk äle ozaq itep [Let us live together as long as possible] Literally, *bergä-bergä* means "one-one", showing togetherness performed on a linguistic level.

Berkemdä ahırına qadär töşenmi [No one fully understands] *Töşenü* also means "to conceive".

Bez qurqınıçsız urında [We are in a safe space] Literally, *qurqınıçsız urın* means "a space without fear". In the Tatar language, a lot of adjectives are formed with negative affixes, e.g. *sez/sız*, which means that something or someone is not there.

Bez zhırlamıy, kem zhırlasıñ? [If we don't sing, who would?] *Zhırlau* is the verb for human singing. There is a special word to signify non-human singing, primarily birdsong, *sayrau*, which shows the importance of music in Tatar culture.

Bezne urap ütmäs äle bähetle qartlıq [A happy oldhood will not escape us] A line from a song by Zhavit Shakirov, a popular Tatar-Bashkir singer from the 1990s. The origin of the word *qart* means "old" in Tatar and is shared with the Chuvash, Mari and Udmurt languages, in which *qart* means "pagan shaman".

Bezneñ zhülärleq isäpläsäñ ülärleq [One would die before counting all the foolish things we have done] *Zhülärleq* means both "foolishness" and "craziness", a common linguistic trope in many languages.

Biek waqıyğa aldınnan küzgä yoqı kermäde [It's hard to fall asleep before important events] The literal translation of *küzgä yoqı kermäde* is "dreams cannot go under the eyelids".

Bu miña yazmağan [It's not meant for me] The literal translation is "it's not written for me". This phrase, together with other idioms using *yazırğa* (to write), signifies the importance of Islamic scriptures in Tatar culture. For example, "mad person" is *akıldan yazğan*, which literally means "written out from mind".

Bu süzlär siña da tiya [That means you too] The literal translation would be "these words touch you too", highlighting once again the understanding by Tatars of the literal materialism of words in our life.

Çıltır-çıltır aga çişmä [The stream flows with a *çıltır-çıltır* sound] *Çıltır-çıltır* means both the sound of bubbling water and the doorbell. In Tatar, the stream flows as *çıltır-çıltır*, the traditional Tatar braid accessory, made of metal, which also sounds like *çıltır-çıltır*, the bell *çıltırıy*, and the phone *çaltırıy*.

Çistartıp aşap beter! [Do not leave anything on your plate!] Respect for food is important. Children are taught to finish everything they have on their plate, but sometimes this is so hard!

Eşegezdä totmağız [Don't hold it in your belly] This advice comes from a relative in Zelenodolsk who practised a very Soviet form of psychotherapy: to hop on the night train and speak about your intimate problems with a random traveller who you will never see again.

Ğomerne däwalap bulmau [Life is incurable] *Ğomer* means "life" and originates from the Arabic *umrah* (lit. "to visit a populated place"), an Islamic pilgrimage to Mecca.

Hakim-apa rähätlänep qaldı, mesken! [Mrs Hakim joyfully remained alone [after the death of her husband], poor her!] This phrase belonged to Flöra and Farida's sister, Elmira, who passed away at the age of 24 after a difficult marriage and birth in the 1960s. *Rähät* means "joy" or "enjoyment". *Mesken* is a very common Tatar word that means "a pitiful person" (whom the speaker, at the same time, has pity for).

Hatın-kıznın eşen tawıq ta çüpläp beterä almıy [Even a chicken cannot peck all the woman's work] The Tatar word for "woman", *hatın-kız*, literally means "woman-girl" and bears a split within itself. Many idioms in the Tatar language highlight the complexity and troublesome character of female labour.

Häerle yul sezgä! [May you have a good trip!]

Hällär niçek? – Ber köy/ber köygä ["How are you?" —"One melody/tune"] An interesting answer to the simple question *hällär niçek*, or "how are you?". Literally, it would be "for one melody", which means that things are as usual, pointing to the musicality of the Tatar people.

Härkemneñ üzeneñ ana tele bar [Everyone has their own mother tongue]

Häzer ük qaytıp zhit [Come back right now] *Qaytıp zhit* is an example of a peculiar Tatar grammar form of double verbs that may sound illogical in literal translation. Literally, the phrase could be translated as "Arrive-achieve right now". Other examples of such double verbs are *barıp qaitam* ("go-return"), *çıgıp kitäm* ("exit-leave") and *utırıp alam* ("sit-take"). All of these are ancient grammatical structures that can also be found in the Altai language.

Ihlastan rähmätemne belderäm [I sincerely express my gratitude] Verbal behaviour in Tatar is dependent on age, religiosity and the area of dwelling. This is a rather old-fashioned expression of gratitude.

Iskä töşerä almıym äytäse süzemne [I cannot remember what I wanted to say] *Is* means both "mind", "memory" and "conscience". *Iskä töşerü* literally means "to bring down to the mind" or "to recall". *Iskä töşerä almıym* means "I cannot take what I recall", or "I cannot remember".

Iya; Zhan iyase; Aqıl iyase; Hezmät iyase; Yort iyase [Master; Living creature; Sage; Worker; House-hold deity] Despite the difference in meaning, all these words derive from the same word, *iya* ("owner") and highlight different perspectives to ownership. *Zhan iyase* literally means the "owner of the soul", *aqıl iyase* "the owner of the soul", and *yort iyase* "the owner of the house".

Jusañ ju, jumasañ juma [If you want to clean, clean, if you don't, don't clean] An old joke, with a slight phonetic distortion of Tatar words mimicking the sounds of French.

Kötü waqıtı [Waiting time] Also, a shepherd in Tatar is *kötüçe*, "the one who waits".

Kük kükri, yaşen yaşni [The thunder rumbles, the lightning flickers] The literal translation is "the sky is skying, the lightning is lighting". It is very common in Tatar to repeat the wording in order to highlight the unspeakable scale of the event.

Kükkä qarap, zhirñe uyla [When looking at the sky, think about the earth] Tatar folk wisdom.

Küñel´ buşatırğa berär keşe kiräk [We all need to give vent to our feelings] *Küñel´*, another word for "soul", is used to speak about the soul as inseparable from the physical body. The derivatives of *küñel´* are very diverse and present in everyday language: *küñelle* means "happy" (lit. "full of soul"), while *küñel´ buşatu* means "to unburden oneself" (lit. "to pour out the soul"), and *küñel´ bolğanu* means "to feel sick" (lit. "the soul is dizzy").

Küp kürgän, küp belgän [The one who has seen a lot, knows a lot] One of the many idioms and expressions that shows the importance of education for the Tatar people.

Küz aldına kiterü [To imagine] The literal translation is "to bring in front of one's eyes".

Maqsatıbız bäysezleq [Our purpose is independence] An important anti-colonial slogan for the Tatar independence movement, in use for more than thirty years.

Mäytäm/Kit, mäytäm/Yuk, mäytäm/Ällä, mäytäm [I say / Go, I say / No, I say / Maybe, I say] The word *mäytäm* is a merge of *min* and *äytäm*, "I say", nowadays used mostly by the older generations and in Tatar theatre pieces.

Menä şulay eşlärsez inde [Please do it this way] *Inde* is a word with a situated meaning, and is mainly used, for example, to soften the tone when making a request.

Min bala taptım [I gave birth] This literally means "I found a child". *Bala tabu* means "childbearing", literally "finding a child".

Min siña ışanam [I believe in you] This means "I believe in you" and "I believe you" at the same time.

Min sine sağınam [I miss you] *Sagış* means longing and in the Tatar language it is closely associated with the colour yellow, which shows the close connection of the culture to nature. *Min sine bik sağınıp kötäm* means "I miss you, awaiting", literally "I miss-await you".

Min sine yuksınam [I am lacking you] *Yuksınu* means to feel the lack of someone or something, somewhere but not inside oneself. *Yuk* is "no". Simplified, *min sine yuksınam* can be translated as "I miss you" or "I feel empty without you".

Minem ayak sızlıy [My legs are nagging] The verb *sızu* means both "an unceasing pain", "a musical sound that goes straight into one's heart" and "the distinct sound of smouldering". In all the meanings, *sızu* points to the whining, lingering character of the experience.

Minem siña açuım kilä [I am angry at you] The literal translation means "I want to be angry at you" as something in the future tense, despite speaking about a current state of anger.

Min monda nişlim? [What am I doing here?] Used both in an everyday and existential sense.

Moñ bulıp kerdeñ küñelgä [It stayed deep inside my soul like *moñ*] *Moñ* is a very particular word for Tatar mentality, a heartwarming sorrow in which one feels a connectedness with the whole world. In Tatar music, *moñ* is the melody of the heart, which cannot be described, only felt.

Närsä bulsa da, uftanma! [Whatever happens, don't worry!] *Uftanma* derives from *uf*, an expression of tiredness and worry.

Nindi hurlıq! [Such a shame!] This phrase has been a very popular saying in the Tatar-speaking media since the beginning of the Russian invasion of Ukraine. *Hurlıq* also means "disgrace". *Hurlıqqa töşte* literally means "to drop the shame", or "to embarrass oneself".

Özgälenä üzägem [My heart is tearing apart] The literal translation is "my centre is tearing apart".

Päri; Päri tue; Päri üpkän [Evil; Snowstorm; A cold sore] *Päri* is an evil (usually female) spirit, a demon, coming from Farsi folklore, that can take the appearance of an animal, a human, or possessed objects. In a figurative sense, it is a bad-tempered person. *Päri tue* (lit. "marriage of the päri") means "snowstorm". *Päri üpkän* (lit. "päri's kiss") means "a cold sore".

Qaber – yahşı ya yaman ğamällär sandığı [A grave is a coffer with good and wicked deeds] Tatar folk wisdom.

Qayğığıznı urtaqlaşam [My condolences] This literally means "I am sharing your grief". *Qayğı* means both "grief", "sorrow" and "worry".

Qaysı zhiren awırta? [In what place does it hurt?] *Zhir* means "territory", "place", "earth", "ground", "soil", "planet" and "spot".

Qot; Qotlaem; Qotlı bulsın; Qotoçkıç; Qotsız [Soul; Congratulations; Be happy; Horrifying; Uncomfortable] *Qot* means "soul, spirit". This word has an ancient Turkic origin and is well-preserved as a part of various words in the Tatar language. All derivative words contain an idea of presence/absence of the soul/spirit of someone or something.

Qunaqlarnı yaqtı yöz belän qarşı alabız [We greet guests with open faces] Hospitality is a very important part of Tatar culture. Whether you are a guest or the host, you should not forget to give *küçtänäç*, "a present to or from the host". The word *küçtänäç* can also be found in the Mari, Udmurt and Chuvash languages.

Qurqmıybız! Bireşmibez! [We are not afraid! We will not give up!]

Sabır itkän, moradına zhitkän [The humble one will achieve the goal] *Sabır* means something between patient, humble, self-controlled and calm. The word came from Arabic and signifies a strong connection of Tatar identity with the Islamic ideal of a religious person, who is, at the same time, patient and full of dignity.

Saqlağız üzegezne [Take care of yourself] *Saqlay* means "to guard", "take care", "protect" and "save".

Sez tınıç yaşisezme? [Are you living in peace?] *Tınıç* means both peace and serenity and exists in slightly different forms in the Chuvash, Mari, Nogai, Kazakh, Qaraqalpaq and Uzbek languages.

Sin minem küz nurım [You are the ray of my eyes] A term of endearment for children and loved ones.

Sin qaya barasıñ? [Where are you going?] *Baru* is a verb that means a purposeful movement in the direction opposite from the one who poses the question.

Suğışka yuk dip äytik! [We say no to war!] A slogan that became an important anti-war statement in Tatarstan after the Russian invasion of Ukraine. The Russian word for "war", *voina*, is banned from usage by the state, leading to a re-emergence in the uses of indigenous languages and as a way to amplify the voices of the indigenous people colonised by Russia until the present day. In Tatar, *suğış* means "war", "battle" and "fight", without distinguishing between the scale of violence.

Tañ tişege [An early morning] Literally, this means "the hole of the dawn". *Tañ tişegen torıp* is "waking up early". This expression is connected to the cosmogenic worldview of the Turkic people, where the sun appears from a hole in the sky.

Tatarğa tılmaç kiräkmi [Tatars do not need a translator] An old proverb from the times before the revolution, when the Kazan dialect of Tatar ("old Tatar") was understood by many Turkic peoples, such as Crimean Tatars, Uzbeks, Uighurs, Kashgars, Qarapaqalpaqs, and others.

Tatlı yokı, tämle töş [Sweet sleep, tasty dreams] A phrase used before going to sleep. As in many other languages, the act of sleeping and of dreaming in Tatar are linguistically differentiated.

Tau-tau vägdä birep kitte [They promised the earth and left] In modern Tatar *tau* is "a mountain", but the original meaning of *tau* is "gratitude". It is a Turkic word that is still used among other Volga indigenous people—the Chuvash, Mari and Udmurt—as "thank you". With the influence of Islam, *tau siña* was replaced by the Arabic *räxmät*.

Tınıp torıyk [Let's have a nap] This literally means "Let's stay in quietness". *Tın* is both "quiet" and "breathing".

Tıñla alaysa, añlamasañ [If you don't understand, listen] Apart from its main meaning "to listen", *tıñlau* also means "to obey" and "to eavesdrop".

Tizräk savığırğa yazsın [Get healthy soon] The literal translation would be "May your quick recovery be written".

Töp nigez haman üzenä tarta [*Töp nigez* is continously drawing towards itself] Literally, *töp nigez* means "the main fundament", "an ancestral home" or a family land, an intergenerational place of birth, life and death.

Tuğan kön belän [Happy birthday] *Tuğan* means "native", not only in Tatar but also, with minor variations, in the Bashkir, Udmurt, Mari, Mordovian and Altai languages. Some Bashkir and Tatar political emigrants of the 1920s and 1930s used *Tuğan* as their surname.

Tuğan yaqnı zhir-suı yam´le [The native lands territories are the dearest] *Zhir-su* literally means "earth-water" and speaks to the love of the land. In pre-Islamic Turkic mythology, *Zhir-Su* was one of the principal gods, the patrons of the land.

Üpkä totma, läkin onıtma [Do not hold a grudge, but do not forget either] In Tatar, the second meaning of *üpkä* ("grudge") means "lungs".

Ütep baruçı/üzıp baruçı [Passer-by] These words are synonyms: while *ütep baruçı* places the accent on the act of passing in the sense of its finitude, *ütä*, in *üzıp baruçı* it is the act of passing in the sense of its longevity, *üzä*.

Üze egılğan yelamas [The one who has fallen on their own will not cry] "To cry" in Tatar is *yelau*, while "to smile" is *yelmayu.*

Uzenä tiñ tormış iptäşen tabu zhiñel eş tügel´ [It is not an easy task to find a life partner for oneself] *Iptäş* means "partner", "comrade" and "friend" at the same time. Tatar is a gender-neutral language; however, feminitives for various professions came into the language under the influence of Arabic.

Vözhdän kütärmi [Conscience can't bear it] The literal translation is "conscience can't lift it". In Arabic, *vözhdän* means "a peaceful soul", which signifies that conscience is life in concord with an inner peace (rather than a feeling of guilt).

Waqıt küpme? [What time is it?] Literally, this means "is there enough time/how much is the time?"

Yañğırdan soñ qoyaş bar, aldaudan soñ oyat bar [Sun comes after the rain, shame comes after the lie] The concept of *oyat* ("shame" or "shameful deed") is connected to the sphere of the laws of ethics.

Yeraqktan işetelgän tawış [Sounds from afar] "Voice" and "sound" are the same word in Tatar, *tawış.*

Yomşak ağaçnı qort basar [Soft trees will be eaten by worms]

Yöräk maem; bäğrem [The fat of my heart] A peculiar expression of tenderness towards small children or loved ones. Originating from ancient Turkic and the nomadic layers of Tatar culture, where fatty food was primarily sweet.

Yulauçılarğa izge yullar bulsın [Safe travels to the community on the road] *Yul* means "a road". *Yulauçı* means "the one on the road". *Yulauçılar* means "the ones on the road together".

Yumartta maya tormas [A generous person will not keep the reserve] *Maya* is not only a "reserve", it is a "necessary reserve". It is most commonly used for the one egg that has to remain in the henhouse so that the chickens will continue to lay their eggs.

Zhan alu; zhan birü; zhan saqlau ["To kill"; "To die"; "To exist"] Literally, this means to "take soul", "to give soul" and "to store soul". *Zhan* came into Tatar from Farsi and means "soul". Unlike Western philosophical dualism, the concept of *zhan* is not opposed to the concept of the body; the presence of *zhan* distinguishes a living body from the dead. *Zhan saqlau* ("to store soul") means "to exist" and is roughly comparable with the Greek notion of bare life, *zoe*.

Zhäy saen bez qaen urmanına zhiläkkä yöribez [Every summer we go to the birch grove to collect berries] A family memory.

Zhir-zhir, köçemne bir [Earth-earth, give the strength] A saying used after finishing the ploughing of the fields, an appeal to the land for a successful season.

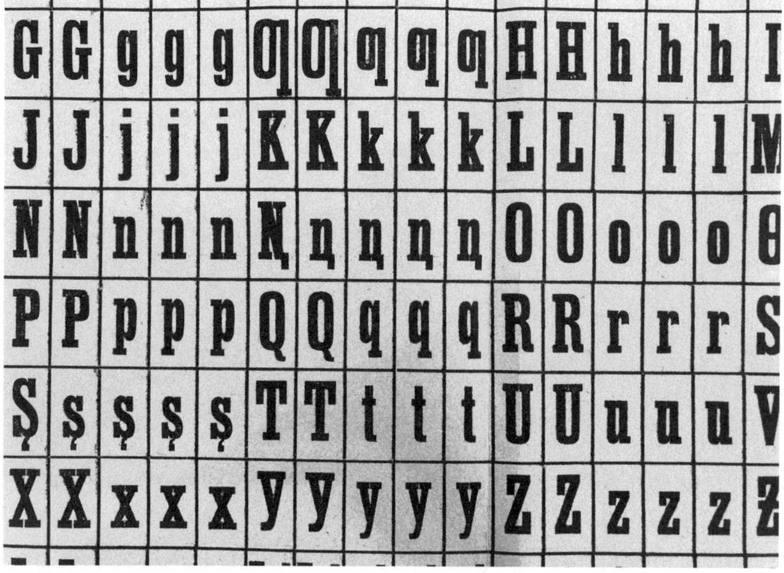

This booklet is published on the occasion of documenta fifteen (Kassel), 18 June – 25 September 2022

It is part of the publication *Jimmie Durham & A Stick in the Forest by the Side of the Road* with Jimmie Durham and Bev Koski, Elisa Strinna, Hamza Badran, Iain Chambers, Joen Vedel, Jone Kvie, Maria Thereza Alves, Wilma Lukatsch, Giulia Grechi, Alessandra Marino Al-Mishlab (ISBN 978-3-7533-0260-7, NUR 640)

Text: Yana Mikhalina & Joen Vedel
Cover image: © Yana Mikhalina & Joen Vedel, 2022
Black and white images: Säyfullin G. Älifba. Tatizdat, Qazan, 1932. Courtesy National Library of Tatarstan.
Editor: Iain Chambers
Proofreader: Nicola Grey
Design: Karoline Swiezynski, inspired by Will Holder's design for *Past Imperfect* by Bik van der Pol, which shaped the collective solution of this publication
Thank you: Rashid Tukhvatullin, Liliya Gabdrafikova, Lidia Griaznova, Alfrid Bustanov, Gölnara Mikhalina and Karen Vedel
Special thanks to: Flöra Zhabbarova and Farida Miññullina

Printed and bound in Belgium by Cassochrome with supervision of ArtLibro Trudy Dorrepaal. Published in an edition of 250 individual booklets (documenta fifteen) to be collated in an edition of 1000 books distributed by Verlag der Buchhandlung Walther und Franz König, Köln. First published by Verlag der Buchhandlung Walther und Franz König Ehrenstraße 4, D-50672 Köln.

Bibliographic information published by the Deutsche Nationalbibliothek – The Deutsche Nationalbibliothek lists this publication in the Deutsche National-bibliografie; detailed bibliographic data is available at http://dnb.d-nb.de.

Disclaimer: In making *Jimmie Durham & A Stick in the Forest by the Side of the Road* we have quotes, images and texts taken from various resources. Information concerning the original authors and sources have been credited as detailed as possible. Despite these efforts, some sources nevertheless could not be identified. Please contact the author in case of questions or objections. The ideas and opinions author unless stated otherwise.

Jimmie Durham & A Stick in the Forest by the Side of the Road has been generously supported by The Office for Contemporary Art Norway (OCA) and documenta fifteen.

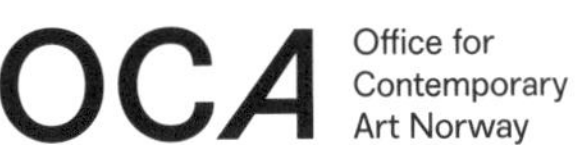

This publication has been realized in the framework of documenta fifteen, June 18 – September 25, 2022

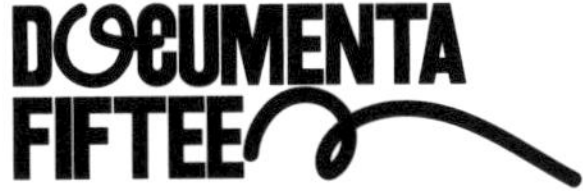

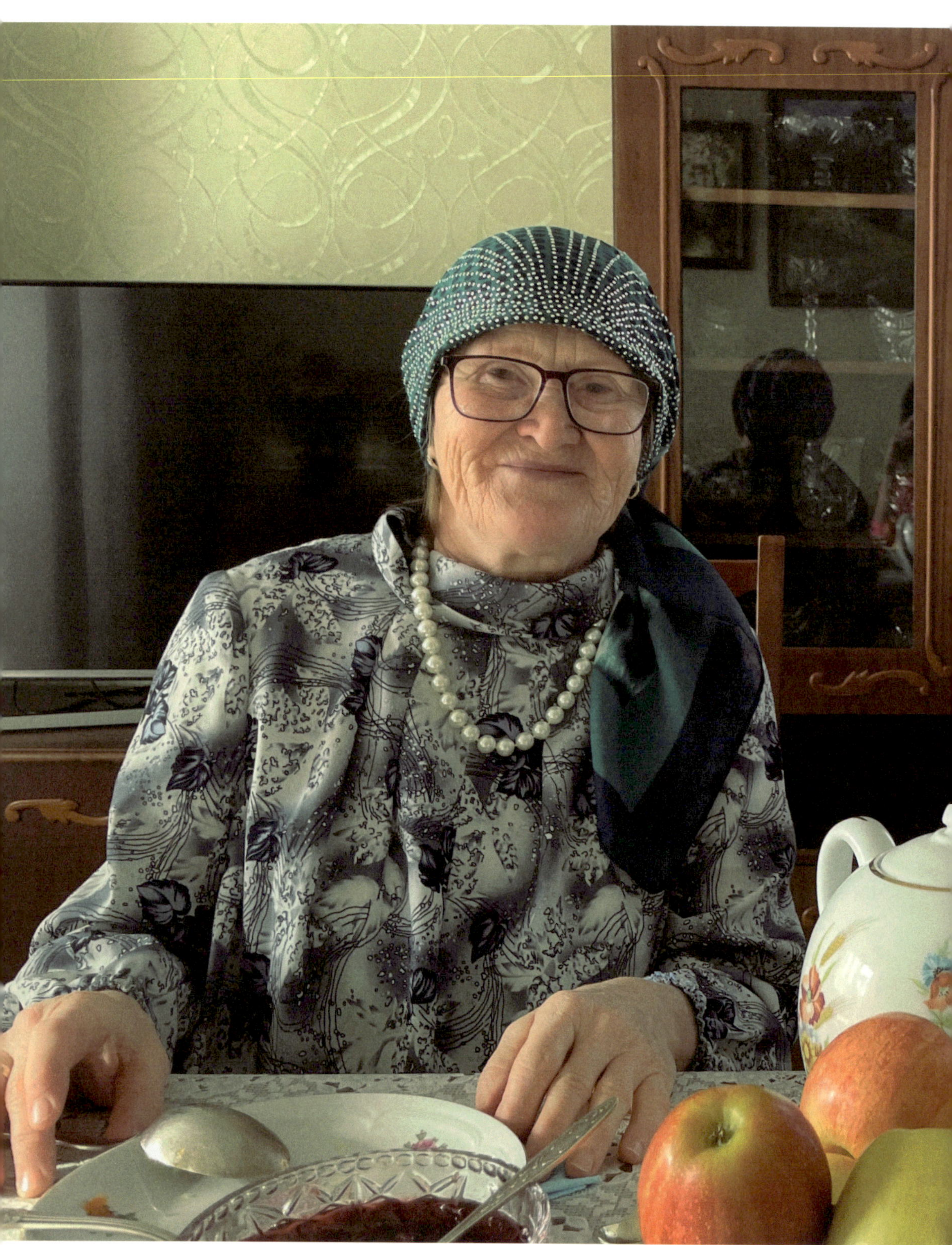

published 15 September 2022

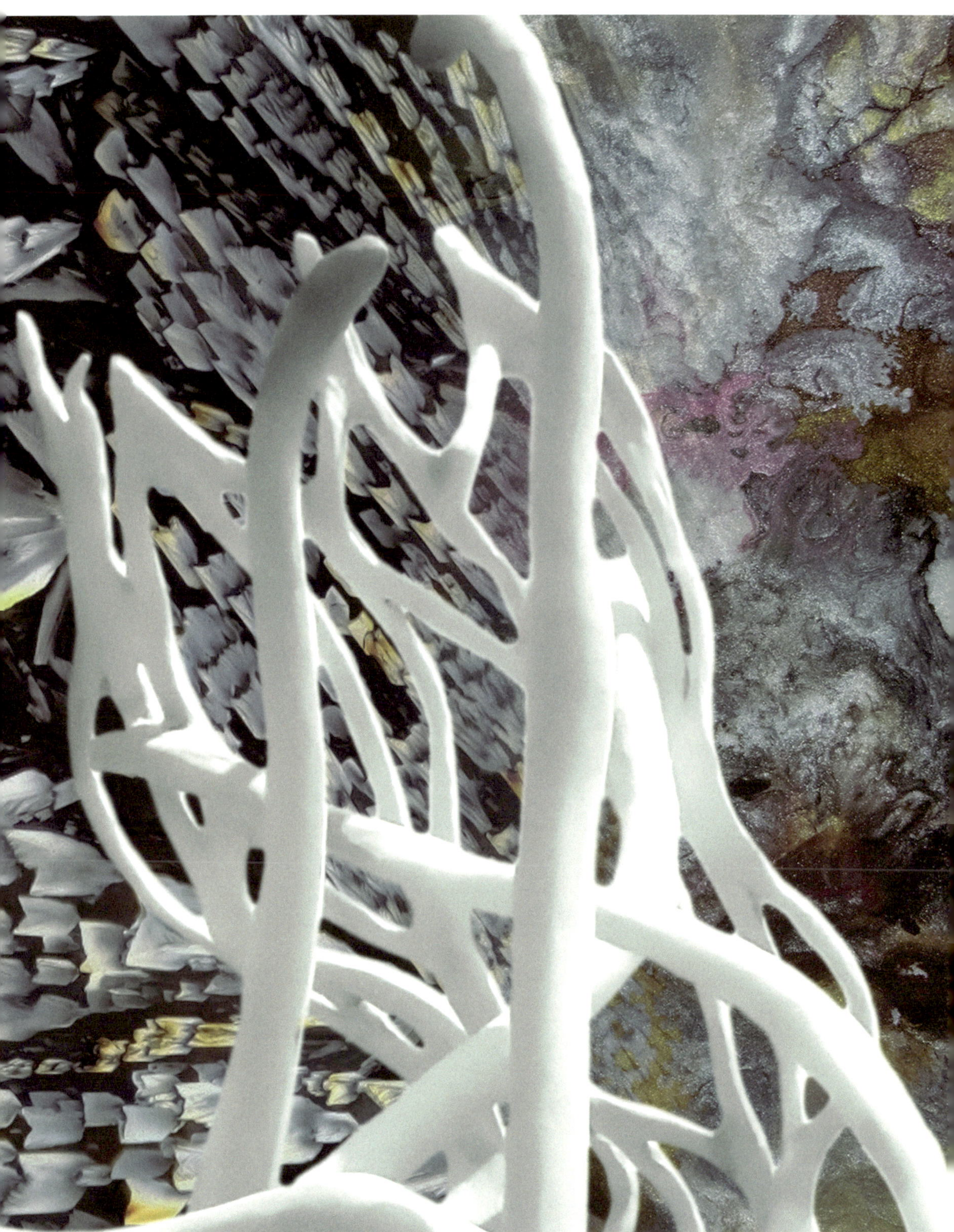
Bewitching Practices
– My Body is a Plant

Elisa Strinna in conversation with Nicole Trigg

Jimmie Durham & A Stick in the Forest by the Side of the Road

Bewitching Practices — My Body is a Plant

Judge me,
Lord, you who know
who I am, who the judges of the
world cannot know. I grit my teeth and
then they will say that I laugh… My heart is exploding.
Lord, send me the angel from heaven to see me and defend me,
let them know that I have told the truth. Commissioner, if you do not let
me down now, you will let me down dead, I am out of breath. Lord, send me the
angel from heaven, Christ, that you may draw out my soul from my body better than false
testimony, and send it where it should go. My heart breaks. Ah, my heart, ah, my head.
Please, let me down a little while, Commissioner, I have told the truth. I am flayed.
Give me a little water because I am dying of thirst. Untie me a little… I can no longer
retain urine, I have told the truth, if you could see my soul. Let me down so that
I can breathe a little. If it is possible, Mister, let me down for I can no longer resist,
I feel my heart bursting. All of you are so cruel, is it possible that none of you will
offer me a spoon that I can put down my throat? Mister, lay the fire
at my feet and get me out of here. Let me burn, for the truth
I have told you, let me away from here where I can no
longer stay, and put me in no more despair.
Take a club, and give me it over
the head, and take away my
worries, I have told
the truth.

—Franchetta Borelli [1]

[1]

Speech attributed
to the accused,
Franchetta Borelli, over
the course of her trial;
Le Streghe di Triora, by
Michele Rosi, self-
published ebook,
1 September 2017;
excerpted and
translated by the
authors.

FRANCHETTA BORELLI,
19 SEPTEMBER 1588, TRIORA, LIGURIA (IT)

Franchetta's story makes me clench all parts of my body, especially my crotch—having just discovered that the torture device known as the wooden horse, or *cavaletto squarciapalle* in Italian (little-horse ball-ripper), consists of a long wooden wedge, point-up, mounted on sturdy wooden legs. The victim is made to straddle it like a log about to be split, balancing on the edge of an axe. The upper body is bound with ropes, while additional weights are attached to each leg. Franchetta was stripped naked, her head and pubic area shaved; she was then posted on the ball-ripper for a total of 48 hours. Her tormentors waited in vain for her to confirm their suspicions, aka 'the truth'.

She was indicted for having worked as a prostitute all her life, well-known in her locality; for then having grown old, and *therefore* being "held to be one of the principal witches that exist there". No further link between prostitution, aging and witchcraft than this is provided. Franchetta was also known in the region as 'una ricca', a rich woman. If she was economically stable at a time of widespread immiseration, it would have been because of her work: rare means for a woman at the time to subsist outside of the bonds of marriage and family. Her refusal to confess incriminated her further; the official who oversaw the proceedings, and later provides the account, declares it 'obstinacy', yet another sign of the devil. She had also been seen to laugh, but never cry, while forced to ride the little horse. And finally, her testimony is described as deceitful and contradictory, again because she failed to validate her accusers' suspicions directly.

Witch trials are famous for the use of a literally annihilating, nonsensical logic, which assures that if you die of torture you may in fact be innocent—though one can never be certain—and if you survive it you are evil, and so deserve to be eradicated. And if you confess to being a witch, no one will argue with you, although some may pity you; and if you do not confess, then you are definitely also a witch, and even more deserving of punishment. Franchetta survived 48 hours of torture by wooden horse, and then they let her go.

The record of the trial ends unexpectedly. At a certain point
the commissioner and attendants become distracted by the
thought of food. Over the course of a few, final hours, they stop
caring about convicting and punishing Franchetta. Indeed,
everything changes when one of the workers evokes the "beautiful brown chestnuts [that] grow in Triora".

From here until the end of the account, everyone—except
Franchetta—slips into a lighter mood, and the commissioner
converses casually with his assistants for nearly an hour. One
of them suggests leaving to prepare a soup, then returning
with it to the prison. The commissioner remains fixated
on coaxing 'the truth' out of Franchetta regardless, until the
worker presses: "I am going to eat plenty [of soup], but this
torture is no good thing; I would rather eat a piece of cake".
Laughing as he spoke, he "seemed to ridicule both his master
and the circumstances".

Food is brought, Franchetta is fed along with the others, and
then she protests: "you ought to have taken me down hours
ago". The commissioner replies: "I'd safely swear you would
have come down without a fight", and he laughs. Something
in between the lines has inspired him to release his grip
on Franchetta's life. The final decree reads: "because [our
Lord] cared little or nothing about [Franchetta], He ordered
she be left alone…"[2]

Chestnuts come to mind and change the atmosphere
completely, making everyone forget who and where they are,
and for what purpose. Returned to their senses, they look
around themselves bewildered.

2
Rosi, pp 133–139

UNA CERTA GIOVANNINA,
8 NOVEMBER, 1588, TRIORA, LIGURIA (IT)

When I read the story of 'a certain Giovannina', my insides
wrung themselves like rags and began to sink lower
in their cavities.

She was arrested after being denounced by others already
accused and incarcerated as witches. When Giovannina "spit
into her hands, then daubed it over one eye to make it appear
that she was crying", she came under further suspicion. So they

held her feet in the fire for a quarter of an hour. She confessed
nothing, before, during or after her torture, and was found
the next morning, three miles from her prison cell: "on cliffs
surrounded by woods that the men who went looking for her,
as they tell it, could barely climb; it seems all the more mirac-
ulous that this woman with ruined feet was able to scale them,
assisted by the devil". She was returned to prison, and the
following morning was discovered dead, on her knees, with
a strap around her neck. The commissary deduced that, given
the feeble weight of the strap, "it appears impossible that
anyone other than the devil could have suffocated her".[3]

The violence between the lines is so obvious that
we cannot (we should not?) even say it out loud to each
other. We expel air audibly and wrinkle our faces, catching
each other's eye. My stomach sank thinking what actually
happened to Giovannina, besides being tortured by fire for
trying to perform, one last time, a woman's role. Kidnapping,
rape, gang rape, murder. *If only* it had been the devil that
plucked her free, gave her flight, then swiftly ended her misery.
Giovannina's bodily autonomy was unthinkable; so too was the
possibility of her suicide.

How to reclaim the demonic grounds that non-conforming
women and other others have historically been relegated to,
marked and terrorised as witches and criminals?

3

Rosi, p 79

01.   AFFILIATION WITH THE DEVIL

It has been estimated that thousands of executions occurred in the
15th and early 16th centuries across Europe. All this in the name
of women's affiliation with the Devil. Instructional texts like the
Malleus Maleficarum (The Hammer of Witches), first published
in Germany in 1486, were widely used to identify and
condemn witches.

I would like to celebrate the life of all of these women. The soil has
transformed their membranes into new and other life. We have been
accused of the most incredible things. We have been charged with
"Copulating with those Devils known as Incubi"; "Depriv[ing] Man
of his Virile Member"; "Transforming Men into the Forms of Beasts";
of making it possible for the "Devil [to] possess Men". We were

7

4

Summary, Jacob
Sprenger and Heinrich
Kraemer, *The Hammer
of Witches (Malleus
Maleficarum)*, 1486

5

Part I, Question 6:
'Why it is that women
are chiefly addicted to
evil superstitions', in
Sprenger and Kraemer,
*The Hammer of
Witches (Malleus
Maleficarum)*, 1486

6

Silvia Federici, *Caliban
and the Witch*, 2004

7

Giorgio Agamben,
*L'Aperto: l'uomo e
l'animale*, 2007, p 45

reputed to "Tear the Male Organ", "Obstruct the Venereal Act" and "Sway the Minds of Men to Love or Hate". In addition, we were accused of being able to "inflict all Sorts of Infirmities", of "Hurting Cattle in Various Ways", of "Killing the Child conceived in the Womb and procuring the Abortion".[4] Each of these condemnations appears as a form of social control in which the male gender aims to secure complete dominance: over healing practices, reproductive practices, practices related to food production, and thinking practices. *Malleus* reads: "When a woman thinks alone, she thinks evil".[5]

As Silvia Federici writes in *Caliban and the Witch*, the question is not only religious but economical.[6] The new bourgeois class constructs women as mothers and wives in a new, 'private' (read: segregated) sphere of domesticity—the 'angels' of relentless social reproduction, which is necessary to the ever-expanding accumulation of capital. The working class becomes capital's instrument, and women are conscripted to the specific role of maintaining and regenerating this mechanism. The social is made to conform to the models of heteronormative families, private property, the institutionalisation of knowledge, and rigid division into social classes. These institutions claim hegemony in perpetuity, operating to suppress all forms of autonomy, the common, and spontaneous affiliation.

Like any other form of cultural repression, it removes us from 'encounters, relationships, interactions'—the essence of life, for me too—that open us up to difference in and beyond our-selves.

It is interesting to reflect on how women, through these condemnations, become identified with the dimensions of instinct and the irrational. The so-called demonic comprises those aspects that tie humans to the animal world. Among other instincts, sexual drives *transform humans into beasts*, making them difficult to control. In a society where social control is becoming integral to economic development, there is the need for a new norm. A new human who, transcending passions, instincts and senses, sublimates the body in a schizophrenic act of alienation.[7] The new body is a mechanism, not an alchemy.

As inscribed by modernism, the human is a mechanism of rationality, functionality, organisation and productivity—of separation. The separation of body and mind, of the rational and the irrational, of nature and culture, remains a cornerstone of Western culture.

> We are trained to believe in life, and history, as progress, and of the
> irrational as something dangerous, linked to chaos. We exist
> in a reality in which those dimensions labelled demonic in the age
> of the witch-hunts, are still disavowed and discriminated against.
> It happens through updated forms of misogyny and racism, neocolo-
> nialism, the savage destruction of the environment, the alienation
> of individuals.

What you are describing is so familiar: the severe discon-
nect between what we do each day, and what we know cannot
continue much longer (what we do each day). I experience
a kind of whiplash looking back and forth between the news
and my life.

Sometimes I go to a place outside of the city, like the
Northern California coast, and I think the news has
to be wrong, or at least the news has left out something very
important. I am thinking about the ecological order, although
to call it an order seems wrong, about which we 'know', and
have categorised (as if to know better), hardly anything. You
go to such a place and you realise how perfect it is, and if you
are wise, how perfect you are among it. And being perfect and
acknowledging the perfection all around, you further realise,
have nothing to do with possessing mastery. You will do even
better if there are animals there, with faces that remind you
of your dreams, who continually acknowledge your presence
as you do theirs. The dog Naia from Albion, California was like
that; I thought I might have hallucinated her long nose out
of another time and place.

I examine my personal experiences with the so-called
demonic, because I think this dimension, these dimensions,
allow us to stop looking for differences *outside* ourselves individually (e.g. male/female, rational/irrational, culture/nature,
etc.), letting us find them within and in relation to ourselves
instead. I think there is absolutely something intuitive to what
I am trying to describe, related to having a body with extra-rational capacities; but I don't believe that our intuitive sensibilities correspond strictly to one of two reproductive anatomies,
even though I acknowledge the reality of hormones and other
(al)chemical factors that contribute to what *feels right* to me,
or you, in a given situation.

I am referring to my own experience because, one, the questions are as big as the world, so they are impossible to answer definitively; and two, because I think the question of method is important. In itself it offers a kind of answer (to the big questions). I think we need to pursue different methods of being and knowing than the leading methods of being and knowing, which are fundamentally violent, alienating, mistrustful, nihilistic…

> For centuries, women in Western culture have been kept away from the male-dominated sphere of cultural production. Only in the last hundred years, and under conditions of enormous discrimination, have we, women, managed to carve out a voice in the social and cultural dialogue. But in the process, the culturally contributing woman's *reproductive* function hardly finds any space. It seems telling that Artemisia Gentileschi, prior to emerging as one of few female artists to gain recognition both in her lifetime and in European art history, was raped at a very young age and publicly shamed. Among other factors, this distanced her from the roles of wife and mother, allowing for the cultivation of her art.

It's hard, in this light, to deny the ongoing impact of binary gender as a concept; whereas sometimes it seems so lax, as if we could each have it all ways at once. I never thought of it in the precise way you put it—that on top of increased generalised precarity, there is added precarity for people with uteruses: for those who have any inclination, or intention, to grow a baby in their body, and for those who have neither the inclination nor the intention, but become pregnant anyway. To say nothing about the ones who want to be pregnant but are not or cannot, and the ones who don't want to be, and aren't, but could be, living the apparent contradiction of their empty wombs in a natalist society.

I never had the intention, but always had the inclination. I feel almost exactly divided in that way–between the social and the biological, is it? If the social is the general confusion (alienation?) I feel on a daily basis with regard to my relationship to the world. I think you're right—I get the feeling that I can't have it all, and that I'd better not try or else be destroyed… When I think about the possibility of having and doing both—the baby, and my thinking and writing work—I don't or can't think: it's unthinkable. I guess, to some extent, this is what everyone who has never been pregnant, and imagines being pregnant, experiences, when trying to fathom the unfathomable: growing another human inside their own physical form, while maintaining a sense of self and autonomous focus. Since the latter is what we are raised to believe that we each have a claim to, and *should* claim, supposedly regardless of our assignments (of gender, race and class) at birth.

Even though I cannot think their co-existence, I would never imagine the one (the 'cultural role') as compensating for the lack of the other (the reproductive role)... they are incomparable and non-substitutable: what I can do and am capable of, provided I can reproduce my *own* life, and what a new human means/is/offers. As I write this I am reminded that the logic is broken—I am not reducible to 'what I can do and am capable of', any more than a child, a baby, is reducible to the bounded social or cultural contribution they may one day make. I talk myself around into remembering that *I* still need mothering, *and* that the mothering I am inclined to do need not be limited to the person or people I can physically give birth to.

Getting back to the demonic, the extra-rational, there is something crucial about confronting and admitting (letting in) the unthinkable: in this case that I could be multiple, and hold/receive more than myself with my physical as well as spiritual, conscious and unconscious being. In this way, I think the possibility and reality of being pregnant, and the attendant feelings of being divided and multiple, constitute an alternative and in certain ways privileged outlook, alongside the patriarchal one, which has been written so that men can enjoy making/having both (proprietary) culture, and (proprietary) inheritors, without conflict or contradiction between the two functions.

02. PLANTS AND KINSHIP – HEALING PRACTICES

8

See 'Coping with
life in isolation and
confinement during
the Covid-19
pandemic', *The
Psychologist*,
18 March 2020

During the pandemic I was reading about how humans can survive in artificial ecosystems and extreme environments such as the North or South Poles or outer space. Designers and scientists are exploring what conditions and practices enable humans to survive isolation, and best cope with sustained uncertainty. These conditions can produce pathologies such as depression, stress, insomnia, irritability, anger and asthenia[8]—some of which I was experiencing. We were living in separate enclosures, physical and mental. We were experiencing the weight of relationships by sensing their impossibilities. In some ways, there was not much difference between living as a polar explorer in Antarctica or as an astronaut in outer space.

You casually traverse the coldness of outer space, looking for connection, as if that non-place were continuous with your experience, a natural segue or next step into the deep… You relay back-and-forth between attention to the very big and distant, and the very local and minute, which leads to breathlessness and claustrophobia, while also stirring up a sense of *too much* breath and space. I imagine the top of my head flapping open to the entire, abominable atmosphere.

Suddenly we were massively confronted with the question of death. We were failing. The modern utopia of human mastery felt defeated. Western medicine and science were powerless in front of non-human agencies.

Coronavirus felt like an extreme symptom of a more general sickness. It felt urgent to think about healing practices. In light of this, all the other forecasts of destruction were taking on a different weight. If we couldn't control a virus, it became that much clearer that we could never handle the disasters produced by climate change, making the Earth's environment hostile to us. In *Withered Season Flowers* I have been filming inside the Ligurian greenhouses. Subjected to drought, and heat, these artificial ecosystems show how the Mediterranean flora would react under extreme climatic conditions.

…the matted, winding stems forming a passageway like the inside of a burrow, through which the camera creeps with no outlet in sight. Although the vine is dead now, too,

it appears to be infinite, and the accompanying sounds
of burbling and tumbling elements (rock, air, water), and what
sounds like breathing, contradict its stillness.

Those species that manage to survive are just a few. What if a more significant part of the planet became an extensive desert? Extreme environments mean isolation. And what does isolation mean to life?

The feeling that I must be the only one experiencing what
I am experiencing, especially when what I am experiencing
is emotionally difficult, was intensified by the pandemic;
I have felt further and further away from a sense of my person
being part of and linked to other beings, other experiences,
other thought processes than my own. So, a kind of psychic
desert in relation to other people... different from an actual
desert habitat, which I find restores my sense of connectedness! This goes back to the point about the ecological: the
logic of the interrelations that constitute and sustain a living
world is very present and close, which is not to say comprehen-
sible, when you are immersed in it directly. Thinking about
the violent transformation of environments and its effects
on human communities, I can say that during the fire season
in California, I have felt a new kind of panic and despair,
distinct from social anxiety. It wears social ties even thinner,
I worry... or else it does the opposite, galvanising us to face
facts: that we rely on each other and other lifeforms to adapt
and survive, making it no longer possible to imagine, incor-
rectly, 'I am in this alone'.

9

Spaceship Earth (2020) is a documentary by Matt Wolf about Biosphere 2, the 1991–93 experiment in which eight individuals spent two years quarantined inside a self-engineered replica of Earth's ecosystem in the Arizona desert.

03. VALERIANA OFFICINALIS

When the pandemic started, I was in Rotterdam. I had just moved to the city, so my social life was almost nil. I was subletting a loft full of plants with huge windows, a sort of open space/greenhouse. I remember watching the documentary *Spaceship Earth*,[9] and thinking of myself as a sort of biospherian.

In this state of isolation, to survive was a question of enduring absence. There was no social space to go to, no spontaneous encounter to experience, no future to imagine. We were all suspended

13

10

Sandro Oddo,
*La medicina popolare
nell'alta Valle
Argentina*, 1997, p 115

in a claustrophobic space of fear. That which is the essence of life—encounters, relationships, interactions—was putting us in danger—it was a paradigm shift. This condition felt exceptional, but also long enough to become a state of reality. Caught in this state of immobility, I decided to look at plants—of all beings, the most rooted.

After four months of lockdown, I managed to return to Italy. I took some time off in Ventimiglia, Liguria, at my grandmother's house. While wandering around steep roads, I noticed an abandoned greenhouse. That was the first of many. Greenhouses are at the base of the modern utopia of BLSS, Bioregenerative Life Support Systems—enclosed artificial ecosystems thought to be independent from planet Earth, considered the future of space colonisation, and the possible future of human life in a devastated earthly environment. In the case of Liguria, these greenhouses constitute the remains of an industry that is today unsustainable. Left alone, their ecosystems transformed into new feral ecologies. They were involuntary experiments of plant survival in extreme climatic conditions. Researching which vegetation could survive extreme temperatures, I began studying the flora of Ventimiglia. From the coast, I went to explore the hinterland in search of other greenhouses. In my explorations, I stumbled on the village of Triora.

There, I found the book *Popular Medicine of the Argentina Valley*, edited by the researcher Sandro Oddo. The book includes transcripts of interviews with women living in the village, among them Amalia Lanteri, Chiara Sasso, Lidia Petricaccio and Maria Rosa Halagian. In the chapter on the 'Nervous System', I looked for remedies for anxiety and lack of sleep. The plants to cure stress were various, such as hawthorn, passion flower, lemon balm, St. John's Wort and chamomile, but among the most relevant to the treatment of anxiety was *Valeriana officinalis*. "The roots have always been known for their medicinal qualities. It could not have been otherwise if its name, as it seems, derives from the Latin *valere*, meaning to heal. In treating anxiety, a tiny root, about fifteen grams, macerated in a litre of cold water for twelve hours, calms the nerve centres and allows a peaceful rest."[10]

Living in the city, and as it was winter, I couldn't find Valerian roots out in the fields. I only found extracts in drops. But I ordered five Valerian plants to put on my balcony. In the meantime, I started a training course with the herbalist Karin Mecozzi, an expert in environmental education and landscape observation. Karin states that all

14

11

Karin Mecozzi,
*Ars Herbaria, Natura e
Cultura Editrice*, 2020,
p 213

medicinal plants have something monstrous and strange about them. A plant becomes medicinal when something is out of harmony in one of its organs or parts. This anomalous dimension is chemically identified as an alkaloid. Alkaloids are a group of secondary and natural molecules containing nitrogen. In humans, alkaloids can induce psychotropic effects, i.e. they act on our systems of perception and consciousness to trigger healing.

The way each plant acts on our perception is very subjective. In these terms, it isn't easy to synthesise the active principle of medicinal plants artificially. This principle is developed through the relationship of the plant to the landscape, and subsequently to the human body, through a phyto-complex mechanism. In these terms, then, understanding which plants are effective is determined by testing, listening to and understanding our inner dynamics in relation.

Valerian is a plant that prefers humidity, part-sun and part-shade. It is perhaps no coincidence that its powers are related to the transition between sleep and wakefulness.[11] It is a very particular plant. It may at first appear common, but is quite peculiar if you look at it closely. The chiselled leaves have non-symmetrical laminae and veins. These irregularities, as well as those of the very pronounced stems, give it a somewhat disturbing appearance, especially in the first phase of growth. Mature branches can reach almost two metres, producing inflorescences with tiny and fragrant flowers, ranging in colour between red, pink and white.

But the most significant scent is that of the roots. In my studies, I dug up the plant's roots several times to observe its growth. Valerian develops some primary roots with a subtle but peculiar shape. They almost look like quills. A much more complex lymphatic system is connected to these roots, and appears as a thin transmission network that envelops and propagates throughout the soil expanding its nutritional range. The scent of the roots is unique. There is something unexpected, intoxicating and repulsive about it at the same time. It is a penetrating perfume, challenging to grasp and, in this sense, mysterious.

Anomaly, asymmetry, contingency, monstrosity, sun *and* shade… I picture it striped. I think all these features point to the potential for dynamism and collaboration, suggesting openness and motility. There is something incomplete about the ontology of Valerian as you describe it. Being incomplete,

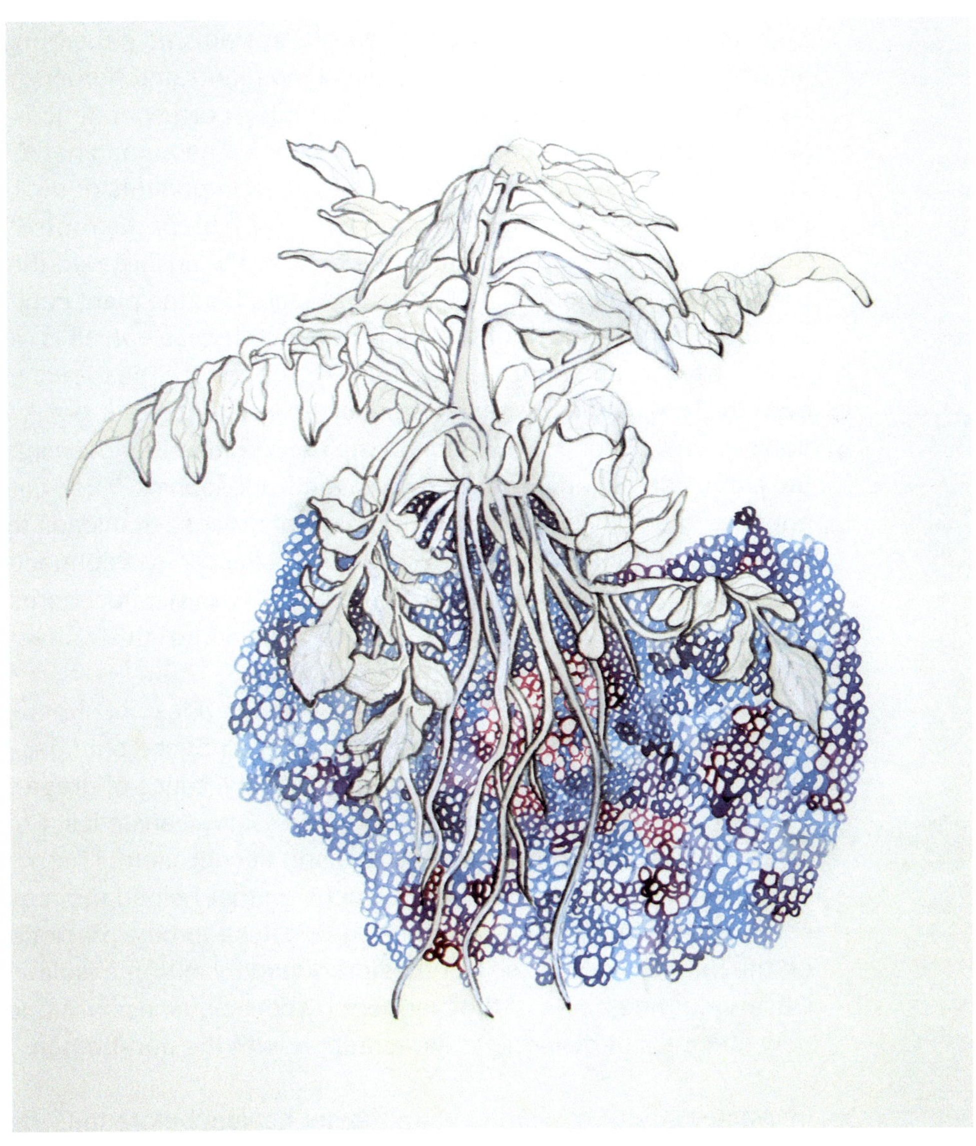

Elisa Strinna, *Valeriana Officinalis*, studio, drawing and watercolor on paper, 36×51 cm, 2022

I think, it is primed to interact; it has negative spaces, unfinished parts; it lures you and repels you at the same time.
It is like an open hand, or claw, or branch, or curtain of moss, etc., ready to tangle, that you brush past and feel simultaneously unnerved and delighted by.

216

12

Ibid., p 38

13

Philippe Nuss,
'Anxiety disorders
and GABA
neurotransmission:
a disturbance of
modulation',
*Neuropsychiatric
Disease and
Treatment*, Vol. 11, 2015,
pp 165–175

14

Wilhelm Pelikan and
Karin Mecozzi, *Le
piante medicinali: La
relazione tra la pianta
e l'uomo*, Volume 3,
1999

15

Ibid.

16

Barbara Ehrenreich
and Deirdre English,
*Witches, Midwives and
Nurses: A History of
Women Healers*, 1973

Valerian makes contact with our nervous systems on a therapeutic level through the roots. Karin explains how plants and humans can be interpreted as tripartite organisms, finding correspondences between their organs and functional designs. The human head, bone structure and nervous system—the mineral components of the human body—correspond to the plant's mineral element, or the roots.[12] Scientifically, Valerian's calming powers have been linked to the valepotriates. At the level of the brain, it appears that the plant can increase the production of the neurotransmitter *gaba*, which is responsible for regulating neuronal excitability throughout the nervous system. The plant activates the reticular formation of our brain reception systems. Strong production of the neurotransmitter *gaba* inhibits the stimuli of fear and anxiety.[13] At an anthroposophical level, Valerian appears to be closely related to the natural process that leads to the formation of phosphorus—a mineral that is deeply interconnected with light, and therefore energy. In the human being, phosphorus acts on the bone system's mineralisation process and positively affects the brain's metabolism.[14]

Unlike other synthetic tranquilisers, Valerian does not suppress spiritual liveliness.[15] Over the period I took it, I noticed changes in my states of consciousness. I began to feel a sense of greater clarity. I was no longer entirely at the mercy of my anxieties. Being less involved, I could trace the causes and accept them. I had a different take on my emotional dimension that helped me tame some inner demons. The plant has shown itself to be a precious ally on the path of healing the traumas produced by extreme isolation. Observing the effects of the plant on my consciousness has opened new channels of dialogue and interaction with the non-human.

In Western Culture, women were master healers before the witchhunts. They took great care in the collection of wild herbs, learning their properties by practical observation. Popular medicine has been categorised as unscientific in order to strip it of its powers. On the contrary, it results from in-depth empirical studies.[16] Healing meant learning about the more-than-human and their/our interactions within the whole, about relationships and correspondences among distinct beings, about how all are secretly related in the circle of life, and how they sustain and support each other. It is a knowledge that is empirical and intuitive, which navigates complexity without aiming to master it. Healers serve as guides, helping us orient ourselves within it.

17

Whereas usually we assume that when we are sick, we should seek the authority of a medical professional, whose knowledge we will have no way of relating to, as if we were not ourselves inside our own bodies. A herbalist told me that one strategy of choosing among medicinal plants, since treatment cannot be standardised, is to identify the plants and tune in. Which plant most compels your attention? That is one to try. Trying is also crucial, no? Accepting that there are no guarantees, that you are learning as you go, that it will take time, and that there is also healing in the process—of trying, of encountering and interacting, studying and preparing and tuning in.

—Elisa Strinna & Nicole Trigg
JULY 2022

REFERENCES

Giorgio Agamben, *L'Aperto: l'uomo e l'animale*, 2007

Barbara Ehrenreich and Deirdre English, *Witches, Midwives and Nurses: A History of Women Healers*, 1973

Silvia Federici, *Caliban and the Witch*, 2004

Le Streghe di Triora [1898], edited and annotated by Michele Rosi, self-published ebook, 2017

Karin Mecozzi, *Ars Herbaria, Natura e Cultura Editrice*, 2020

Philippe Nuss, 'Anxiety disorders and GABA neurotransmission: a disturbance of modulation', *Neuropsychiatric Disease and Treatment*, Vol. 11, 2015, pp 165–175

Sandro Oddo, *La medicina popolare nell'alta Valle Argentina*, 1997

Wilhelm Pelikan and Karin Mecozzi, *Le piante medicinali: La relazione tra la pianta e l'uomo*, Volume 3, 1999

Nathan Smith and Emma Barrett, 'Coping with life in isolation and confinement during the Covid-19 pandemic', *The Psychologist*, https://www.bps.org.uk/psychologist/coping-life-isolation-and-confinement-during-covid-19-pandemic, 18 March 2020

Jacob Sprenger and Heinrich Kraemer, *The Hammer of Witches (Malleus Maleficarum)*, 1486

This booklet is published on the occasion of documenta
fifteen (Kassel), 18 June – 25 September 2022

It is part of the publication *Jimmie Durham & A Stick
in the Forest by the Side of the Road* with Jimmie Durham
and Bev Koski, Elisa Strinna, Hamza Badran, Iain
Chambers, Joen Vedel, Jone Kvie, Maria Thereza Alves,
Wilma Lukatsch, Giulia Grechi, Alessandra Marino
Al-Mishlab (ISBN 978-3-7533-0260-7, NUR 640)

Text: Elisa Strinna & Nicole Trigg
Images: © Elisa Strinna
Editor: Iain Chambers
Proofreader: Nicola Grey
Design: Karoline Swiezynski, inspired by Will Holder's
design for *Past Imperfect* by Bik van der Pol, which
shaped the collective solution of this publication

Printed and bound in Belgium by Cassochrome with
supervision of ArtLibro Trudy Dorrepaal. Published
in an edition of 250 individual booklets (documenta
fifteen) to be collated in an edition of 1000 books
distributed by Verlag der Buchhandlung Walther und
Franz König, Köln. First published by Verlag der
Buchhandlung Walther und Franz König Ehrenstraße 4,
D-50672 Köln.

Bibliographic information published by the Deutsche
Nationalbibliothek – The Deutsche Nationalbibliothek
lists this publication in the Deutsche National-
bibliografie; detailed bibliographic data is available
at http://dnb.d-nb.de.

Disclaimer: In making *Jimmie Durham & A Stick in the
Forest by the Side of the Road* we have borrowed quotes,
images and texts from various resources. Information
concerning the original authors and sources is
credited in as much detail as possible. Despite
these efforts, some sources nevertheless could not
be identified. Please contact the authors in case
of questions or objections. The ideas and opinions
are the authors' unless stated otherwise.

*Jimmie Durham & A Stick in the Forest by the Side
of the Road* has been generously supported by
Mondriaan Funds and documenta fifteen.

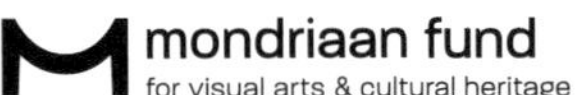

This publication has been realized in
the framework of documenta fifteen,
June 18 - September 25, 2022

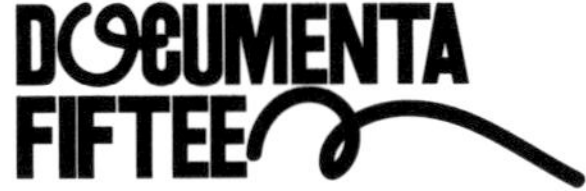

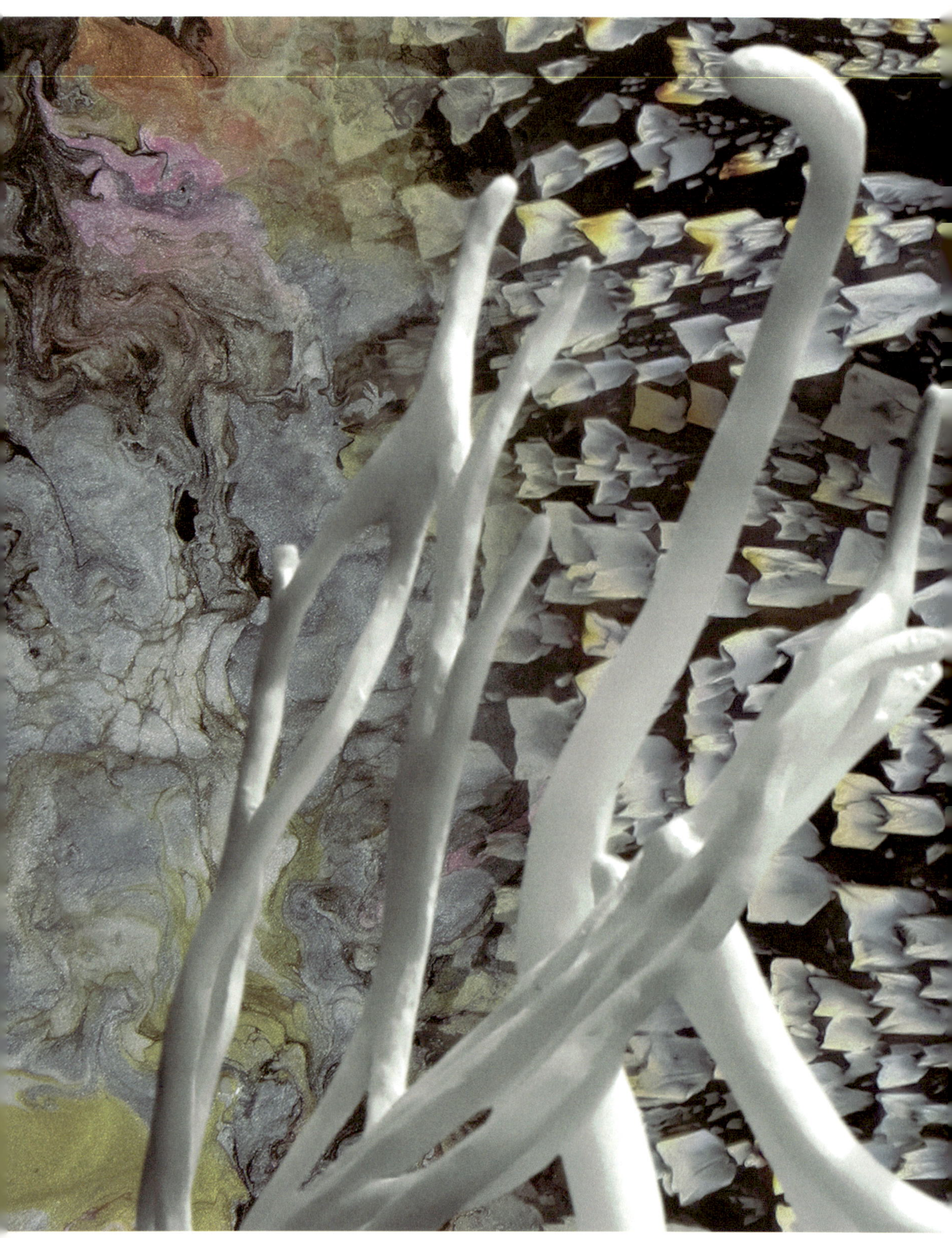

published 15 September 2022

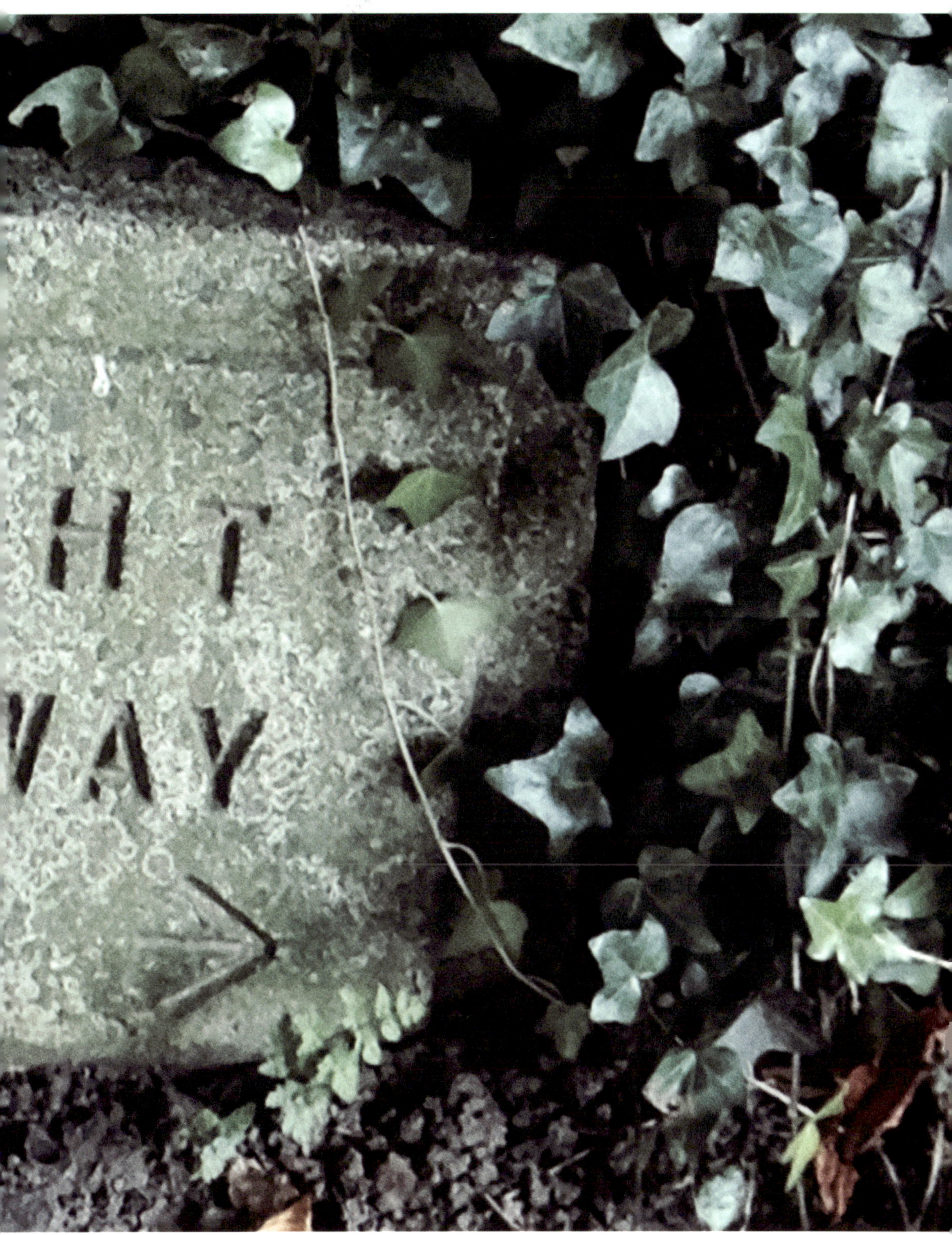

Jimmie Durham & A Stick in the Forest by the Side of the Road

THE COLONIAL CLOCK AND CRITICAL REPAIR ' …looking for connections
that cannot, may be, should not, be made' (Jimmie Durham)

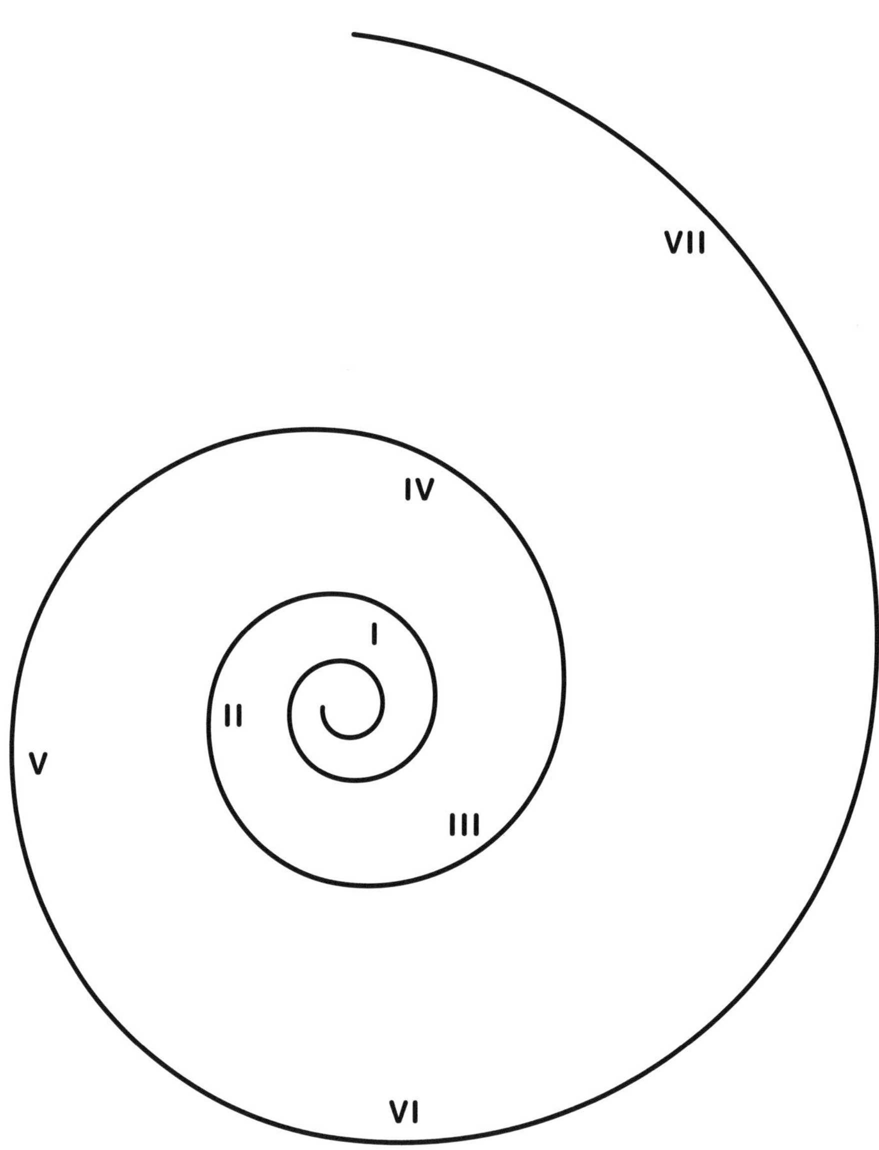

THE COLONIAL CLOCK AND CRITICAL REPAIR
' …looking for connections that cannot, may be, should not, be made'
(Jimmie Durham)

"The world needs an epistemological change that will rearrange desires"

Gayatri Chakravorty Spivak,
An Aesthetic Education in the Era of Globalization

I

What do we mean by 'repair'; is it simply about mending, restoring
and fixing an object or situation and setting it back to work? Is it
merely about acknowledging that something is not functioning
correctly? For example, is it a condition triggered by racism, sexism,
social inequality and historical injustice that needs to be adjusted to
make amends? Or does it point to deeper processes and perhaps something even irreparable. The concept is ambivalent. It suggests setting
things right to continue as before. But it also evokes an idea of temporary residence and gathering to repair from the storm (called
progress, as Walter Benjamin would have put it). In the second case,
the critical repair is not simply about making amends, restoration and
moving on. Rather, it can also suggest confronting the *impossibility*
of moving on, of being blocked and abused by powers that refuse to
register an untended state.

Bearing this in mind, we could deploy the idea of repair as being more
than a transitory fix. For it also acknowledges the impossibility of
ever returning to a previous state, one that is presumed to be pristine,
innocent and uncontaminated. The world remains broken. Its reas-
sembled fragments lead to something more complex than the lost
'original'. The artist and the critic now become collectors. They know
there can be no turning back to a disappeared totality or vanished
community. There is no cure. Instead, we acknowledge a wound, and

a cut is conceded. It leads to the critical responsibility of caring for
the damage. We adopt another body of understanding and weave
together the threads of another carpet of coherence, "a reminder
of complexities beyond the human" (Maria Thereza Alves).

We choose to think of art not simply as a sociological or historical
phenomenon but as an interruption and critical language. Art evades
capture in the straitjacket of explanations policed by disciplinary
protocols. Instead, it explores, excavates and expands the world.
Rather than an illustrative instance of history or sociology, art as
history, as sociology. It sustains a language that takes us to the edge
and beyond...

"The rigid and restrictive underpinnings
of disciplinary thinking becomes apparent
when we notice that categorisation
—*specifically the method and methodology
of sustaining knowledge categories*—
is an economised emulation of positivist
classificatory (thinking that is produced
in the shadows of biological determinism
and colonialism)."

Katherine McKittrick

Occidental art and aesthetic practices are about location and the powers that have permitted their universalisation. So how do we unpack the violent mechanisms of that universalisation? Seeking to register the world and renovate its languages, we discover inherited concepts are increasingly out of joint.

Today, the cancellation of distance and the insistence on immediacy — of the repressed past, negated bodies and unredeemed histories — is increasingly pursued in contemporary art. As a critical space, such art proposes an insistent mediation on uprooted cartographies, displaced objects, interrupted lives and broken archives. The proximity and prospects of other cosmologies, of different manners of worlding the world, breach the premises of our vision; they interrogate our aesthetic grammar and expose the confines of our moral agenda. Cutting time and refusing established chronologies, this art returns us to histories we think are past and unable to connect to the present. On the contrary, we encounter their contemporary pertinence and refusal to fade away. The seeming anachronism of matter out of place, assumed to be safely back there, locked up in a superseded time, becomes a contemporary critical interrogation. Occidental humanism turns out to be fundamentally hostile to those it has structurally excluded. Nevertheless, those it has abandoned in a refused past return to the necropolitical present. They confront us with the traces of attempts to resist the eradication of the rights to exist and persist by collecting, registering, and beading together other lives and forces (Bev Koski).

Maria Thereza Alves, commencing from the neo-classical Villa Pignatelli on Riviera di Chiaia in Naples, has deliberately linked colonial Mexico to the modern Mediterranean. The full name of the villa is Villa Pignatelli Cortés. It is directly tied to Hernán Cortés's invasion of Mexico in 1519 and the genocidal colonisation of the Americas. It announces the "connection and flows of monies from Mexico to Naples that began when Hernán's granddaughter, Catalina Vigil de Quinones, married Juan Alonso Pimentel, Viceroy of Naples in 1602". In the fog of colonial amnesia that invades the present, the white neo-classical building is usually called Villa Pignatelli: the colonial reminder of Cortés falls away. From the conquest of Mexico to the gold that adorns the Counter-Reformation

Baroque churches of Naples, the sacking and despoliation of
Mexico set the conditions for both modern European wealth
and indigenous poverty.

Deep histories connect the destruction of indigenous culture and
ecological damage across the centuries. These follow the dismantling
of native land and water management to meet the needs of trans-
Atlantic capital accumulation in the sixteenth century. The artist
resets the Valle Xico Community Museum — located in the metro-
politan area of Mexico City that was donated by the Spanish Crown
to Cortés — as a critical counter-space. The local community seeks
to maintain their rights and culture through the museum, which
houses over 5,000 pre-invasion artefacts. As an unregistered colonial
archive, the indigenous Mexican museum offers a brutal contrast to
the placid European cosmopolitanism of the exhibits and musical
concerts that Villa Pignatelli Cortés regularly hosts in contemporary
Naples. As reparation, the artist proposes that the Neapolitan institution invite the Valle de Xico Community Museum members every
year to carry out research and to provide an artist-in-residency
grant. This proposal will, of course, go unheard. However, the question remains, the interrogation insists.

II

The conceptual establishment of 'art' and 'aesthetics' emerged from
the entanglement of European rationality and Occidental global
hegemony. It is necessary to consider and contest the privileges of this
perspective if we wish to free discussion of art from its present enclosure. At this point, we could deploy the idea of art providing and
provoking a critical apparatus or disposition. It would mean to mess
up and refute the rationalising distance between the subject and
object of the Occidental tradition.

At the heart of the aesthetic programme of modernity is the connection of art to ideas of truth. To take that argument seriously and then
world it suggests a path towards another paradigm or constellation.

Borrowing from Antonio Gramsci, Sigmund Freud and Black
Quantum Futurism, we could shift the temporal axis 180°. Cutting
into time means contaminating the flat homogeneity of 'progress'
with the stratified temporalities of the subaltern, the unconscious
and the refused. To consider such turbulent rhythms and depths that
render the past contemporary is to confront the abstract accumulation of capital with its planetary violence.

The past lives on as a persistent interrogation. It betrays the colonial
constitution of Occidental modernity: in the open cut of Palestine/
Israel, in the deafness to indigenous rights, the abject body of the
contemporary migrant, the after-life of slavery, in missions to colonise space. Unauthorised archives and unregistered lives are always at
work between the colonial clock and critical repair. This unrecorded
past spills out to challenge the current order. It can be caught in the
diversity of Mediterranean sounds, the culinary complexities of food,
recipes and journeys of taste, and the diverse modalities of receiving,
representing and living the planet. For sensitive excavations of cuisine
and local *savoir* can draw us into intricate pleasures and understandings not only of food but also of pursuing possibilities that refute
a homogenous arrangement of taste and the senses (Wilma Lukatsch).

All of this leads towards 'subaltern', 'minority' and 'indigenous'
rearrangements: a planetary remixing of the contemporary world...
Beyond the white myths of present-day cultural institutions, it
suggests a relocation involving the abandonment of the stereotypes,
categories and places already prepared for the 'natives' of a still
persistent colonial rule (Frantz Fanon).

Outside the academic shelter of definitions, we encounter the slide
from product to process, from an isolated aesthetic value to the
collective call of ethics: from the work of art to the workings of art.
In this movement through the world, we look and listen again, to
register in sensory materialities what sustains while cracking the
inherited mould of 'art'.

Digging deeper: this is also a response to other epistemologies, other
forms of knowledge, different constructions and cosmologies. These
other specificities undermine an imposed universalism. If the West

has become the world, it is also unwound, dissipated and fragmented in places and practices it cannot permanently authorise. Best to linger in this opening and not rush to establish the security of another definition.

To insist on the transit of translation in the transformative becoming of art conjures up communities on the road. Not to say that there are no longer artists, but there is a recognition that they are now suspended and sustained in wider nets. The sources of the work lie further down the road, beyond the present aesthetic regime and its historical and political formation.

To step outside of tradition — which includes the institutional practices of Western art — is to look and listen again. Acknowledging a complex sensory experience means diluting the premises concentrated in ocular hegemony. The world mapped and rendered transparent to the sovereign subject's will is thwarted. In the exercise of measured distance and controlled positions, maps and perspective, lie the political 'realism' of European colonialism: its epistemic violence and the unilateral appropriation of the globe.

Returning to the abandoned world of 'artificial deserts', where intricate processes tap into the material complexities of a world unfettered by human agency and arrogance, is an invitation to concentrate on what has been wasted and discarded for a particular order to be represented (Elisa Strinna). Every act of representation is simultaneously an act of repression.

In proposing *an art beyond art*, we admit the diffusion of critical processes that exit the categories prepared for them. What lies between institutional recognition and the risk of not being admitted sustains an uprooting. We begin to learn from unlearning in the ongoing pedagogy of auditory and visual languages that intercede to decompose and recompose an unfolding archive in the montage of the present (Joen Vedel). Meanwhile, artworks never stop working. Roots become routes amongst the sticks in the forest.

The epistemic violence of a uniform art and universal aesthetics is confronted by histories from below, from the multiple souths of the world, from margins that propose new centres seeking "justice against epistemicide" (Boaventura de Sousa Santos). Maps are extended, interleaved and fray. Responding reveals that history is never merely of the past. On the cusp of what never simply passes, we catch the echo and afterlife of the repressed accounts of marginalised cultures accumulating in the constitution of the present. For example, Cape Town, South Africa, is also a Muslim city. We are invited to look AND listen long enough to catch the limits of our authorisation of the world. It is now exposed to other rhythms and lives generated within the colonial continuity of the present (Hamza Badran). Along with the other monotheisms of Judaism and Christianity that emerged from the Middle East, Islam, since 711, is also a European religion. In being unrecognised, ignored, refused and unregistered, such histories come to meet us from the future (Jacques Derrida).

In the commodification of the planet and the commercial capture of art, the unruly supplement of an emergent narrative disseminates doubt, disturbance and depth. The subsequent mix loosens the grip of commodity fetishism while "…all social analysis is revealed as montage" (Michael Taussig). The time and geography of the nation, its institutional and exhibition spaces, are crossed by unacknowledged accounts. The latter are not simply counter-histories. They do not represent a separate or autonomous alternative. Instead, they insist on their right to participate in the planetary mix. They challenge the asymmetrical relations of power that have subordinated them to the existing state of affairs.

To respond to these other narratives means to travel beyond the endorsement of Europe and North America. For some of us, this means losing part of our baggage. It involves a passage from the relative comfort of an established language to the inescapable violence of the modern world that assures that comfort only for some.

All can be reasoned, but not all can be reduced to the rationality of a single point of view. The world is saturated and sustained in power relations, but not all forces are equal.

III

On the street at night: it is warm but not too humid. Nairobi is over
1,600 metres above sea level. We are strolling on Electric Avenue in
the Westlands district. This is the heart of Nairobi clubland. The
volume is incredible. It is impossible to converse in this musical
warfare even out on the street. Between cars and pedestrians, sounds
battle each other seeking their auditory claim on the territory. We
stop to take a beer outside on the sidewalk. Meanwhile, music bellows
out of an open door. We walk down some steps into a sonorous density
so thick as to reverberate through the body, denuded of words
or explanation.

Does this sonic interruption propose a different or an emergent
public sphere? In bringing me to my senses it undoubtedly sustains
a dynamic social space. We could even suggest that a form of citizenship, perhaps elsewhere formally denied or truncated, is here publicly
proposed in sound. Such transitory geographies of musical belonging
connect us to the altogether more complex unfolding of the immedia-
cies of the world. Drawn into multiple temporalities and spaces, I am
linked to what I can never fully comprehend. I am carried beyond the
rational conversation that seemingly typified the eighteenth-century
coffee house and the public promotion of debate proposed by Jürgen
Habermas. That particular sense of the communal sphere and associated model of citizenship is contaminated and remixed down here in
sub-Saharan Africa (and certainly not only there). In the diverse
urban spaces of Nairobi and Naples, Lagos, Luanda and Lisbon,
spacetime is lived, shaped and reconfigured in practices and processes
that scratch, bend and splinter the presumed model of European
provenance. They render explicit the problematic relationship
between citizenship, social space, everyday culture and democracy.

Here, European and extra-European scenarios are unsuspectedly
conjoined. Caribbean and Turkish diasporas in Bristol and Berlin,
illegal immigrants in the backstreets of Naples, rapping in Arabic,
further underline that other versions of community, citizenship and
modernity are at work. Sharp distinctions between public and private
spheres, patrolled in differences of class and gender, come undone.
Just as in Kenya, where everything is modern — both the ubiquitous

cell phone and the poverty, the midnight car wash in the club complex and the urban slum — democratic participation is often independent of the formal manifestations of official politics. In noisily taking the lid off the institutional can, the contents of modernity that can be heard and seen in a Nairobi night invite us to reconsider our lexicon, uncoil our certainties and take a further walk in the world.

The democracy and citizenship claimed in the West depend on the subordination and exclusion of bodies and histories that inhabited the colonial world and today live in the postcolony. Our 'freedom' has been historically dependent on the extension of non-freedoms (slavery, indenture, genocide) elsewhere. The liberal formation of modern European democracy on both sides of the Atlantic is riddled with the perversities of power and possession that form its citizens as the bearers of planetary injustice. The rule of law, inscribed in the universal claims of a property-owning class and its political economy to legislate for the world, reveals the arbitrary and unilateral powers of a European-derived sovereign will on the planet. It also exposes that very same logic to both translation and treason. Elsewhere *within* modernity, the terms of the polity are not merely a charade to be played by dictators and oligarchs while pursuing their particular interests. Ideas about citizenship, democracy and public life are everywhere taken up and embodied by subjects engaged in the multiple languages of modernity. Traditions — including those of the West — are transmitted, transformed and translated.

IV

With this history in our eyes and ringing in our ears, there lies the promise of a radical reorientation. We turn away from a European idealist tradition located in Hellenic roots whose presumed purity guarantees whitewashed origins and the exclusive custody of modernity. Now there is the need to reach for another compass.

What might this mean? I will take an example from thinking with the Mediterranean. In discussing the historical and cultural formation of the basin, one approach, often seemingly progressive, involves continuing research to widen and deepen the picture. It consists in adding

forgotten and negated elements to the narrative, returning to the
archives, and retrieving additional knowledge. A colonising method
continues to accumulate cultural capital in the endeavour to render
the world transparent to our will. The other, which I propose, is to
consider the premises whereby the Mediterranean, crudely "ours",
has emerged to obfuscate the histories and cultures of its African and
Asian shores. The latter approach is not about additional accumulation to set the record straight. Instead, without simply overturning the
predominant European take, it seeks to configure the Mediterranean
in the light of what was repressed precisely to permit a particular
representation to pass as universal.

So, turning to art would suggest that we should not be interested in
simply extending the artistic and aesthetic canon to incorporate the
previously excluded. Instead, there is something more at hand.

We shift from *representation* to *registration*. With that, I mean to
mark the impossibility of reducing anything to a single perspective.
I now find myself speaking in the vicinity of cultural and historical
complexities that precede and exceed me. These breach my control
and powers of representation.

The sense of the world today is overwhelmingly constituted through
its European appropriation, most directly emphasised in white settler
colonialism (USA, Canada, Australia, New Zealand, South Africa,
Israel). Likewise, understandings of art and aesthetics have emerged
from a colonial matrix. They, too, are deeply imbricated in the coloniality of power and its necessary fracturing.

V

A unique perspective that confirms the viewing subject at the
centre of the world sustains the Romantic understanding of the
artist. A talented individual lends her or his vision to our eyes. If
contemporary neo-liberal individualism reinforces this inheritance, it also clashes with most artists' lived experiences... The
latter find themselves in the differentiated precariat that constitutes the modern workforce. International relations in the existing

art world only recognise singular exceptionality. Such is the aesthetic
and commercial norm. It produces stars and astronomical figures
in the market. However, the socialisation of art production in
collectives, collaborations and networks directs us towards a very
different political economy.

Against the prevailing institutional logic of museums, galleries and
biennales, looser arrangements and transitory communities of artists
and critics — such as the situation created at documenta fifteen — insist
that aesthetic value cannot simply be mirrored by capital. Processes
and not merely products, transitory experiments and experiences,
rather than collectables, conduct us towards different evaluations.
The global market is sequestered for a period. Its mechanisms are
temporarily rendered vulnerable to other questions and agendas.

An economy of art practices and procedures, as opposed to the
vertical directives of institutional aesthetics and commercial
authority, can also be built via horizontal connections. The latter
produce communities seeded in pooling resources, methods and
ideas. We are talking here about the continuing communality and
shared benefits of 'lumbung'. In these processes, an understanding
of power emerges in collecting and connecting rather than brutally
exercising it. To practise art out of place is to push institutional logic
and cultural management out of synch. So, we move from consid-
ering the artwork restricted to art history and commercial concern
to registering a critical practice. Although seized by capital, art
sustains a shattering supplement which reconfigures the present
through a negated past that can never be recovered nor fully known.

Against the odds, such art works the gap. It sustains the tensions and
contradictions that render its language critical. If, while pushing up
against the white (supremacy) walls of the modern museum and art
gallery, such art does not escape capture in the institutional frame,
it nevertheless disturbs its premises. It has led to some of the most
significant debates in contemporary culture, practising the reach
of art while reworking the concepts and grammar of the present.
Refusing to harmonise, reciting what has yet to be registered and
narrated, such art propels us into another history.

VI

Out of joint: art is in the world but is not merely a mirror. Art is
an anachronism: for it pushes accredited History out of alignment.
Before the image, the artwork, I confront a time that is not simply
mine (Georges Didi-Huberman). As Adorno once put it, this means
"to blow open what cannot be absorbed by concepts, or what,
through contradictions in which concepts entangle themselves,
betrays the fact that the network of their objectivity is a purely
subjective rigging."

History splinters into turbulent constellations to challenge the organisation and explanation of time. The past is continually constructed and
underway, querying the presumed integrity of documents and facts that
presume to endorse a transparent chronology. The 'facts' have to be
retrieved and elaborated; the 'documents' identified and interpreted.
The explanation, the narrative, no matter how neutral or scientific it
pretends to be, has to be shaped and configured. The nature of historical time yoked to Occidental subjectivity is now exposed to coordinates
that challenge the 'objectivity' of its universal presumptions.

Art at work proposes a constant re-membering of this challenge.
It sustains a continual return to that rift and performs a cut that
reminds us that history is always a work in progress. The door can
never be shut on the past precisely because the present continues to
charge the questions that ignite its authority. So, to think of the past
is to think of current configurations. As Walter Benjamin beautifully
characterised origins, it is "that which emerges from the process of
becoming and disappearing". There is no stable source but rather
a "whirlpool in the river of becoming".

Critically unpacking and decolonising present languages — from
historiography to art criticism, from aesthetics to sociology — depends
on recognising such an interruption in time and knowledge. Acting
against normative interpretations involves pushing them out of joint
and insisting on the anachronistic. To register what resists and
persists in the times of others means to implode the present. What has
been repressed, negated and denied now claims the past and, with it,
another future.

The insistence of the subaltern, slavery and structural racism, forced diasporas, feminism, gender, and sexual rights provoke the disruptive quality of previously unauthorised and invisible histories. Such a replay and amplification transports us beyond disciplinary boundaries. Recent artistic work and research, often coming from unacknowledged archives and margins, now puncture the boundaries between the empirical and the inventive. The stubbornness of established 'facts' and institutional narratives evaporate in critical imagination and practices that deliver a more complex sense of the present.

In the slide from speaking for to speaking alongside (Assia Djebar, Trinh T. Minh-ha), I arrive at a place of listening. The 'white man's burden' (sic) of the curatorial gaze is challenged, turned inside out, or refused. The Occidental drive for knowledge, appropriating the world as intellectual property to render it transparent to sovereignty and capitalist accumulation, brushes up against the right to opacity (Édouard Glissant). For if we are all within the planetary frame that sustains difference without separability (Denise Ferreira da Silva), differences insist. Asymmetrical relations of power persist; they refuse to accede to my comprehension.

This is the death of a certain anthropology and the Occidental management of disciplinary and border control. Of course, both persist, but their premises are now historically and politically un-sustainable, even if they continue to exhibit and explain the world. Cultural measurement and historical comparison become part of an altogether more mobile and unstable landscape. In an anthropology of anthropology, we begin to witness the treadmill of 'progress' spinning off its axle. The linear dictatorship of historical reasoning splutters. Perhaps the modern museum and art exhibition is the subconscious site of mourning for the death of such a world now in ruins. Elsewhere, indigenous communities, subaltern and marginal-ised cultures, despite the genocides, negation and structural violence, still exist, resist and live on. And art now charts the failure of the machinery of existing institutions to represent the world. Such a 'failure' — of the museum and the art exhibition *and* also of a countervailing art project like documenta fifteen — is not to be refused. Instead, it can be understood as an opening where it

becomes possible to register something more. In falling short of the
desire to capture the world, another unauthorised space emerges.
Considered a negative sign for many institutions, this space borders
on incomprehension and nonsense. For artistic processes attuned to
the planet's hum, it proposes care and critical responsibility for
a becoming that fuses aesthetics with ethics.

Others usher in the future by refuting existing categorisations.
Rather than adjusting the archives or renovating the disciplines,
it becomes a question of undoing the colonial constitution of the
present. Existing capital and cultural accumulation are ready to be
redistributed. It inaugurates the communal outreach of 'lumbung'.
If there is no 'democratisation without decolonisation' (University
of Colour), the museum and the art show now secedes control.
Objects valued in isolation are no longer the point of arrival. The
exhibition complex withdraws and hands its spaces over to others.
But, of course, it will not placidly relinquish its powers and is
destined to continue as the site of a ruin.

VII

The ultimate context of these considerations is what Ros Gray and
Shela Sheikh call the *wretched earth*. The persistency of the earth,
despite its reduction to instrumental exploitation and wrecking on
the part of human agency, increasingly announces itself. 'Freak'
weather, rising sea level, plastic islands and polluted rivers are both
the signs of the poisoned planet choking in our presence and the
increasing combination of deeper rhythms and resources in
its response.

But is this simply about an unequal relationship between humans and
nature? Of course not. A wealthy minority produces the vast majority
of the world's pollution. The political economy of 'progress' has
ransacked the planet only for a few. The classification and management of the world — from its plant life to its populations — was never
a neutral affair. Motored by capitalist accumulation and overseen by
Occidental governance and culture, the world has become a planetary
plantation system and rubbish dump. This connection is sharply

revealed in the modern emblem of the cell phone and computer: both in the assembling of materials and resources in its production and in the manner of its disposal. It has created terrifying geographies of the abysmal and the obscene. Land, location and territory are divided between those without choice, condemned to structural poverty and anonymity, and those who believe they can remove themselves from the escalating apocalypse.

The complex terrestrial ecology of movement and mutation produces illicit maps via the continual migration of human bodies, animals and plants. In a temporary borrowing of stones and plants, natural objects and processes interrogate us and, refusing to acknowledge our presence, displace our mastery of place and time (Jone Kvie). We tap into worlds that refuse to be passive objects, lying there to confirm us on our way. Here in Kassel, we have planted an apple tree in Jimmie Durham's memory: both testify to what has passed and indicate what can still come about. We draw energy from this theatre of mourning: acknowledging who and what we feel we have lost while simultaneously finding renewal through saying farewell to a particular disposition of art. Despite the terrible world raging out there, artistic research and critical repair still propel us beyond the bounded immediacy of the present into further becomings.

The above draws from discussion, projects and proposals in the Jimmie Durham & A Stick in the Forest by the Side of the Road *collective. I want to thank everyone involved for such an enriching experience and journey.*

REFERENCES

Theodor Adorno, 'The Essay as Form', *New German Critique*, 32,
Spring–Summer, (1958), 1984

Maria Thereza Alves, *Thieves and Murderers in Naples: A Brief
History on Families, Colonization, Immense Wealth, Land
Theft, Art and the Valle de Xico Community Museum in
Mexico*, 2020

Walter Benjamin, *The Origin of German Tragic Drama*,
(1928) 1977

Jacques Derrida, *Archive Fever: A Freudian Impression*,
(1995) 1996

Georges Didi-Huberman, *Confronting Images: Questioning the
Ends of a Certain History of Art*, (1990) 2009

Assia Djebar, *Women of Algiers in Their Apartments*, 1992

Frantz Fanon, *The Wretched of the Earth*, (1961) 2004

Edouard Glissant, *Poetics of Relation.* (1990) 1999

Ros Gray and Shela Sheikh, 'The Wretched Earth: Introduction',
Third Text 151–152, March–May 2018

Katherine McKittrick, *Dear Science and Other Stories*, 2021

Denise Ferreira da Silva, 'On Difference without Separability',
32nd Bienal de São Paulo – Incerteza Viva, Catalogue.
Edited by Jochen Volz and Júlia Rebouças, 2016

Boaventura de Sousa Santos, *Epistemologies of the South: Justice
against Epistemicide*, 2014

Gayatri Chakravorty Spivak, *An Aesthetic Education in the Era of
Globalization*, 2012

Michael Taussig, *The Nervous System*, 1992

Trinh T. Minh-ha, *Reassemblage*, 1982

University of Colour:
https://www.facebook.com/universityofcolour/

This booklet is published on the occasion of documenta
fifteen (Kassel), 18 June – 25 September 2022

It is part of the publication *Jimmie Durham & A Stick in
the Forest by the Side of the Road* with Jimmie Durham
and Bev Koski, Elisa Strinna, Hamza Badran, Iain
Chambers, Joen Vedel, Jone Kvie, Maria Thereza Alves,
Wilma Lukatsch, Giulia Grechi, Alessandra Marino
Al-Mishlab (ISBN 978-3-7533-0260-7, NUR 640)

Text: Iain Chambers
Image: © Iain Chambers
Editor: Iain Chambers
Proofreader: Nicola Grey
Design: Karoline Swiezynski, inspired by Will Holder's
design for *Past Imperfect* by Bik van der Pol, which
shaped the collective solution of this publication

Printed and bound in Belgium by Cassochrome with
supervision of ArtLibro Trudy Dorrepaal. Published in
an edition of 500 individual booklets (documenta
fifteen) to be collated in an edition of 1000 books
distributed by Verlag der Buchhandlung Walther und
Franz König, Köln. First published by Verlag der
Buchhandlung Walther und Franz König Ehrenstraße 4,
D-50672 Köln.

Bibliographic information published by the Deutsche
Nationalbibliothek – The Deutsche Nationalbibliothek
lists this publication in the Deutsche National-
bibliografie; detailed bibliographic data is available
at http://dnb.d-nb.de.

Disclaimer: In making *Jimmie Durham & A Stick in
the Forest by the Side of the Road* we have quotes,
images and texts taken from various resources.
Information concerning the original authors and
sources have been credited as detailed as possible.
Despite these efforts, some sources nevertheless
could not be identified. Please contact the author
in case of questions or objections. The ideas
and opinions author unless stated otherwise.

*Jimmie Durham & A Stick in the Forest by the Side
of the Road* has been generously supported by
documenta fifteen.

This publication has been realized in
the framework of documenta fifteen,
June 18 – September 25, 2022

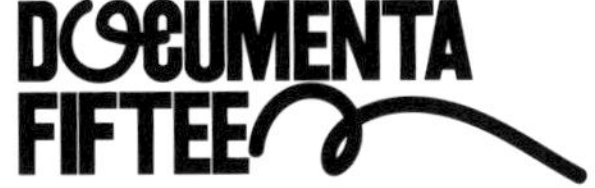

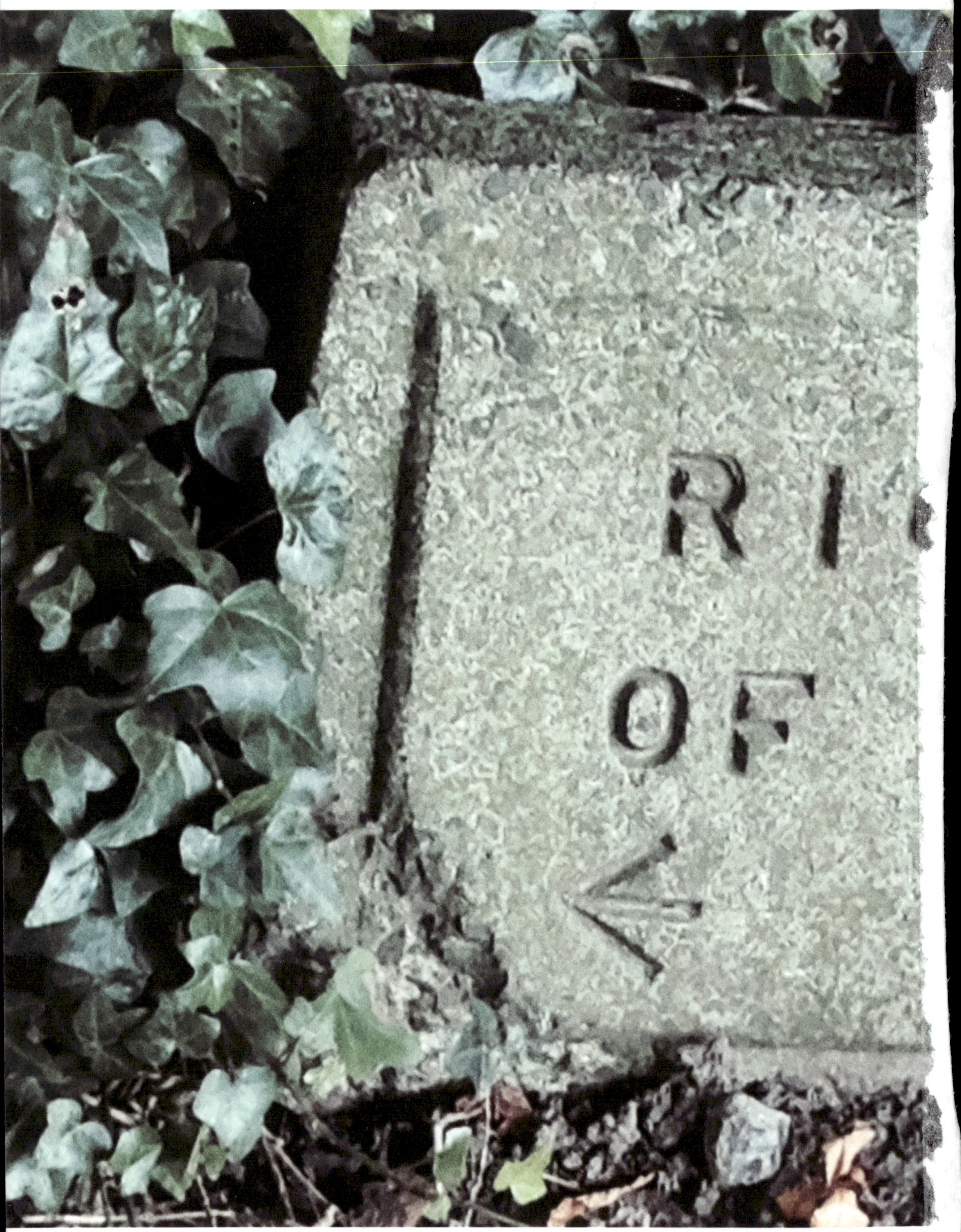

published 15 July 2022